XIII WINT

REFLECTIONS ON RUGBY LEAGUE

Edited by Dave Hadfield
Foreword by Michael Parkinson

MAINSTREAM
PUBLISHING
EDINBURGH AND LONDON

*In memory of John Jackson, a much-missed friend
and Rugby League enthusiast*

This edition 1995

First published in Great Britain in 1994 by
MAINSTREAM PUBLISHING COMPANY (EDINBURGH) LTD
7 Albany Street
Edinburgh EH1 3UG

ISBN 1 85158 743 8

A catalogue record for this book is available from the British Library

Typeset in Baskerville by Servis Filmsetting Ltd
Printed in Great Britain by Butler & Tanner, Frome

CONTENTS

CONTENTS

FOREWORD
BY

MICHAEL PARKINSON

Had I my time to come again I would make two major changes. First, I would learn the game of golf when I was a child so that I might be spared the agony of learning how to swing a club in middle age with creaking joints and thickened waist. Secondly, I would pay more attention to the game of Rugby League instead of dedicating my winters to the fortunes of Barnsley FC.

Sadly, as is often the case in Rugby League, geography played its part in my choice. People who assume that the game is strong anywhere above a line drawn through where Yorkshire meets Derbyshire should think again. When I was a kid in Barnsley I had as much chance of meeting a rugby player as I had of standing behind Mamie Van Doren in Bailey's Chip Shop. Rugby was a distant rumour coming from faraway towns like Wakefield and Leeds which, in those days, were as remote as space stations. By the time I had my appetite whetted I was working in London, and Wembley had become an annual pilgrimage – as much, it must be admitted, to hear the accents and the humour of my youth as to watch Rugby League.

Over the years I have come to love the game, the men who play it, the people who watch it and, so help me, even those who are responsible for running it. My enthusiasm has been sustained during annual trips to Australia where, although the game is glitzier and presented in a more showbizzy style, it still possesses the same big heart and unsullied character.

XIII Winters tells it all with great style and, above all, passion. Reading of the men and the moments, I was both delighted at a yarn well told and frustrated that, for one reason or another, I had not the same intimate acquaintance with the game and its players.

Neil Tunnicliffe's story of his love affair with Wakefield Trinity is both funny and sad, like love affairs should be. Huw Richards's account of trying to sell Rugby League to Londoners is a reminder of what the game has to do in the future if it is to blossom and prosper beyond the confines of the M62 corridor. But the gem is Dave Hadfield's 'A Tangerine Machine', his account of reporting on the fortunes of Blackpool Borough in 1978–79. This is where *Field of Dreams* meets *Monty Python's Flying Circus*. It needs a talented observer with a keen ear and a sardonic eye to make me laugh as much as I did reading Mr Hadfield's marvellous essay.

If anyone asks me in the future what attracts me to Rugby League, I will recommend they read *XIII Winters*. It is a reminder of the joy and fulfilment a sport can provide when players and spectators are shaped by a common clay, united by the love of a great game. I am still learning about Rugby League. What follows is an important part of my education.

INTRODUCTION

Part of the idea for this book was shamelessly filched from the plethora of personal confessions which detail unhealthy obsessions with another game. Very nice, I thought as I waded through various pre-Hornby, post-Hornby and sub-Hornby volumes about the effects that football can have on your life; but they're all about the wrong sport. Football, even down to a relatively humble level, is a vast, impersonal machine that doesn't know you exist. Its players live on a different planet from that inhabited by almost everyone who watches them and, while attempts to bring those two worlds together might be readable, they are doomed and, ultimately, rather sad.

Rugby League is something else again. Its players are just as good at what they do as anyone who pulls on a shirt for Manchester United or AC Milan – indeed, the physical demands upon them are far greater – but you can go to the bar after the match and find yourself standing between two internationalists, all of you trying to attract the barmaid's attention. The limit of their celebrity is that they might get served first, but who could begrudge them that? Part of the claustrophobic magic of the code is, as one contributor to this book points out, that you can marvel at the skill and courage of men who go to the same barbers.

I recall a story about one Wigan player who got a bit above himself when he was refused a drink after time in a town-centre pub.

'Do you know who I am?' he asked.

'Just a minute, everyone,' shouted the woman behind the bar. 'We've got a lad in here doesn't know who he is.'

The vast majority of Rugby League players remember who they are. It isn't just the fact that they get less media attention than their footballing cousins, either. In Sydney, where more column inches are devoted to a single sport – and that sport is Rugby League – than anywhere outside Italian soccer, the players still keep a grip on their roots. It isn't that there is anything intrinsically virtuous about them; it's just that no one has yet devised a better sport for knocking the bullshit out of you before it takes over.

They tell me football used to be like that. If it was, it was before my time. Such a nominally amateur game as Rugby Union should be like that, but its leading players seem increasingly cosseted from the real world. The unique thing in my experience about Rugby League which all the contributors to this book love is that it combines excellence on the field with an integrity to its community. And, before I'm bombarded with whippets and cloth caps, let me say that this is not a specifically northern trait. It transcends geography, it is timeless and it is one reason why, if people will look beyond cultural superficialities, Rugby League can establish itself in far more countries during its second century than it has during its first. There are no whippets or flat hats, as far as I could see, in Papua New Guinea, but a sport that can make a man a hero yet still leave him with his feet firmly planted on the ground does more than any political ideology to bind that country together.

So the idea dawned that we should put together a volume which would capture the sense of intimate involvement that characterises the game. There has been one book – the Yorkshire Arts Circus's acclaimed *When Push Comes to Shove* – which has done this through the medium of myriad short reminiscences from scores of people immersed in the sport in all capacities. For a series of longer, more considered insights, I have turned to people who write for a living, either on a full-time or part-time basis. Because all of them are, or have been, paid to write about Rugby League, it should not be inferred that their affection for the game is any less genuine than the man or woman on the terrace. They are all, in their different ways, fans as well as writers. Indeed, it's another aspect of our game's strange alchemy that it blurs that distinction as well. In another sport, the emotional attachment which the writers in *XIII Winters* chronicle would seem affected or, at best, inappropriate. In Rugby League, it is the most natural thing in the world – because that world is small, intimate and full of people who know each other by their first names.

The contributions are, by design, a mixed bag. Some are from people who were born into the game; others, like me, were converts in their youth, or later. Each was asked to write about the season at a particular club which means the most to them – the one with the most resonance or significance, or the one which typifies their particular love affair with the sport. But we like tinkering with the rules in Rugby League, so there have been a few departures from that pattern. It seemed only right that Paul Fitzpatrick should write about the 1982 Kangaroos, rather than about a club, because the couple of months that they were in Britain were clearly a Road to Damascus experience for him. Although I can imagine how well it will go down in St Helens, it also seemed justifiable for us to have two pieces on Wigan, from Mel Woodward and Paul Wilson, because the contrast between the two says a lot about those two impostors (that's triumph and disaster, not Woodward and Wilson) and the sheer impossibility of treating them just the same. Peter Wilson's addition to the line-up enabled us to draw upon the heartache and humour that go into running an amateur club. In Rugby League, there's no reason why Jay the Brick and Big Dog should not share a volume with Brett Kenny and Graham Steadman. Martin and Simon Kelner have been allowed to pool their Swinton memories, but there is no law against that. The worst excesses have all been mine. Not only have I been the greedy boy at the party by writing two pieces, but I have split one of them between two clubs. My excuse is that Blackpool Borough, Newtown and Parramatta comprise the membership of a mental super-league that cannot be split by promotion or relegation. If that will not suffice, I claim editorial prerogative, droit de seigneur, and the medieval rights of tillage and cullage.

Although facts have been checked where possible, it is personal recollection rather than historical accuracy which has been our priority here. Contributors have been given a free rein to recount events as they recall them. Some readers will recall them differently, but we hope that will be part of the enjoyment of the book. I may still spend the rest of my life fielding corrections about the number of drop-goals in the 1969 Lancashire Cup final and the precise length of Alf Macklin's sideburns, but I would like to avoid that fate if possible.

In apportioning gratitude, I have to start with the team at *Open Rugby*, whose support has been crucial to this project. In a game whose other qualities have sometimes been counterbalanced by a hyper-sensitivity to honest criticism, it is often forgotten how much unpaid work for the development of Rugby League goes on in that small office in Leeds. Not by dilettantes like me, who drift through every blue moon, I might add, but by Harry Edgar and Trevor Gibbons – both of whom contribute splendid chapters here – and by Joanne Lumley.

Equal thanks go to Neil Tunnicliffe who, apart from his own atmospheric piece on Wakefield Trinity, has prepared all the copy for publication with his customary care and diligence. We are also grateful to Michael Steele for the cover picture, and to Michael Parkinson, a glittering example of a person whose good taste and discrimination were bound to lead him towards Rugby League eventually, for kindly agreeing to write the foreword.

Mainstream Publishing have been enthusiastic supporters of the project since the idea was first put to them, and they do an excellent lunch. Most lunches, however, have been eaten over the typewriter at home, so my family have had even more than usual to put up with. Special thanks to the two fully paid-up Rugby League fans in the clan: Lucy, who thinks there should be *more* chapters on Wigan; and Sam, who can't understand why his personal highlight, Hugh Waddell giving him his sandwiches, isn't included. You can't please everyone, but I hope others will find something to chew upon and relish.

Dave Hadfield
May 1994

A TANGERINE MACHINE

Blackpool Borough 1978–79

Dave Hadfield

My memory is vague on this point but, if it wasn't John Corcoran who narrowed his eyes and said, 'You know the trouble with you, don't you? You're writing us into the first division', then it should have been. It wasn't meant as a compliment, either. No slap on the back and thank you for your support. It was more a matter of 'Okay, smartarse, who's going to make up all the winning money we won't be getting? You? Eh? Eh? You?'

There was no answer to the implied question. Not like the time when he told me, with ill-disguised bitterness, that if he'd had my size to go with his temperament and ability he would have taken on the world and won. I thought I had the answer to that. But John, I told him, if you were as big as me you wouldn't be as nasty as you are. It was a good debating point and, if we had been at the Oxford Union, I would have been one-nil ahead (Hadfield, drop-goal). At Borough Park, Blackpool, though, it was more the equivalent of dropping the ball, on the first tackle, behind your own try-line. I would undoubtedly pay for it in an unguarded moment in tick-and-pass. But I didn't care; I was in the middle of a tangerine sea-mist, in which anything was possible. Even promotion. Even back-chatting John Corcoran and living to tell the tale. Anything.

It was all nonsense, of course. You couldn't be written, talked or wished from second to first division. The only way a side like Blackpool Borough could make that leap was by winning an improbable number of games against opponents who, whatever their limitations and tribulations, were almost all richer in ability, resources and tradition. And yet there were times when we all seemed to be engaged in some con-trick or conspiracy. Not Watergate, or even Whitewatergate; perhaps, in tribute to Blackpool's airport, Squiresgate.

Not that the Borough hadn't had their moments. Or, to be nit-pickingly precise, their moment. It was a while coming, though – more than 23 years after the Fosdykean figure of Sir Fred Emery was instrumental in establishing Rugby League-on-Sea. At the risk of sounding like that great Blackpudlian, Alistair Cooke, I can never think of Sir Fred without recalling the making of the film *Valentino*, starring Rudolf Nureyev, which was largely shot on location at his home on the Fylde – that is the sort of man of substance he was. In return for the use of his house, Sir Fred was guest of honour at the world première of the finished product in Blackpool. He was already around 90, and *Valentino* was not a high-water mark in cinema history, so he spent much of the evening nodding happily on the front row, only to wake up at the precise moment that Nureyev – contrary to all his instincts, as we now know – was doing energetic and unspeakable things to his leading lady on the baronial dining-table. 'Good grief,' said Sir Fred, 'I ate my breakfast off that.'

Borough had spent most of their history getting similar treatment from the rest of the Rugby League to that which Michelle Phillips (for it was she) was getting, in simulated technicolour, from Nureyev. They had, however, one brief, delicious experience of turning the tables. In what was then the Player's No. 6 Trophy in 1976–77, Borough beat Barrow, Halifax, Workington at Workington, and Leigh, in a dense Blackpool fog, in the semi-final. *The Evening Gazette*'s picture of the side walking out for the final against Castleford at Salford is as dazzling as any black-and-white photo could be. As if determined to outshine his team's tangerine-black-and-white, Borough's coach, Jim Crellin, is wearing flares, an eight-inch check jacket and kipper tie. Spectators are shielding their eyes.

Blackpool lost, of course – it wasn't that much of a fairy-tale.

But they went down with great credit by only 15–25, and 'Smiler' Allen, the Borough hooker, shared the man-of-the-match prize with Gary Stephens. One of the small delights of a career writing about the game since then was being able to extract an admission from John Joyner, when Castleford next appeared in what was by then the Regal Trophy final in 1994, that Borough had given them an infinitely tougher time than Wigan.

It is in the nature of these unlikely moments of glory, however, that they can often usher in even worse times than those which made the idea of any glory so unlikely in the first place. So it was at Blackpool. The team slid down the table very much like Ms Phillips, finishing with only Doncaster below them. Half of the side that played Castleford drifted away through being sold, lost or mislaid – among them Allen and the second division's player-of-the-year, Ged Marsh – and Crellin resigned.

Matters were no better the following season. Under their new coach Joe Egan – doomed, long after he receives his free bus pass, to be known as 'Young Joe' – Borough couldn't win a game. I had, by this time, become a reporter on *The West Lancashire Evening Gazette*, a truly remarkable organisation in those days, in the shadow of Blackpool Tower. And the perk that went with this job, if you wanted it, which no one else did, was the opportunity to cover the Borough home and away. But that wasn't enough for me. For some reason that I can't fully understand even now, I needed to immerse myself in the club. It was perhaps a variant of the primitive urge that sends the truly depressed to Blackpool to throw themselves under the wheels of trams. It wasn't enough to watch the Borough and write about them. I had to train with them, I had virtually to live at Borough Park, sections of which I spent the journalists' strike that winter painting.

Some of that handiwork would probably still be visible to this day, because I very much doubt whether it has been painted since. Even in those days before Borough were scandalously driven out of their natural home, the Park that bore their name was a highly effective antidote to the idea that there is necessarily any glamour in professional sport. There was certainly little glamour in training there without any floodlights on a winter's night, with only the occasional patch of semi-gloom created by the lights in the directors' tea bar to suggest where your team-mates might be. No wonder that the set moves rarely came off when people could actually see each other.

And then, breaking into that darkness just as though Red Rum or Diana Dors had flicked the switch to turn on the Illuminations, there was Albert Fearnley. Blackpool Borough were not unused to men of Rugby League pedigree around the place: Brian Bevan and Billy Boston had, after all, ended their playing days there – although I can't pretend that the Last Resort saw the best of them – and Tommy Bishop pretty well launched his career beside the seaside. But having a big wheel like Albert steering the ship was something new. As a player, he had been part of the Halifax pack of the 1950s which he now claims proudly to have been the dirtiest ever. As manager, not merely coach, of Bradford Northern, he had directed their revival in the early 1970s. He was still – good grief – national coach. He was, on the face of it, an extraordinary capture for a club like Blackpool.

Soon after his arrival, he and I went on a prolonged drinking session at a sea-front pub and he convinced me that, in some mysterious way, we were going to get Blackpool Borough into the first division. The details weren't exactly explicit – Albert always asked Blackpool barmen 'Is it strong?' before committing himself to any particular beverage, and what we were drinking that day certainly was – but the approximate manner in which it was meant to work was this: he was to provide me with vast quantities of exciting stories with which to make my fame and fortune; I was to make sure that all this assorted fact, fiction and bullshit got headline treatment in *The West Lancs Evening Gazette* and beyond; and we would thus make the Borough (a) popular, and (b) successful. With the Irish Sea thundering towards us in foaming waves from one direction, and the extra-strong lager doing much the same from the other, it all seemed perfectly feasible.

Of course, he would need a few players, although Borough did have some already. There was a minibus-load from Wigan who bombed up the M6 and the M55 for matches and training sessions in the dark. Apart from the occasional jewel like Jimmy Molyneux, however, they did not tend to be the upper-crust of piedom, more like the crumbs. It was a syndrome that imposed its own limitations as well. A decision once had to be made not to sign a particular Wigan-based player because the bus was already full.

As befits a man of national stature, Albert spread his net wider, and his first signing was his most inspired and crucial. Bakary Diabira had been a bright young prospect at Bradford, albeit one with unusual antecedents. His mum was from Hull, his dad was from Dakar in Senegal, and Bak had been born in Bordeaux. Albert had first signed him as a Northern colt from a youth club on Humberside, and he had clearly been a favourite protégé. You only had to see him with a rugby ball in his hands to understand why. You will have heard of players who could almost make the ball talk. There was no 'almost' about it with Diabira. I'll swear that at one session the Mitre Multiplex – if that's what we were playing with in those days – piped up and pleaded, 'For God's sake give it a rest, Bak!' He could not only thread a needle with a pass, he could embroider one of those Victorian samplers with 'Home Sweet Home' and nail it above the fireplace. Before a match, he would sit around casually spinning the ball on the index finger of one hand, roll it down one arm, round the back of his neck and along the other arm, finally spinning it with equal non-chalance on the other index finger. It wasn't a case of showing off, either. He was merely getting to know an old friend once more, the way that you or I might grab the ball in two fists, throw it against the changing-room wall and, with luck, catch it. I still have no doubts about it: Bak Diabira had, by a distance, the best hands I've ever seen on a rugby player.

The knees, regrettably, were something else entirely. When you saw them, devoid of their layers of strapping and protection, it was all too obvious why a lot of his fancy handling routines were performed sitting down. They were only recognisable as knees because they happened to be half-way up his legs. There was nothing that was easily identifiable as a knee-cap. Indeed, it seemed that everything that could be removed, had been removed. It had not been a job for surgeons; it had been one for house clear-ance specialists. The souvenirs he had of all this activity were scars that looked like maps of the Blackpool tramway network in the days when it consisted not just of one route down the prom, but also included numerous branch lines to the suburbs and the Fylde countryside.

Those knees had wrecked his career – in fact, there was enough damage there to wreck several careers – after just a handful of first-team appearances at Bradford. So it came as some-thing of a surprise to Bak when his phone rang one night and a vaguely familiar, gravelly voice said, 'It's your dad!'

'My dad's in Africa.'

'Not that dad! Your proper dad! Albert!'

Naturally, he told Albert that his knees were more knackered than ever, and there was absolutely no chance of him making a comeback, certainly not for a club with no money and no prospects, on the wrong side of the country. Equally naturally, he was in the home changing-room at Borough Park the following week, resplendent in tangerine-black-and-white and yards of elastic bandage, spinning a ball on his fingertip.

It would be an exaggeration to say that Fearnley and Diabira immediately transformed Blackpool Borough. In fact, the club ended the 1977–78 season in a familiar position – one off the bottom of the second division, with only Halifax below them, and perennial strugglers like Huyton, Doncaster and Batley all above. But a team was taking shape. Alongside Diabira and serviceable players who were already on the books, such as Molyneux, Paul Gamble, Jimmy Hamilton and Doug Robinson, Fearnley spread trifling amounts of money around the League to procure players who could, in the immortal phrase, 'do a job' for him. There was Norman Turley, a beanpole full-back from Warrington, who became a highly-effective loose forward. Norman, then as now, rarely shut up and he formed a great double act off the field with Alan Fairhurst, a clever stand-off from Leigh, who never spoke. There was Corcoran, there was Peter Clarke – as mean an hombre as ever hooked – and there was Norman Brelsford, a veteran winger whose little girls were always there in perfectly-matched Sunday best whenever their dad was playing. Albert specialised in picking up good players who were cheap because they were, to all intents and purposes, crocked, but who could be patched up to do the proverbial job. Tony Redford was one in that mould: he had wrecked his back, maudlin as it sounds, carrying a coffin after the Golborne Colliery Disaster. I saw him in South Africa last year, and his back is really bad these days – but he did a job.

Looking back on it now, what an astonishing job they all did. The season didn't begin all that well, with a home defeat by Swinton, followed by a loss at Dewsbury. By far the highlight of September, in fact, was an unlikely visit from the 1978 Kangaroos, something that could be put down jointly to the influence of Reg Parker, a former Great Britain tour manager and a Blackpool director, and the general feeling that it might suit the Aussies to start off with a nice training canter by the seaside. What a mis-calculation that almost turned out to be, when the Borough went into a shock lead (Diabira, drop-goal) before the tourists sneaked home 39–1, with memorable performances from the likes of Steve

Rogers, Bob Fulton and Les Boyd – who had a typical Les Boyd-style confrontation with Molyneux. Ian Heads's history of Australian tours, *The Kangaroos*, notes that 'Bak Diabira, a black half-back with a cracked shoulder and a wonky knee, produced some magic for the locals.' Only one wonky knee? Come on now. He would have given his right arm to have only one wonky knee.

I find even now that writing about matches during Borough's *annus mirabilis* makes it very difficult to avoid slipping into partisan mode, the one-eyed stance that is the stock-in-trade of local sports journalism. If I had this disease in a more acute form than the average hack, then I blame Fearnley. I did things I shouldn't have done. I sat in for his pre-match motivational diatribes and, had I thought it was worth a single extra point on the scoreboard, I would gladly have marched up to the press box and ripped off the head of the unsuspecting reporter from *The York Evening Press* or *The Halifax Evening Courier*.

Memory can play tricks, though. My recollection of these times was that I was unfailingly supportive to the side, whatever their fluctuations of form. Browsing through the cuttings library at *The Evening Gazette* for the purpose of this chapter, however, I discovered that, when they let me down, I could be as bitter and vitriolic as a spurned suitor. I could recall having a bit of a dig at one or two players. I could even remember being hit by something that felt like a meteorite one starry training night at Borough Park and coming round to find a prop I had never particularly rated asking me: 'Whose soddin' place do you reckon's in danger now, then?' But what surprised me was the feeling of having been betrayed that seeps out of some of the match reports before they got into their stride that season. I'd fallen for my own propaganda: I expected them to win – not just occasionally, but on a regular basis.

The most surprising thing was that they went very close to fulfilling that wholly unrealistic expectation. Between defeats by what was then known as New Hunslet on 15 October and 15 April, Borough lost just one League match. That isn't quite as impressive as it sounds, because it includes seven weeks without a game on either side of Christmas – and we think the fixtures are a mess now – several draws and a Challenge Cup defeat by Dewsbury. But it was impressive enough. Even the defeat was a defeat in name only. I still bristle with indignation at the very thought of it. The record books might say that Hull FC won every one of their 26 matches in the second division that season, but they speak with forked tongue. They might also relate that Hull beat the Borough 14–13 at the Boulevard in their closest game of the campaign. But those who were there know that Blackpool won and would have been officially recognised as having done so but for having a perfectly good try from Paul Machen disallowed on some flimsy pretext, and being caned for a seven-point try when Molyneux – the odd stand-up scrap with Les Boyd aside, the most gentlemanly of players – was unjustly accused of sliding in late on a try-scorer. Although this was only mid-November, Hull were already being tipped to go through the season unbeaten. For a Humbersider like Diabira, the disappointment of missing out on a long-delayed moment of triumph by such a narrow and unfair margin was too much. He wept inconsolably in the Boulevard changing sheds afterwards, and I didn't blame him.

That match was the one hiccup in a remarkable autumn and spring – we managed to side-step most of the winter – for the Borough. The Hull travesty apart, they showed a startling facility for snatching a win by a point or two or, failing that, scrambling away with a draw. The key to that ability to salvage a result was their mastery, unequalled before or since, of a neglected aspect of the game. People get very sniffy about drop-goals. They are wrong: drop-goals are one of the crowning glories of the game and, in second-division matches alone, Blackpool Borough popped over 36 of the little beauties. In all matches, the total was 42, with the main contributions coming from Turley, who landed 18 of the record 97 that punctuated a long and varied career, Fairhurst with 16, and Diabira with a modest but stylish six. Towards the end of the season, when the situation became a bit wobbly, Borough signed another drop-goal specialist, Colin North, and he duly chipped in too. It is many people's belief – and even Albert Fearnley remembers it this way – that Borough scored more drop-goals than tries that season. That isn't quite true, but it was a close-run thing, and there was plenty of sniffing and sneering as a result.

That didn't worry anyone at Borough Park one whit. Nobody there was going to start quibbling about how games were being won and, while you couldn't claim that they were being carried along on a wave of public frenzy, Borough's gates, according to their Silver Jubilee history, went up from 900 to 1,236. (This is the same brochure that won the Nobel Prize for Understatement when it commented that 'Mr Fearnley was also publicity-minded and got support through the local press'.) There were setbacks, like

Diabira breaking his nose, a disaster area of his anatomy I haven't mentioned so far, for the 14th time, and Jimmy Hamilton busting his leg at Bramley. That, believe it or not, denied him a trip to Australia on the 1979 Lions tour. It might sound unlikely that an unknown second-division prop, who couldn't even drop goals, could be a tourist, but this was the era of selection committees who operated under the motto of 'you pick one of mine, I'll pick one of yours', and Reg Parker had a bit of clout. Besides, Jimmy could hardly have done much worse than some players who did make the trip. It might have been worth taking him with his leg in plaster, but we will never know. What I do know is that, after his professional days, he lost around six stone and played stand-off for the Heysham Atoms in the North-West Counties. A man of stature, and the best cheat at training I ever saw.

These occasional problems on the field were nothing to what was going on off it. The club's financial affairs were under police investigation, and its chairman eventually went to jail. The bankers were screaming for the overdraft to be paid off, and only a loan from the Rugby League bought them off. And all was not well with Albert. There had been a warning when he needed to take time off with 'nervous exhaustion'. There was a court case, which did not result in conviction, after an incident at Shipley Baths. Worst of all, they made him a director at Borough, whereupon an accountant looked at the club's books and told him to get out of town quick. With five weeks of the season left, Fearnley resigned as director and team manager amid tired and emotional scenes at Borough Park and went to Keighley.

Bak Diabira took over the coaching – he had already been doing a good deal of it – of a side with an excellent chance of promotion to the first division. This was the era of four up from second to first at the end of every season; sadly for those who took that leap, it was also the era of four down the following year. That jammy Humberside team whose name I temporarily forget were clearly going up as unbeaten (huh!) champions, with New Hunslet, tuning-fork goalposts and all, trailing some distance behind in second place. The remaining deck-chairs on the *Titanic* were in dispute between York, Dewsbury, Borough and Halifax – vastly improved under the coaching of another volatile Yorkshireman, Maurice Bamford.

It was traditionally that time of year when teams who knew what would happen to them in the first division started to lose a few surprising matches. But Borough, hard-headed realists like Corcoran and Clarke aside, were too innocent, too inexperienced at reading the implications to make the necessary calculations. As a consequence, they went into the last month of the season extended by the severe winter looking certain to carry the tangerine-black-and-white into the upper echelon for the first (and only) time. As a strip, it undoubtedly deserved to be in the top flight. Although originally based on the tangerine worn by Matthews, Mortensen and Co. down the road at Blackpool FC, it was actually a far richer hue. It made the colour worn at Bloomfield Road and the muddy orange favoured by Holland look like fruit that had been left all winter on a greengrocer's shelves to fade and go manky. If the footballers wore tangerine, Borough's shade on the citric spectrum would be better described as Jaffa or Outspan – something with a lot more juice in its soul.

Rightly or wrongly, though, the world's smartest shirt isn't enough to ensure automatic promotion. You have to win a few matches too, and Borough's May schedule began with what should have been a routine trip to Doncaster. In the bad old days (i.e., anything more than six months before), Borough had always been able to console themselves with the thought that, however bad they got, they were never quite as bad as Doncaster. It wasn't simply that Doncaster had so often cushioned Blackpool by getting in between them and the hard, flinty floor at the bottom of the second division. It was also the way that Tatters Field (before it was transformed into Tattersfield) made Borough Park look like the Houston Astrodome. On my first visit there with Borough the previous season, I had asked about the whereabouts of the press box and was told that I would have to hang on a minute because they were in the process of evicting a family of gypsies who had taken up residence. I got in eventually, but the lingering aroma of baked hedgehog was off-putting in the extreme. Along with Alt Park, Huyton, where I once saw the local scallies steal the corner-flags during a match, it was a place we could feel superior about, so it was perhaps inevitable that we should go there on a Monday night, luminous in our promotion-seeking Outspan-ebony-and-ivory, and get beaten 8–11.

A clear case, you might suppose, of the Borough climbing too high and getting vertigo and nosebleeds as they contemplated struggling vainly to cling to an even higher ledge the following season. But, in truth, they didn't have to try to play badly that night. They were just naturally wretched, and even the clothes-peg sellers and fortune-tellers shunned them. Despite that, there was an atmosphere on the coach back to Blackpool reminiscent of Carnival in Rio, Mardi Gras in New Orleans, or Glasgow holiday fortnight without the violence. So frisky was the mood that one player, now a grave and respected eminence within the game, was stripped naked and had all his clothes, socks and shoes included, thrown out of the window on the M6. Disappointment can affect men in strange ways. The victim himself reacted by tip-toeing to the front of the bus and – presumably for a dare, although I've never been sure – thrusting part of his person into the ear of a very elderly director, who had been fast asleep but suffered a very rude awakening. The name of the perpetrator is one of the two I shall leave out of this account in order to protect the guilty. The other is the player who handed out little blue pills before games; pills which, when taken in combination with the bottle of Cyprus cream sherry that Cliff Darbyshire always packed with his kit – I don't think they can touch him for that – might not have made you play any better, but certainly stopped you worrying about it.

But I digress. This mighty team of which I sing had gone to Doncaster and lost. Three days later, they went to Halifax and lost again. Mick Murphy, the globe-trotting prop with the French moustache who had been talked out of retirement to replace Hamilton, was so disgusted with his form that he promptly went back into retirement. Among the other good excuses for failing to win promotion were injuries to Fairhurst, Gamble, Clarke and several others – including, predictably and most seriously, Diabira. It was generally acknowledged that winning their last three games would be beyond them and that their promotion dream would be quietly put to sleep at York the following Sunday. Instead, they went there and won 18–14, with Murphy un-retiring once more, a previously unconsidered Maori called Dave Bristow having a stormer at scrum-half, and Turley dropping three goals. Even better, promotion rivals Dewsbury suffered a typically fishy result by losing at Huyton, which meant the Borough merely needed to win their last two games, both at home, against Halifax and Whitehaven, to take the great leap into the unknown. Halifax were beaten 11–3, with Murphy again doing the damage in the forwards, and only Whitehaven stood in the path of the Tangerine Machine.

By this stage, however, the secret was out. The bizarre possibility of Blackpool being promoted had reached the ears of the game's establishment – and establishment, from where we stood, meant everyone except us, Doncaster and Huyton. Ray Dutton, the former Widnes and Great Britain full-back who was then player-coach at Whitehaven, put the prevailing view of the 'haves' neatly into words: he hoped that his mob would beat Blackpool and stop them going up, 'because they would make the first division a mockery'. Typing that phrase 15 years later gives me a surge of indignation matched only by recollections of that bloody travesty at Hull. To Borough that Sunday in late May, it was worth a couple of extra drop-goals at the very least.

I can remember very little of that afternoon, beyond the stark fact that Borough won 22–9. I had spent the morning fretting not about whether Blackpool could squeeze into the first division, but about how to squeeze all my earthly possessions into one suitcase and one old training hold-all. Just like a few of the canny, unromantic old pros at this stage of a promotion season, I'd already decided that I wasn't going up with them and I wasn't staying in Britain with Margaret Thatcher as Prime Minister. Oh yes, I'd felt like pulling the plug on such a minor enterprise as working my way round the world, but I'd fought off the temptation. (The paper had actually advertised my job covering Borough, and nobody wanted it.) That Sunday afternoon is a blur of charges for the try-line and last-minute dashes to the station, of note-taking and leave-taking. Diabira, still sidelined by shoulder, knee, nose or all three, was carried gingerly round Borough Park by fans. By fans! I could remember the time, not much more than a year before, when there weren't enough of them to carry his bandages, let alone the man himself. They sang 'One Bak Diabira, There's Only One Bak Diabira' to the tune of 'Guantanamera'. They worked their way through the whole team, in fact, although 'One Billy Lomax . . .' didn't have quite the same ring.

One last match report filed, this time for the *front* page, and I was in the queue that wound around Blackpool North Station in huge, end-of-holiday spirals. I didn't have the one thing that I'd promised myself I would get – a genuine, sweat-soaked, tangerine-black-and-white shirt. I had to make do with a sadly-faded tangerine specimen from one of the kit's aberrant phases until, transported to America by Freddie Laker, I bought a Denver Broncos jersey because it was the nearest thing I could get.

I did carry something worth having, though. Albert might have decamped to Keighley – soon to take Diabira with him, incidentally – but he was still an influential bod in the world of Rugby League. I had thought a letter of recommendation from him might open a few doors, and I read it on Laker's Skytrain. 'David Hadfield is a very knowledgeable person on Rugby League football,' he began, lying from the outset. It got worse. After tributes to my monumental integrity and match-winning performances in the 'A' team, it seemed to me that this was a testimonial which was designed not so much to open doors as to kick them down. He could not, however, end without a reference to one night out, when I had made the mistake of drinking at his rhythm and had narrowly avoided arrest and disgrace when apprehended on Whitegate Drive. 'Unfortunately,' he concluded, 'he does have a tendency to pee down grids in the middle of the street.'

I folded it and put it away. And that, half-way to New York, was that.

I phoned Albert Fearnley at his present home in the Rugby League hotbed of Felixstowe to compare notes for this piece. It happened to be his 70th birthday. 'That promotion season?' he said. 'We were robbed at Hull, weren't we? Jimmy Molyneux never touched that bloke.'

Years after that season, I was asked to indulge in the harmless pastime of picking my 'dream team'. Molyneux was alongside Mark Graham in the second row; Diabira elbowed pretenders like Peter Sterling and Alex Murphy out of the scrum-half position. I realise now that I was making ridiculous selections and that I got the side hopelessly wrong.

I should have picked Fairhurst, Turley and Corcoran as well.

GETTING WORKED UP WATCHING BAMBI

Fulham 1985–86

Huw Richards

You might call it *The Year of Living Dangerously* if Peter Weir had not already annexed the title for his film. But then, living dangerously has been the characterising habit of Fulham/London Crusaders. More exceptional were those seasons that might instead have been subtitled *Years of Living with a Modicum of Security*.

But they were never nearer the edge than this time. And not only Fulham. Swansea City FC, for more than 60 years a genetic defect passed down the male line of the Richards family, also expired briefly just before Christmas 1985. To lose one favourite team may be classed as misfortune, but losing two smacks of being terminally jinxed. Slightly different outcomes to the crises at both Chiswick Polytechnic Ground and Vetch Field could have launched a new variety of sports blackmailer penning letters like this:

Dear Mr Lindsay,
    I am a former supporter of Fulham RLFC and, following their demise, I am seeking a new Rugby League club to follow. You may also be interested to know that I am a former supporter of

Swansea City FC. Wigan are among the clubs I now have under consideration, but I would be willing for a small consideration to follow Hull Kingston Rovers.

Yours etc . . .

Subsequent London managements do indeed appear to have secured survival by not entirely dissimilar tactics, although their implicit threat was that of expiring embarrassingly on the front steps of Chapeltown Road, and thus ending League in London. But the mood was different in 1985. Southend and Bridgend had been axed in the close-season, and the League's attitude to expansion echoed Churchill's immortal order: 'Give all possible help short of actual assistance.'

It was hard to imagine a world without Swansea City, but all too easy to visualise one without Fulham – you only needed to remember back before 1980. And growing up in Shropshire in the 1960s and 1970s was hardly conducive to expecting to be able to watch live League, even without the inbuilt suspicion of the code that comes with Welsh ancestry. This, after all, was the code that had denied Keith Jarrett and Maurice Richards to Wales and stopped Stuart Ferguson from scoring masses of points for Swansea – a view which conveniently overlooks the reality that the main losers of the schism of 1895 had been England. In a parallel universe, Twickenham has no doubt had Alex Murphy rather than Nigel Starmer-Smith at half-back (and, if it is genuinely a better world, there will be a guarantee that neither is allowed ever to enter a commentary box).

But while there was no youthful grounding in League and its traditions of the sort contemporaries in Leeds, Whitehaven and Widnes were receiving, there was always television and the inimitable tones of Eddie Waring. Yes, I know that Reg Bowden's view that Uncle Eddie 'has done for this game what Cyril Smith has done for hang-gliding' was one of the milder comments. But, as outsider rather than *aficionado*, I enjoyed his commentaries, whose humour and infectious enjoyment of the game did as much as the quality of action on show to suggest that League would repay attention. The suspicion remains that the real counts against him were *It's a Knockout* and Mike Yarwood rather than anything inherent in his commentaries.

Fuller initiation came on 15 August 1975 – the day on which Phil Edmonds spun the Australians out at Headingley. The first live match: Cas versus Wakefield Trinity in a pre-season friendly, result long-forgotten. But, even to a non-initiate, it was obvious that John Joyner could play a bit.

A live competitive match had to wait a further five years, when a fortuitous combination of circumstances allowed me to attend Fulham's fabled debut, the 24–5 beating of bemused Wigan – although this, like the Second World War, is one of those events whose real winner becomes less clear as time goes on. A seed of affection for the new London club was undoubtedly planted that day, but took time to grow. Living first in Oxford, then Cardiff, limited further visits to Craven Cottage, although one weekend in London coincided happily with a match against Doncaster. The game itself was less notable than a Donny team sheet which took cosmopolitanism to impressive lengths by the inclusion of Sygfusson and Pflaster, and the casual precision of the high kick that brought a letter crashing down from the masthead on the Eric Miller Stand – 'possibly the first time, but certainly not the last, that somebody kicked L out of Fulham,' in the words of fan, Dave Ballheimer.

Those years even provided a rival for my nascent League affections. My next Fulham game would be the infamous 'Battle of Stamford Bridge', in which Tom David broke the record for most tries scored by a prop in one season, and the other 25 players combined in a collective bid for the 80-minute punch-throwing, foul-play and ungentlemanly-conduct record – and I was there as a Cardiff supporter. Still, it is perhaps as well that the Cardiff Dragons experiment failed – it felt more than a little schizoid to regard Cardiff City as proof of the earthly existence of Evil Incarnate on Saturdays, and then to support them on the following day.

Fulham also provided first opportunities to report the game – these three matches establishing credentials which might not have impressed *The Halifax Courier* or *The Wigan Observer*, but which were regarded as heaven-sent by Hayter's Sports Reporting Agency. Largely staffed by Londoners, they were inordinately grateful to have a new recruit who claimed to understand this strange game they played down at Craven Cottage and, what is more, was prepared to go and report it on Sundays. One thing led to another: first *The Rugby Leaguer* needed a Fulham correspondent; then the match programme needed someone to ghost the manager's column and write the away team profile and, finally, a new editor. All in the space of two years – albeit a progression firmly rooted in the principle enunciated by a *Daily Star* copy-taker, who explained the need to nominate a Fulham 'Star Man' after a particularly dire performance: 'You've got to give it to somebody.'

The programmes for 1985–86 sit red-bound on my bookshelf – a long-dormant intention to preserve them finally fulfilled in late 1993 when the Open University's regulations for the submission of doctoral theses forced a visit to a bindery. The conjunction of Ph.D. thesis and club programme was more appropriate than it might seem. The thesis concerned *The Daily Herald*, a newspaper that attracted intense loyalty from dedicated supporters, but was plagued by the financial consequences of its inability to win a con-sistently large following, and forced into endless short-term crisis management measures. Only a failure of nerve about the likely reactions of academic examiners stopped the inclusion of Fulham/London Crusaders RLFC in the acknowledgements. Still, if there is a better training in empathy for enterprises suffer-ing such problems than monitoring the club over a decade, I have yet to hear of it.

Like any contemporary document, the programmes bring back memories. In part, naturally enough, of the process of pro-duction – shuffling papers on the kitchen table, chatting on the phone to manager Roy Lester on his return from away matches, turning those conversations into his column, and gently remind-ing contributors of their deadlines. Then the trip to our printers in West Hampstead and discussion of lengths and layout. They did a quality job – Colin Welland said that, while most League pro-grammes appeared to be printed on recycled toilet paper, ours was 'more like *World of Interiors*'. Though it is open to question whether *World of Interiors* would have retained the same centre-spread feature for an entire season.

But what it really brings back is the extraordinary atmos-phere of mid-1980s Fulham – a weird blend of rootlessness and wild enthusiasm summed up beautifully by *Open Rugby* humorist Arthur Ardbottom: 'I hear some coaches are showing their teams *Rambo* to get them motivated. Those Fulham fans could get worked up watching *Bambi*.' Fulham's attitude towards League was not unusual, but its context was. Other club identities are built around the collective lives and memories of their host communi-ties – the common experience of living and working in or near Bramley, Leigh or Whitehaven, and the memories and legends passed down through generations of supporters. Identities so created are what rescue clubs when they get into trouble: those roots generate public reaction, and wealthy local men alleged to have gained illicit entry to matches by crawling under fences in their impoverished youth emerge as saviours.

But there are no such roots at Fulham. London is too large, impersonal and uninterested; while *The Evening Standard*'s abysmal attitude may suggest otherwise, there is no London conspiracy against League, merely indifference. Most Londoners simply don't know what Rugby League is. If there was a common core of memory at Fulham it related to Johnny Haynes. (Fulham FC season ticket-holders were given tickets for the Wigan game in 1980. Those who came, saw and were conquered included Roy and Barbara Close – who bought the RL operation from Fulham FC in 1984 – and Supporters' Club stalwarts, Ron and Mo Snares.)

Nor were there alternative sources of League lore ready to recount tall tales about the feats of Billy Boston or Clive Churchill and of great teams of the past. There were relatively few transplanted northerners assuaging an exile's itch for Widnes by spending alternate Sundays at the Polytechnic Ground; and the hoped-for invasion by hordes of Aussies from their bed-sits in Earl's Court had never happened at Craven Cottage, three stops down the District Line, so was hardly likely to happen when a far more awkward journey to the wilds of Chiswick was involved. Colin Welland was a regular, and club sponsor Richard Lawton's father Alfred could remember watching Wagstaff and Rosenfeld at pre-1914 Fartown. But they were the exceptions.

Most Fulham fans might never have heard of Billy Boston or the Yorkshire League or realised that Wakefield Trinity were once the best team in the country. But many were prepared to travel several hundred miles by coach to support their side, then give up their summer weekends to get the Polytechnic Ground fit for second-division rugby.

Too bad there was no budding sports sociologist or active club marketing and commercial operation to run the survey which might have told us who the club's fans were, and what it was that had captivated them. But the attractions of the game itself were reasonably clear. At the same time as enjoying the devil's advocate role in debates between supporters of rugby's two codes, a Union fan could not but be impressed by League's simple directness, the quality of handling and tackling, and the virtual guarantee of entertainment. Over a decade, there have been few irredeemably dreadful games – even if Fulham/Crusaders' performances have too often fallen into that category.

It wasn't just the game, but the warm, welcoming atmosphere around it. Soccer practised exclusion, with everyone confined to their hermetic roles – press in the press box, players on the pitch, directors in their box, coaches and managers in the dugout, and fans on the terraces – never meeting except in the ludicrous ritual of the post-match press conference, wherein managers gave clichéd answers to predictable questions to be misquoted into shock-horror headlines for the following morning's papers. At Rugby League you were allowed to report the game rather than rehashing quotes, and if you wanted to talk to a fan, a player, a coach or a committee member at Fulham all you had to do was walk into the bar after the game. There was a fair chance of finding them all in the same group.

Earlier in the 1980s, League had been promoted as the 'Man's Game For All The Family' and, while the sparse crowds at the Polytechnic Ground doubtless sheltered the odd husband escaping his family on Sunday afternoon, they also included numerous couples – not only the Closes and Snareses, but the Barlows, the Lambs, the Warrens, and several other family groups. The common denominator was enthusiasm. As supporter Sandra Barlow put it: 'There are a lot of people here with whom I've nothing in common but Fulham, but they're the best and dearest friends I've got.' In default of an underlying identity, the motley, diffuse crew who made up Fulham's following found one in themselves.

There were never enough of them, of course. The club appeared to have dropped into London's collective memory hole when it moved from Craven Cottage. The ease with which the capital loses sight of things was brought home to Roy Lester by telephone calls at home from people wanting to know where Fulham were now playing. Lester was understandably nonplussed that they could locate a private number in Leigh, but mislay an entire rugby club in London.

Even today, the confession in London of an interest in League is liable to evoke the response: 'Whatever happened to Fulham? Are they still playing? Not at Craven Cottage any more, are they?' If the club had received a fiver for every conversation of this sort over the last decade, its finances would have been the envy rather than the despair of Chapeltown Road.

Fulham's fans were a working illustration of the proposition that there is no enthusiast like a convert. Possibly the most spectacular example was Bob Evans, a City worker who had never even seen a League match until he walked past Craven Cottage and had his curiosity aroused when he saw that the visitors were York, his birthplace. Fulham by themselves rapidly proved incapable of satisfying his new interest; by the mid-1980s, he was so ubiquitous a figure on northern grounds that he was suspected of the ability to attend three games at once. Visiting Sydney in 1987, I was introduced to every League person I met as 'a friend of Bob Evans'. Nobody needed any further explanation.

And the hard core of converts thrived on adversity: the more Fulham struggled and their fellow-Londoners declined to take notice, the more determined they were to sustain the club. Roy Lester got it right when he compared Fulham to a religious minority. Quite how right would be shown in later years, when the club started to display the downside of religious minorities – schism, factionalism and internecine warfare. But at this time the positive side – warmth, boundless enthusiasm and common purpose – had the upper hand, underpinning the supporters' faith that the game could be made to work in London.

It was a questionable faith, though. Sports habitually disseminate down from rich to poor between and within nations: hence the vogue for American football and the spread of soccer from upper-class Victorian England to the world. It was hard to see a game which emanated from and identified with the industrial North colonising the wealthier half of the country. The subsequent choice of 'Crusaders' as the club name seemed cruelly apt – the original Crusaders had after all captured Jerusalem on their first outing, just as promptly lost it, and then spent the next two centuries devising more and more improbable and disastrous ways of failing to get it back.

But theories are made to be disproved, and I had in any case come to like the game for itself. And, while the northerner who enjoys League is likely to have a choice of allegiances within a 20-mile radius, for the Londoner it was Fulham or nothing – which created a rather strong vested interest in the club's success. If the demise of Cardiff Blue Dragons had averted one form of schizophrenia, reporting Fulham imposed another. Half-fan, half-reporter, the allegedly detached and analytical observer constantly battling for supremacy with the Fulham fan biting his nails as they held on to a narrow lead. The nail-biter had plenty of outings: 16 of 20 home second-division matches between November 1984 and mid-January 1986 were settled by 10 points or less. Partisanship wrestled with the temptation to over-compensate – not that partisanship mattered overmuch in *The Leaguer* when every club had its own correspondent, few of whom were noted for their rigorous objectivity.

The Leaguer problem, in pre-fax days, was deadlines which required the despatch of copy before the weekend. Thus, in September 1984, Roy Lester gave his view of newly-appointed assistant player-coach Ken Green: 'He's a great bloke, a model professional, and a wonderful influence on our younger players.' All perfectly true, although its impact may have been somewhat diminished by Ken getting sent off on the intervening Sunday. And, in 1985–86, it seemed a player had only to be featured in *The Leaguer* to disappear from the side – returning Welsh international forward, Martin Herdman, fell victim so comprehensively to the Curse of *The Leaguer* that he never played for the club again.

Most articles were based around interviews with Roy Lester, the archetypal good pro turned coach and manager. Tim Lamb, a sane and sensible chief executive during the troubled late 1980s, would comment: 'Part of the trouble with this club is that there are too many people who think that they are Fulham.' It was never suggested that Roy suffered from this particular malady, but nobody ever had a better claim.

He had been the first player signed by Fulham – and, much as Sheffield's first signing, Daryl Powell, has personified the immense virtues of that admirable club, so Roy epitomised the best of those early Fulham days. He inherited the managership in June 1984, at the point when the unquestioning faith of the early years had been battered by Fulham FC's abandonment of League, Roy Bowden's departure, and the court case which declared the bulk of the squad free agents. Left with just four players, Roy put together a squad that ended 1984–85 in seventh place in the second division.

But his impact was far wider than being just another good coach. When a club has roots as shallow as Fulham's and suffers the knocks it took in the summer of 1984, it needs more than just results. Roy Lester's decency and humanity helped restore the club's faith in itself. The fans had idolised Bowden, but their response to Roy had an extra element of personal affection and empathy.

They recognised a fellow-spirit. Many of them volunteer workers for the club, they responded to the lack of pretension showed by a manager who was happy to pick up a mask and welding torch when the public address system needed repairing. The dedicated professional, devoted to getting the basics of the game right, was also a romantic who found inspiration in the challenge of taking the game to previously uncharted areas. He had an unashamed love of Rugby League – nobody since Michael Colin Cowdrey has been given more appropriate initials – and would gladly share that enthusiasm with anybody. This made him immensely approachable to fans and press – our Sunday-night conversations frequently turned into 40-minute discussions on the club and the game as a whole. They were hugely enjoyable, stimulating exchanges as well as great experience, for Roy had the insights of a sensitive, thoughtful man. For me, without much of a League background, they were a sort of second-chance education in the game. If I ever moved from remedial literacy to GCSE standard, those conversations with Roy were the main reason.

As half-fan, half-reporter, it is too easy to identify uncritically with someone you like and respect. But, even in hindsight, there was little to criticise – hardly a poor signing, one or two inspired ones, and acceptable results. And as one fan put it: 'I don't know if he's a great coach, but I do think he's a great man.'

A long-distance coach as well. Not least of Fulham's oddities was that the squad, still northern-based, had to travel much further for home than away matches. Roy himself had travelled 25,000 miles on club business during the 1984–85 season. There were, importantly, some familiar faces among his fellow long-distance travellers.

Fan loyalties focus largely on a club's identity rather than on its players. Sandra Barlow was typically perceptive a season and two near-closures later, when a vastly-changed Fulham side opened their Chiswick season by going down 14–62 to Sheffield Eagles, saying: 'Most of them are complete strangers, but they were all heroes to us today, just for being Fulham.' That principle would be tested to destruction in future seasons, as fans found the opposition more familiar than their own team in early-season outings. It never was too clear who was playing during the Ross Strudwick era, when the ingenuity applied to import quotas led to one forward ostensibly changing colour between games.

But continuity reinforces identification. So there was a warm welcome for established favourites such as Charlie Jones, the epitome of the 100-per-center, and Steve Mills, an elusive winger of inoffensive temperament – except at Batley, where he was sent off twice. Perhaps it was something to do with the slope. These two had been at Fulham since the Craven Cottage era, together with Widnesian Tony Kinsey, on his day a passable Harry Pinner impersonator; Welsh wing, Adrian Cambriani, teenage golden boy of the first season; and Alan Dearden, last reminder of the playing roots in the great Widnes sides of the 1970s. Another survivor, giant prop Shaun Hoare, had one of those careers cursed by 'potential'. Fulham had spent £30,000 on him – taking him in preference to Henderson Gill – and there were occasional hints of latent talent and power. He certainly looked formidable enough, but was maybe too mild-mannered to be a top forward – his name had been misspelt Sean for three years at Fulham before he was moved to protest. Much less retiring was skipper Harold Henney, a Cumbrian always termed 'larger than life', and quite substantial in reality, who had revitalised a fading career at 33. Similarly venerable but even tougher was Ken Green, who prepared for one match by falling off the roof of a house.

Among the younger players, Chris Wilkinson, a slight but resilient outside-half who had been snapped up from a pub side in division seven of the North-West Counties League, was the team's goal and tactical kicker. Centre, Frank Matthews, had been the victim of a broken leg and a car break-in on the previous season's New Year's Day visit to Southend Invicta, while Norman Barrow had yet to learn that his destiny would be a career with Runcorn Highfield. We were still somewhere short of the time when Swinton secretary, Steve Moyse, would compare the sounds coming from the Fulham dressing-room to rehearsals for the remake of *Crocodile Dundee*, let alone the 'backpacker club' days of the early 1990s. But the Aussies were beginning to arrive.

Injury ruled out George Bryan, an amiable utility back from Queensland who had left his mark in club lore by sustaining frost-bite in an excruciatingly ice-bound cup-tie at Halifax and saying: 'I wouldn't mind if I hadn't rung home and been told that it is 102° in Mackay.' But scrum-half Michael Davis, a lethally incisive attacker unmatched until Mark Riley joined Crusaders in 1992, had returned together with Parramatta club-mate, Don Duffy – cheerful, friendly, relaxed, and invariable leader of the tackle count. So too had the diminutive prop, Andy Key, hero of a solicitous female fan who shrieked 'don't hit him, he's only little' whenever he was in possession. She need not have worried; he could look after himself.

They were joined by Glen Nissen, a Penrith youngster destined to win Most Valuable Player honours in a Sydney Grand Final, but never really effective during a five-month stay. More successful in the short term was Mick Glover, hooker and refugee from Bridgend, who was diagnosed by club doctor Mike Irani as suffering from a complaint rare in professional sportsmen: 'He's such a nice chap, he finds it difficult to generate real aggression.'

And, praise be, the demise of Southend sent us two Londoners. Bob Mordell was one of many Englishmen capped once at Union against Wales, but so long ago that most League followers had forgiven him. And Peckham builder, Frank Feighan, scorer of an immortal televised try against Castleford in Invicta's hopeful earlier days, would cap this effort for Fulham fans in the following season with a length-of-the-pitch interception in that massacre by Sheffield.

Others would arrive during the season. Classiest of these was blond Oldham back-rower Alan Platt – stylish, accomplished, and an excellent kicker. Most memorable was Dave Bullough, a tearaway forward signed from Bramley after a fund-raising campaign by the supporters. Dave showed excellent timing with a devastating first-half display on the afternoon when the fund was launched, but justified all too literally the campaign's 'Wanted!' posters by getting sent off three times in 16 appearances. And on-loan prop, Billy Platt, he of the General de Gaulle profile, who clearly wanted to sign and subsequently took out his rejection by invariably playing brilliantly against Fulham. One cup-tie a couple of years later was preceded by an only part-joking man-of-the-match panel debate: 'Shall we give it to Platty now, or wait till they've played?' And he won. Roy could have saved his successors a lot of trouble by signing him.

As important as players in establishing an identity is a proper home – and the Polytechnic Ground was Fulham's third (fourth if you counted a couple of games at Wealdstone FC). The previous season, the first post-Craven Cottage, had been spent in South London exile at Crystal Palace – a bit like the Manchester Arndale Centre, without the crowds and the charm.

The Polytechnic Ground itself was far from ideal. The grand-stand was a draughty relic of the days when ferro-concrete was considered aesthetically pleasing, there was uncovered grass on the other three sides, and it was a struggle to accommodate 1,000 on wet days. It was none too easy to get to, either – unless you were Tim Lamb, who lived just up the road. (Tim, ironically, would be instrumental in moving back to the unloved Palace a few years later.) It was certainly inadequate for first-division rugby, although what to do about first-division rugby and crowds regularly in four figures were unhappily to be academic issues for the rest of the 1980s. But it, and above all the second-floor bar that ran the length of the stand and hosted many a match-day post-mortem, felt like home in a way that the Palace could never be.

The previous season's seventh place from scratch created high expectations which looked justified when the first two second-division matches were won and Wigan were scared nearly to death in the Lancashire Cup at Central Park. Wigan's dominant start and finish were decisive but, for an hour in between, Fulham matched them, leading into the last 15 minutes. The Wigan fans were astonishingly generous and appreciative, perhaps taken in the same way I was – disbelieving for the first hour, then stricken by appalling tension in the final quarter as the possibility dawned that Fulham might just hold on. They didn't, but Roy Lester said it all in his column the following week: 'I was a proud man at Wigan.'

But then reality dawned. Batley's Carl Gibson exploited vulnerability to real pace with a hat-trick, and the fixture list generously allotted consecutive early-autumn clashes with division two's top five. Davis sparked only intermittently, Duffy was dogged by injury, and an honest, persevering team lacked the pace and power needed to break out of mid-table.

But there were still days when anything seemed possible. A team capable of collapsing dispiritedly against a solid but hardly inspired Bramley could also hold Leigh – on their way to several records – until the last minute, and demolish promotion-chasing Rochdale with a stunningly fluent first half on Australia Day. Still fondly recalled is the defeat of previously unbeaten Whitehaven. In the absence of a local derby, the Cumbrians, a mere 338½ miles away by rail, fulfilled the psychologically necessary role of hated rivals, sustained by the shared yo-yo syndrome that made them the only opponents common to all six seasons so far, and the rooted belief of our fans that Whitehaven was somewhere near Spitzbergen, only colder. Haven in turn regarded Fulham with the suspicion accorded anywhere you are likely to be ripped off. Maybe they had a point. With scores level in injury-time, Wilkinson sent Davis over in the corner. Far be it from me to suggest that the referee made a mistake, but our American foot-ball-conscious fans were unanimous in nominating Wilkinson 'quarter-back-of-the-year' for his interestingly-angled pass.

Mid-season, mid-table – and the onset of the winter freeze remembered for the way unfancied Halifax took a grip on the first-division title by playing through when others suffered postpone-ments and were eventually derailed by fixture pile-ups. Fulham were similarly afflicted. A home cup-tie against Barrow suffered multiple postponements and was eventually played, by League order, at Wigan. Barrow won 26–14. There was no second-division action at Chiswick for ten weeks – but the weather was only partly to blame.

It hardly took financial genius to recognise that the club was scarcely viable on gates of less than 1,000. But a phone call in early March still came as an immense shock: 'It says on Ceefax that Roy Close has decided to close Fulham – is this true?' YOU WHAT! All too true.

The next few weeks were a blur of telephone conversations, frantic speculation, and grasping at implausible straws. It was like waiting for news of a sick relative – you could persuade yourself that all this activity was helping, but it was really a matter of sitting tight and hoping for the Seventh Cavalry. In the midst of this came the match at Huddersfield, doomed to perpetual postponement until the players, in another Swansea parallel, offered – Davis apart – to play for nothing. At this distance, you can't blame Davis: a club may be life and death to fans, but it is an employer to the professional player. And how many of us love our employers? But, at the time, it seemed an affront to the collective spirit embodied in his team-mates' gesture (one illustration of the changed atmos-phere by late 1993 was the solid fan support for the players in dispute over unpaid wages in the period before the Broncos' take-over). Other end of the popular esteem scale was on-loan Warrington prop, Mal Yates. He had no stake in the club's future, and this was his only game for Fulham. But he played anyway, as did Frank Feighan – who promised to walk up the M1 to Fartown if there was no other way of getting there.

That wasn't necessary. But, in place of their normal coach, the bulk of the squad piled out of a battered black minibus. Were we really playing away? There was scarcely an unfamiliar face in the bar an hour before kick-off, and the roar of appreciation when Roy Lester, complete with club blazer and a slightly dazed expression, walked in must have disturbed Fartown's numerous ghosts. It would be his last match in charge.

The Fulham contingent of around 100, a quarter of the total crowd, assembled noisily in the venerable grandstand – their high spirits evoking genuine puzzlement in an elderly steward, who asked: 'What the 'eck are you closing for? We could do with some of this.'

But the whole Fulham experience was an education in the truth that enthusiasm can do only so much. The same went for a match memorable only for its circumstances. Fulham, borne on a wave of emotion, began well and Frank Feighan's try, forcing his way through tacklers to the line, was a classic of will-power over logic. But Huddersfield knew far better how to cope with a pitch that reflected their club's understandable nostalgia for the times around the First World War – any Ypres veteran will have recognised the conditions. The match was lost, 8–14.

And that, it appeared, was that. The following week's match was postponed and a closure meeting set for 1 April. The phone lines went on buzzing, but it was impossible not to feel that we were talking merely to keep our spirits up. But the Seventh Cavalry did arrive, in the shape of Paul Faires, the former Kent Invicta chairman. And the sense of a new era was confirmed by the initial decision that a northern-based squad was uneconomic, and that the team should be run from Chiswick and built on local talent. Such a move had to come eventually; it was the only real long-term option. But its immediate consequence was the departure of Roy Lester and his replacement by Bill Goodwin, former coach of Invicta. Professional sport is, we are often reminded, an unsentimental world – but emotional farewells would be made at the Supporters' Club annual awards night and disco on Challenge Cup final weekend, when Roy received a special presentation from the fans.

By then it was clear that 1 April was an entirely appropriate starting date for the new regime – although who was fooling who was never quite clear. If previous experiences had been unusual, the rest of the season was downright surreal.

One factor in this was a giant fixture pile-up – there were four home matches *after* the Challenge Cup final. Since the weather was good and the matches meaningless, except insofar as they fulfilled the club's outstanding commitments – Fulham were final opponents for four clubs – there was a loose, carefree air that contrasted with the tensions of a few weeks earlier. Two hundred and eighty-six points were scored in the last six home matches, shoehorned into 21 days along with a couple of away trips.

With American football, particularly the Chicago Bears, the fashion of the hour, Faires announced that Fulham were also to be known as 'The Bears'. This experiment was rapidly dropped when ribald laughter greeted the playing by the disco truck – which, complete with cheerleaders, had replaced the creaky old public address – of 'The Teddy Bears' Picnic' after the opening score against Mansfield. Other tries – announcer Mike Jones resisted Faires's suggestion that they be termed 'touchdowns' – were greeted with bursts of 'Another One Bites The Dust' (yes, Keighley were among the visitors exposed to this).

Still, there were some good ideas amidst the general wackiness: persuading referee Cliff Hodgson to wire for sound as an aid to crowd understanding for the match against Doncaster was a genuinely imaginative innovation, even if its output consisted largely of whistling sounds and suggestive rustlings.

But what the club actually lived on during this period is a matter of conjecture – air, mostly hot, would appear the most likely answer. The talked-of sponsorship deals never quite materialised. And the printers tired of waiting for their cheque, so there was no programme for the visit of Huddersfield – a clear breach of League regulations for which we attempted to compensate by producing a retrospective, complete with teams and match report, for sale at the following game.

But simply being there was what mattered. There was hardly an unhappy face at Chiswick after the revival game against Doncaster, even though it was lost 12–14. Nobody was happier than Bob Evans, concentrating so hard on tackle counts that he missed Doncaster's second try and believed Fulham had won.

Faires in turn closed the club in the summer, but the interlude – and southern players such as Brian Hunter, Russ Gibson, Eddie Tinsley and Tony Cooper, who put in brief stopgap spells – had served their purpose. The only alternative to Faires in April had been closure, but the close-season found fresh rescuers in Tim

Lamb and Richard Lawton, who restored rationality, even if they found results and crowds even harder to come by than their predecessors. The sick relative had lived, although the following years would turn some thoughts to euthanasia.

This season was the end of Fulham's Age of Innocence. The threatened closure in 1984 could be put down to loss of interest by an organisation, Fulham FC, whose commitment was, naturally enough, to another sport. But three near-death experiences in the space of two years could not be explained away, and they took their toll. Years of adversity and insecurity inevitably followed, remorselessly grinding down energy and tempers in London, and overdrawing the rest of the game's once-inexhaustible stock of goodwill towards the club. The financial backing needed to shift horizons from survival to development was a long way off – in 1986, the Brisbane Broncos had still to be invented.

No wonder everybody laughed at 'The Teddy Bears' Picnic'. It was fun, but never remotely a picnic. 'Here Comes Your 19th Nervous Breakdown' would have been more like it.

HUW RICHARDS is from Bridgnorth in Shropshire, but feels like he is from Swansea because of the spelling of his first name. His middle name is versatility because, as well as his Swansea City and Fulham/Crusaders affiliations, he also reports on some pretty ordinary Rugby Union. He works for *The Times Higher Education Supplement* and brings up a unique double in this book, having also contributed to *My Favourite Year*.

SOMETHING ROTTEN IN THE STATE OF WIGAN

Wigan 1966–67

Mel Woodward

Atherton isn't the kind of name that makes the hairs on the back of your neck stand on end. Not unless your name happens to be Merv Hughes, that is. Apart from having an England cricket captain and a North Queensland tableland named after it, it's fair to say the South Lancashire town has pretty much kept its head down over the centuries. There was the odd skirmish in the Civil War; a miners' riot in the 1890s; and the world's second-oldest railway used to pass through it before being ripped up to make way for the Bolton-Leigh freeway.

So there you have it; a potted history of my home town. Not exactly riveting stuff, is it? But growing up there wasn't all bad news by any means. In fact, Atherton had one extremely big thing going for it: it was near Wigan.

It didn't take me long to find my way to the forbidden city. In my pre-pubescent years, I spent countless hours train-spotting near the Springs Branch locomotive sheds. (There's a Rugby League writer in Australia called Neville Hill. With a name like that, I assume he must have had a similarly misspent youth at the equivalent location in Leeds.) Then, when steam engines started to be seriously outnumbered by diesels on the west coast main line in 1964, it was simply a matter of changing buses at Hindley instead of Platt Bridge to get to Central Park.

I could hardly have picked a better time to become a Wigan fan. The remnants of the great team of the late 1950s and early 1960s were still intact, and my first season ended with a trip to Wembley and an epic Challenge Cup win over Hunslet. The trouble with starting your supporting career like this, though, is that you think all seasons are going to be the same. A return to Wembley and a 2–21 thrashing by St Helens the following year quickly disabused me of that notion.

The 1965–66 season was a bizarre one for Central Park regulars. The team had played some superb football that year and, as late as 14 May, were still in with a chance of winning the League and the Cup. But a Championship semi-final defeat by Halifax was followed a week later by the Wembley débâcle – and, to rub salt in the wounds, it was deadly rivals Saints who finished up doing the double instead. At the time, it seemed like one of Wigan's darkest hours. Twelve months later, it almost seemed like the good old days.

It occurred to me the other day that a whole generation of Wigan supporters must have grown up in the last decade without knowing anything but success. By the same token, that same generation can never have sampled the delights of the Central Park Shuffle. The Shuffle, for the uninitiated, is that singularly Wiganesque ritual which involves thousands of fans streaming out of the ground like migrating birds 20 minutes before the end of an impending home defeat. Nowadays, because Wigan hardly ever lose at home, it's rarely seen. During the 1966–67 season, though, it was almost as common a sight at Central Park as a meat and potato pie.

Wigan had had bad years before, and they've had bad years since – most notably when they dropped into the second division 13 years later. But what made this particular season so unusual was the quality of playing personnel at Central Park at the time. Apart from George Fairbairn's weekly re-enactment of Custer's Last Stand, the 1980 relegation team didn't really have a great deal to offer. But in 1966, by my reckoning, Wigan had the services of 14 players who were, or who later became, Test players. That's the kind of international representation more readily associated with the great Central Park outfits of the present-day and post-war eras. What's more, the team that year contained some of the most famous names ever to play the game, yet they could only finish 17th in the old one-division system.

After the cataclysmic end to the previous season, we should have realised that many of our heroes were past their sell-by date. But, probably because we were only looking through one eye, we didn't see the big picture. And we certainly didn't realise that lurking around the corner was a momentous rule change which would ruthlessly lay bare the deficiencies in the team.

As the Cumbrian-born editor of a monthly Rugby League magazine gleefully reminded me recently, Wigan's 1966–67 season began with a 0–16 midweek defeat at Whitehaven. This abysmal curtain-raiser maintained my record – which stands to this day – of never having seen my team win at the Recreation Ground. Come to think of it, I only ever saw them win once in the old county of Cumberland.

In those days, the Cumbrian away games were a real endurance test. The M6 only went as far as Carnforth, and the rest of the journey was over the tortuous Lake District road network. For Saturday games, supporters' coaches – or saloons, as they were invariably known in Wigan – left at 9 a.m., which could test the mettle of even the most devoted fan. The story goes that one legendary supporter, known to all and sundry as Little Eric, turned up one wintry morning to find that the Unsworths stagecoach had already left for Workington. Displaying admirable coolness under enormous pressure, he made his way to Central Park to cadge a lift on the team coach. Now Eric was almost as big a local celebrity as Billy Boston, and he hadn't missed a Wigan game, home or away, for donkeys' years. But all that counted for nothing when he reached the ground and asked for a lift, only to be told by a Wigan board member to sling his hook. So Little Eric never got to Workington and traipsed home, a broken man. Speaking as someone who once missed a game at Bramley because his mother hid his trousers, I think I know how he felt.

Eric was one of several locals who were afflicted with that peculiarly Wigan disease, HACPS – Hanging Around Central Park Syndrome. Maybe it's because the ground is so near the centre of town. Maybe it's because Wiganers just can't go a week without some contact with Rugby League. But, in my experience, it's virtually impossible to go past Central Park at any time of any given day without spotting someone hanging around outside the ground for no apparent reason.

At any other Rugby League ground, loitering is always done with intent. If you see someone waiting outside Headingley, for example, it's almost certainly an Aussie backpacker looking for a game. At Wilderspool, it's probably someone on their way to strip lead off the stand roof. At Central Park, people hang around because . . . well, because it's Central Park. Graham Lowe was made painfully aware of this phenomenon when he arrived for his first day at the office in 1986. As usual, there was an HACPS sufferer outside the ground, and he took the opportunity to put the new coach right about one or two things. Well, one thing, actually. 'It doesn't matter what you do, as long as you beat St Helens,' said the forthright fan. 'And if you do it at Wembley, so much the better.' History records that the nonplussed Kiwi regained his composure sufficiently to grant the fan both wishes simultaneously three years later.

I must admit the possibility that Wigan might one day whitewash Saints at Wembley did not enter my mind as the Unsworths saloon crawled through Milnthorpe on its way back from Whitehaven that Wednesday night in August. It's strange, isn't it, how a trip home from an away game seems to take five times as long when you've just lost. Maybe that explains why so many Leeds fans seem to age prematurely. But, with the first home game of the season looming on the Saturday, I consoled myself with the thought that things could only get better.

Things, in fact, got considerably worse. The Halifax team that had given Wigan the run-around in the Championship three months earlier returned to Central Park to repeat the dose. Then a midweek trip to Leigh ended in tears. Alex Murphy had taken over as coach at Hilton Park, although a dispute with Saints at least meant we didn't have to put up with him as a player for a few months yet. The Comics (as they were affectionately known in those days) did, however, have a full-back called Colin Tyrer, who scored all their 18 points that night. When Wakefield Trinity made it four defeats out of four the following Saturday, it began to dawn on even the most optimistic fans that something could just conceivably be rotten in the state of Wigan.

In retrospect, some of the pack formations in those early games make bizarre reading. Billy Boston, for example, started the season in the second row – an experiment which was, thankfully, abandoned after only two games. By September, things had got so bad that Wigan even took the extraordinary step of taking a Liverpool City forward on loan.

Then there was the hooking position. Compared to the Wigan board's blind spot on this subject, Lord Nelson had 20/20 vision. In those days, scrums had yet to become the gentlemen's agreements they are today, and you couldn't just bung a half-back into the front row and tell him to get on with it. So when Colin Clarke was suspended for the 1966 Challenge Cup final, Wigan had been a tad disadvantaged by the absence of a specialist reserve hooker. The reason they didn't have a reserve hooker was simple: they'd sold the vastly experienced Bill Sayer to St Helens for peanuts earlier that year. When Bill mopped up the scrums for Saints that day at Wembley, you could say the powers-that-be at Central Park had got their just deserts.

Bill had been unloaded on the grounds that he was too old and slow. So, when the board finally got around to replacing him, they did the obvious thing: they signed someone who was even older and slower. Apparently, Len McIntyre had been a bit of a dasher in his day. By the time he signed for Wigan, that day was long gone. Battle-scarred gnarly that he was, Len had an uncanny knack of reading play and being up in support. The trouble was, he was the last player you wanted to see up in support, and many a promising move ground to a halt when the opposing cover defence sauntered over to halt his crab-like progress.

The combined age of the Wigan front row at Wakefield that August, when Len lined up between John Barton and Brian McTigue, would have tested the capacity of a medium-sized computer. Fortunately, Colin Clarke returned from Great Britain tour duties to put us briefly out of our misery by inspiring the first win of the season, at home to Leigh. I say 'briefly', because further ignominy was lurking just around the corner.

One of the greatest Rugby League scandals of recent years was the way Blackpool Borough were allowed to wither on the vine. Not just because it meant the demise of one of our most popular clubs, but because it deprived League fans of the one truly great away trip, apart from Wembley, the game had to offer (fans didn't go on Lions tours in those days). Wigan's annual visit to Borough Park was even better, because it usually coincided with the Blackpool Illuminations. It was one of the most predictable days of the year, which invariably went along these lines:

Board saloon in Wigan;
Arrive at ground;
Enjoy romp at Borough's expense;
Gorge on fish and chips;
Ride on tram;
See lights (usually from inside pub);
Re-board saloon (not quite as steadily as first time);
Get home late;
Pause to reflect on near-perfect day;
Enter coma.

In 1966, however, someone rewrote the script without telling us. Borough won. And won fairly comfortably, too, by 20 points to 10. I seem to remember the post-match festivities weren't quite so convivial that year.

It was still only early September, but the thought had already crossed my mind that Wigan might not pick up any pots that season. As it turned out, my pessimism was misplaced. Curiously, while their Championship season was falling about their ears, Wigan were putting together a highly respectable Lancashire Cup run. Not for the first time in their history, the sniff of silverware got the adrenalin flowing, as Leigh, St Helens and Warrington were despatched in successive rounds. And so it was off to Swinton for the final against Oldham.

Station Road, which I understand is now a *bijou* housing estate, wasn't the happiest of hunting grounds for Wigan in those days. The Swinton side was always stacked with Wigan-born players with a point to prove, and two of the club's greatest modern disasters (the 1968 Challenge Cup semi-final against Leeds and the 1971 Championship final against Saints) occurred on the ground. So any scraps at Station Road were gratefully accepted, and Wigan duly picked up their umpteenth Lancashire Cup with a 16–13 win. To be honest, the final score is just about all that sticks in my mind about an undistinguished game. That, and the fact that it was one of the last games ever played under the old unlimited tackle rule.

In Australia, there's a popular belief among St George fans that the four-tackle rule was introduced to destroy the domination their club had enjoyed since the mid-1960s. While this conspiracy theory might be a little paranoid, what can't be disputed is that Saints' 11-year run of Premierships did come grinding to a halt in

1967. The new rule wasn't exactly designed with Wigan in mind, either. With unlimited tackles, our ponderous pack could sometimes hold its own. Under the new regime, our forwards spent long periods chasing shadows – something they were singularly ill-equipped to do.

I can't remember which rules were in operation when Rochdale Hornets came to Central Park in late November that year, but a 10–13 defeat plumbed new depths of humiliation in an increasingly desperate season. Which brought us to the annual excursion to Liverpool.

In common with all teenagers throughout history, we didn't know we were born in those days. We used to moan about what a dump the Knotty Ash ground was, how you got showered with rust if a goalkicker landed a conversion on the roof of the tin shed behind the posts. Yet, compared to some of the 'stadiums' City's more recent manifestations have occupied, it was like Old Trafford. But the trip to Liverpool was undoubtedly one of the lowlights of the season, a counterbalance to the garden of earthly delights enjoyed on a day out in Blackpool. To make matters worse, the fixture had recently lost its traditional 'romp' status, and Wigan had been distinctly lucky to scrape a 13–12 win the year before.

In December 1966, they were even luckier – although one Wigan player certainly wouldn't remember it that way. An otherwise totally unmemorable match sticks in the mind for two incidents: one which bordered on farce, the other which ended in tragedy. Even by the abysmal standards of the times, Wigan were serving up a particularly large helping of tripe at Knotty Ash that afternoon. More by good fortune than by good management, they were clinging to a 10–8 lead late in the game, when a City forward made one of the cleanest breaks you'd ever wish to see. Mentally, the Wigan players must have already been in the Royal Oak, because there wasn't a defender within 20 yards of him. Gruesome headlines in that night's *Football Pink* sprang to mind, as the solitary predator strode inexorably for the line. Then it happened. Just as he approached the 25, he just . . . well, sort of fell over. Quite extraordinary, as David Coleman would say. I seem to remember the player was called Cork. But, on this occasion, he certainly didn't float. On the contrary, he was rapidly submerged by a posse of Wigan defenders who'd suddenly remembered that the Royal Oak didn't open until half past five.

After the game, theories abounded as to the cause of the City player's mishap. Was he wearing the wrong size boots? Was it sabotage by Knotty Ash anarchists? Had a disused mineshaft suddenly opened up (like the ones Wigan built a new stand on a couple of years ago)? I prefer to believe that some supernatural force had decided that Wigan couldn't be beaten by Blackpool, Rochdale *and* Liverpool in the same season, and had intervened to prevent the ultimate disgrace. Whatever the reason, Wigan got away with the points – but lost one of their most promising players in the process.

David Stephens had arrived at Central Park a year earlier from a Rugby Union club in Castleford, of all places. His signing was highly unpopular with the press, because it meant that Wigan then had three players called Stephens on their books. But the fans took to him, because he added a much-needed touch of youthful dash to what was becoming a rather staid threequarter line. David was really a centre, but Wigan often used him on the wing, his position that day at Knotty Ash. When he went down in a two-man tackle late in the game, it looked harmless enough. But he must have struck a particularly glutinous patch of mud because, as the rest of his body was driven towards the grandstand, one leg stayed where it was. The result was just about the worst leg injury imaginable – a double fracture, of the ankle and the thigh – and certainly the worst injury I can ever remember seeing. David could have been forgiven if he'd hung up his boots there and then. But, displaying the single-minded approach to horrific injuries that characterises Rugby League players (David Marshall springs to mind as a more recent example), he attempted a comeback the following season. But he played only a handful of games before heading back home over the Pennines.

Wearing the No. 1 jersey for Wigan that day was a bloke called Ray Ashby. As a former Liverpool player, he knew every blade of grass on the Knotty Ash pitch (not that there were many blades of grass to know). There's no way he would ever have disappeared down a pot-hole on his way to a certain try. Ray was a top full-back. So top, in fact, that he once achieved the singular distinction of representing Great Britain while playing for City. Wigan duly took note, and signed him to replace Rhodesian (as Zimbabweans used to be known in the days of white supremacy) John Winton. Ray, of course, will be forever remembered for his contribution to the classic 1965 Challenge Cup final, when he shared the Lance Todd Trophy with that immaculate Hunslet stand-off, Brian Gabbitas. A sensational break from deep in his own half that day led to one of the great Wembley tries, scored by that other Rhodesian/Zimbabwean, Trevor Lake.

Ray was one of my favourite players. Unassuming, utterly dependable, and with an unfailingly cheerful demeanour, he rarely had a bad game for Wigan. One of the club's more recent custodians, Steve Hampson, was straight out of the Ashby mould. Ray was one of several full-backs of that era who liked a chat with the fans behind the sticks. (The brilliant Paul Charlton was another – although, because he was Cumbrian, we could never understand a word he said.) As he was retrieving the ball from a kick at Huddersfield one day during the winter of 1967, Ray asked a bunch of us shivering at the Scoreboard End if we'd like a snowball. Maybe it doesn't quite rank with the story of the Wigan fan who once gave the great Puig-Aubert a swig of his coffee at Central Park, but it was nice of Ray to ask.

As it turned out, that game at Fartown was one of the last Ray played for the club. Maybe the board thought he was getting on a bit; maybe they decided to discipline him for offering fans a snowball. Whatever the reason, they signed Colin Tyrer from Leigh a couple of weeks later. Ray's days were immediately numbered, and he played just a few more games in the cherry-and-white before heading down the well-worn path to Blackpool the following season. But at least he was given the opportunity to play out his career with a certain amount of dignity – which is more than you could say for Frank Parr.

Frank – or Frankie, as he was always known to the fans – was my other favourite player of that era. Although indelibly etched on most people's minds as a Wiganer, Frank actually came from Leigh, where he played scrum-half in the same school team as Colin Tyrer. (Also in that side, at loose forward, was a lad called Clive Powell. Clive was regarded as a good prospect, but unaccountably threw a promising League career down the drain when he went to London and changed his name to Georgie Fame.) In those days, Rugby League clubs didn't sign 12-year-olds. The nearest thing we had to cradle-snatching then was the midnight-on-the-16th-birthday signing. This was a cloak-and-dagger operation reserved for only the most promising juniors. (Shaun Edwards got the same treatment on his 17th birthday – although, with a BBC film crew parked in his front room, that signing hardly came into the cloak-and-dagger category.) In the best Wigan tradition, Frank was duly snapped up under cover of darkness one night in 1960, and went on to become one of the club's most durable post-war players.

With his distinctive strutting gait, Frank was the kind of scrum-half that Eddie Waring used to delight in calling, *ad nauseam*, a 'cheeky chappie'. But beneath his fresh-faced appearance lurked a fierce competitor, as more than one highly-rated opponent found to their cost. Not just opponents, either. During his 12 years at Central Park, Frank saw off a never-ending stream of rivals for the No. 7 jersey. Whenever he established himself in the first team, a new scrum-half would inevitably be signed, as if the club was never quite convinced of his ability. But Frank always came out on top in the end, and reclaimed his rightful position.

When Eric Ashton made it clear that Jimmy Nulty was his preferred half-back in 1972, though, Frankie decided it was time to move on and asked for a transfer. Barrow had their eyes on him, but lost interest when one of the Wigan board told them Frank couldn't drive. Whether this was yet another classic piece of direc-torial ineptitude, or some kind of sinister plot to freeze him out of the game, it had the same result. In fact, Frankie *could* drive – it was just that he didn't own a car at the time. By the time he found out about the Barrow bid, he'd missed his chance of a move. So he walked out of Central Park and never played again – a sad end for one of Wigan's great unsung heroes.

The world was a very different place in 1966. Wigan Athletic were where they belong – in non-League obscurity; the England soccer team had just won the World Cup; a Labour government had just been re-elected. Wigan was a different place, too. That ridiculous bypass hadn't been built, and Central Park hadn't been cut off from the town centre. Where the road to nowhere now stands, there was a classic little sweet shop where we used to stock up on Uncle Joe's Mint Balls on the way to the match. Now long gone, of course, along with my favourite Wigan pub, the Park Hotel, demolished around the same time to make way for a strat-egically important slip road to a multi-storey car park.

Central Park, too, would have looked unfamiliar to the modern-day fan. The old wooden Douglas Stand, with the pre-carious press box perched on its roof, was still in place. The Powell Street End was uncovered terracing, with the Boys' Pen a poignant reminder of the days of huge crowds, and a proper scoreboard next to the pavilion. The original Edison cylinder version of *Entry of the Gladiators* still greeted the teams as they made their way down the old tunnel. There was no electric blanket for someone to forget to switch on. Most conspicuously of all, there were no floodlights. Which meant that, if you staged a Challenge Cup replay, it had to be played on a midweek afternoon.

In theory, especially in an era of relatively high employment, this was a recipe for disaster at the gate. In practice, it was quite the opposite. The last time it had happened at Central Park was in 1961, when the gates were closed on a crowd of more than 40,000 for a first-round replay against Leeds. Things weren't quite so frantic when Wigan played Warrington on a February Wednesday in 1967. But an attendance of 25,000 wasn't bad going for the worst season in living memory.

If ever there was a game that graphically underlined the advantage for a Rugby League fan of going to school in a soccer town, it was this one. At any seat of learning within shouting distance of Central Park, my feeble excuse about going to the dentist would have been rumbled immediately. In Bolton, where Rugby League was about as familiar as Mongolian folk-dancing, it was accepted without question. (Strangely enough, my teeth always seemed to need urgent attention whenever we played at Barrow on a Friday night, too.) Still, I reckoned I could learn a lot more in an afternoon at Central Park than I could from meandering around a Rugby Union field. So, having made my apologies to the games teacher, I joined the massed ranks of the dentally-disadvantaged for my first and only afternoon Cup replay (they installed floodlights the following season).

What a cracker it was, too. Inspired by Eric Ashton at full-back, Wigan had come back from the dead to snatch a sensational draw at Wilderspool the previous Saturday. On that Wednesday afternoon, though, there was only one team in it. Sir Eric – as we used to call him in deference to his MBE – was again superb at the back, as the Wire were cut to shreds by a real old-fashioned Cup performance. Then, as now, the merest sniff of Wembley was enough to send Wigan fans into paroxysms of barminess. And, so convincing was the lads' victory, a third successive trip to the Twin Towers seemed a formality.

Alas, the euphoria lasted just 12 days. The Salford side that would shortly become a force in the game may have been only in its embryonic stage, but it was still more than good enough to dispose of Wigan. So, on 25 February, we were out of the Cup. And that, effectively, was the end of the season for us. Victory at Rochdale was followed by five defeats on the trot. And even a home win over the mighty Liverpool City – this time achieved without divine intervention – wasn't enough to snatch a place in the top 16.

So when the Championship play-offs kicked off in April, Wigan, unbelievably, weren't involved. As the season elsewhere reached its climax, Featherstone Rovers beat Barrow at Wembley to win their first Challenge Cup. Wakefield Trinity – after a 'water-splash' draw at Headingley, which should really have been the perfect preparation for Wembley the following year – beat St Helens at Swinton to take their first Championship. If the League had split in two at that point, instead of six years later, Wigan would have found themselves in the second division 13 years ahead of schedule. As it was, they turned things around to such an extent that, only five months later, they were capable of beating the 1967 Kangaroos on an unforgettable night at Central Park.

I don't get down to the old ground much these days; it's a fair hike from Sydney, and Unsworths don't run saloons. And, of course, as a strictly impartial journalist, I take no interest in Wigan's results. Unless you count staying up until three in the morning frantically trying to tune into the World Service, and running up an international phone bill that would service the debt of a Third World nation, that is.

Sydney would just about have the edge over Atherton, I suppose. In fact, you might think it was the perfect place for a League fan to live. But I'm not so sure. After four years in the colonies, I still haven't found a drinkable pint. I've yet to unearth a decent pie. And I'm still waiting for an Aussie full-back to offer me a snowball.

MEL WOODWARD was once told by his history teacher – the father of the jailed solicitor and *cause célèbre*, Angus Diggle – that he was only the third laziest pupil he had ever taught. He has devoted the rest of his life to disproving this calumny and has naturally gravitated to Australia.

A FOREIGN COUNTRY

Australia 1982

Paul Fitzpatrick

The past, as L. P. Hartley observed in his prologue to *The Go-Between*, is a foreign country: 'They do things differently there.' Is the past also a land of deception? Were the 1982 Kangaroos all they were made out to be?

Statistics alone insist that they were. They were the first Australian tour side to win all their games, blazing their way unchecked across the English Rugby League heartlands and, more predictably, across France. Twenty-two games played, 22 won, many of them by crushing margins. They scored 166 tries and conceded nine. Only Wigan, Bradford and Hull of the club sides gave them anything resembling a match. Great Britain were no match for them at all.

Four years later, Wally Lewis's Kangaroos won all their games – 20 as against 22 – as well, and in the opinion of some critics were the superior force. But they did not capture the imagination of the public the same way as Max Krilich's handsome troops. Those who come up with a first always hold the advantage. A multitude of fine athletes have run sub-four-minute miles since 1954. But how many are remembered? Roger Bannister's name, though, will never be forgotten.

It is not the statistics, though, for which the 1982 Kangaroos will be remembered, but for the quality and freshness of so much of their play. But it runs deeper than that. The Kangaroos registered the sort of shock to the English Rugby League consciousness that the Hungarian soccer team administered to English football in 1953.

Ron Greenwood, later to manage a succession of cultured West Ham United sides as well as England, was never the same man after watching Puskas, Hidegkuti and Kocsis flitting through the mist of that November day at Wembley. The Hungarians challenged his preconceptions. They forced him to look at soccer in new ways. The 1982 Kangaroos had a similar effect on Phil Larder, then the sport's recently-appointed National Director of Coaching. That was the measure of their impact. They were so good, they made you wonder what game you had been watching before.

When they arrived in the autumn of 1982, I had been covering Rugby League for *The Guardian* for a little over four years. Before that, my experience of the game had been non-existent. I had never played it nor taken any interest in it. Code 13 meant no more to me than pelota or pigeon racing, croquet or curling.

Like most converts to it, I was soon addicted. The game's pace, skill, courage and non-stop movement made a welcome contrast to so much of the dreary soccer I was obliged to report on at that time. Soccer was a game in decline. It was dull on the pitch and in the grip of the hooligan off it. The generally civilised behaviour of Rugby League followers came as refreshing relief.

Widnes were then the power in the land. They won their first League Championship in 1978 and embraced such good players as Doug Laughton, Reg Bowden, Eric Hughes, Keith Elwell, Mick Adams and Kenny Gill, one of two players to make a special impression on this greenhorn. Bill Ashurst was the other.

The Challenge Cup final of that season, the first I had seen, was a classic of its kind. Leeds 14 St Helens 12, this after a stirring fightback by the Yorkshire club who looked destined for an afternoon of acute embarrassment when they went 0–10 down (tries then worth 3 points) early in the game. With tension mounting, and time running out, John Holmes and David Ward dropped the goals that kept the Challenge Cup at Headingley.

Over the next four years, writing about cricket was my main responsibility, but I saw plenty of Rugby League as well, enough to convince me that there were few more exciting or entertaining team sports. Not the least of the great games of this period was the 1982 replayed Challenge Cup final at Elland Road between Widnes and Hull, two of the best clubs in the business. It was fair to conclude after a match that burned with the brilliance of a kerosene lamp that there was not a lot wrong with English Rugby League football.

There had, though, been evidence of a growing discrepancy between the international capabilities of the Australian and Great Britain Test sides. The series of 1978 showed Australia as a young, vigorous, emerging nation; Britain as an ageing and over-physical force. Tony Fisher, hooker in that formidable front row of Hartley, Fisher and Watson in Australia in 1970, was brought back at the age of 36 for the third and final Test at Headingley. He was flattered but felt it was a massive step backwards. The Lions tour of Australia the following summer was a calamity from which journalists returned with many embarrassing tales to tell.

I saw neither of the last two Tests of 1978 nor anything of the 1979 tour and, although alarmed at some of the stories, remained largely in ignorance of Great Britain's shortcomings. These were then further underlined by the 1980 Kiwis. They played some wonderful football, their desire to keep the ball 'live' producing some thrilling and sustained passing movements. It might have been a good thing for Britain if they had lost that series. But, after going a Test down, they squared the series at Headingley, and a draw was enough to quieten the alarm bells.

The warnings should have been heeded. That they were not was understandable to a degree, because there was still so much good club rugby to admire.

What, then, was the mood of the English game in the autumn of 1982? It was not, to be fair, one of complacency. One journalist, watching the Kangaroos posing for the cameras at Headingley soon after their arrival, spoke with more prescience than he knew when he said: 'I'm delighted the Kangaroos are here. But I'm terrified at what they might do to us.' And that was about right. There was a sense of anxiety. Few people were expecting a close series. The portents suggested it would be unequal. But no one could have foreseen how ruthlessly the English game was about to be exposed.

The happenings between 10 October and 28 November should have prompted the longest post-mortem examination in the game's history. So many aspects of English Rugby League were shown to be inadequate, the preparation of the Great Britain side naïve in comparison with the Australians.

It should not have been that way, of course, between the sport's two strongest nations, but there were reasons why it was so. Rugby League in Australia, in Sydney and Brisbane in particular, had evolved into a high-profile, confident, wealthy sport, enjoying saturation coverage in newspapers and radio and on television. For all its tradition and achievements, in England it was a game struggling for media recognition, short of money, decidedly part-time, and still firmly in the shadow of its more powerful neighbour, Rugby Union.

That was no solace, though, as the Kangaroos proved themselves superior in every facet of the game. They were fitter, stronger, quicker. They were better technicians and more naturally gifted. Their tactical awareness was more acute, their powers of concentration more developed, their discipline more mature. They also had in Frank Stanton an exceptional coach directing their operations.

'Cranky Frankie', as he was known, was not the man with whom most of his players would have chosen to spend 12 months on a desert island. Some of them did not like him at all. But, to a man, they respected him. And the strict discipline that he demanded he received. Ray Price, that inexhaustible lock forward who had toured with Stanton's Kangaroos in 1978, had some interesting things to say about him in his autobiography, *Perpetual Motion*.

'It was pretty obvious why Stanton was called "Cranky",' says Price. 'On the 1978 tour, Stanton was like an old-fashioned English schoolmaster. He ruled with an iron fist . . . Stanton's other common nickname was "Biscuits" which he had acquired as a red-headed half-back on the 1963 Kangaroo tour . . . But "Biscuits" and "Cranky" were about the best names he ever got. A lot of players called him a whole lot worse.

'But as long as you played hard and did the right thing under his many rules, he was all right. Frank Stanton proved a master at keeping us fit, united and hungry.' Price was then referring to the 1978 tour. But that judgement held good for 1982 as well.

Some players on the 1982 tour could not believe how strict

Stanton was and were astonished to be told that he had mellowed almost beyond recognition from 1978. But, whatever Stanton's strengths or weaknesses, he was a formidable adversary. He was single-minded. He knew his job. He knew what he wanted. And he had the players to carry out his strategies.

Great Britain's players were under the much more benign regime of Johnny Whiteley, an outstanding Great Britain loose forward in the late 1950s and early 1960s, and Colin Hutton. They were honourable and likeable men, and knowledgeable. But they were in charge of hopelessly inadequate forces.

Hutton, as manager, was obliged to maintain a public front. But, at the end of the series, he admitted privately that he knew the fight would be unequal. Hutton was one of the few men at that time who had taken the trouble to visit Australia to assess the strength of the opposition. His public opinion was that Great Britain had nothing to fear. His private view was that they had everything to fear: that the English game – if these things can be so measured – was seven years behind Australia. There were times over the coming weeks that it seemed like light years.

At the end of the devastation, Hutton made a plea: 'Do not blame Great Britain's failings on team selection,' he said. He had a point. He felt that to put all the responsibility for Britain's failings on the selectors would be to overlook the real problems. This was fair enough, but it did not exonerate a selection system which had become a laughing stock.

Choosing teams by committee had long been abandoned in English soccer. Yet it was still in fashion in English Rugby League in 1982, and it was a mess. The response to the first Test defeat at Hull was to sweep that bunch of British failures out of the way and bring in another lot; and similarly after the second Test defeat at Wigan. By the end of the series, 33 different players had been used, and only the black winger, Des Drummond, had played in all three Tests. Stability, an essential ingredient of any successful team, was absent.

The embarrassment reached its nadir before the third Test at Headingley when David Topliss, the Hull stand-off, was made the third captain in the three-match series (this after Warrington's Ken Kelly was told that he had the job). But then the selectors could not find Topliss, who was eventually tracked down on holiday in Majorca. It would be unfair to suggest that Topliss had tried to get as far away from the battlefield as possible. There have been few more courageous or committed stand-offs. But this episode was yet another example of how little grasp the selectors appeared to have on affairs.

At the end of the tour, English Rugby League resembled a devastated war zone. Little that was worthwhile had been left standing. The land was scorched and bare. The vanquished troops would carry the scars for the rest of their days. Long-cherished myths had been exploded, particularly that one about British players possessing skills that Australians could never hope to acquire.

Who were these guys who wrought such havoc? Unlike the Pinkerton men who so doggedly pursued Butch Cassidy and the Sundance Kid, they were not total unknowns, although your average Rugby League follower in 1982 was much less familiar with the Australian game than he is today. Video was still something of a novelty, there was no BSkyB to bring weekly offerings from the Winfield Cup, and it was not every day that you would bump into a subscriber to the Australian magazine *Rugby League Week*.

Ten of the party, in fact, had toured in 1978, Max Krilich, the captain, among them. Not a lot, though, was known about the rest. By the end of the tour, that was still true of some of them. On all sporting tours, some figures are destined to remain in the shadows, and this one was no exception. Who can now recall in any great detail the contributions of Rohan Hancock, Don McKinnon, Ray Brown, Greg Conescu, or even Gene Miles, who was such a big influence four years later with Wally Lewis's Kangaroos?

But what memorable talents were to emerge as well. By the completion of the tour, there were players who had won an imperishable place in the minds and hearts of English fans. And the subsequent achievements of these players – and I refer in particular to Peter Sterling, Brett Kenny, Wayne Pearce, Eric Grothe and Mal Meninga – were proof that that admiration was not misplaced. They were all to become great players – and the adjective 'great' is not used lightly.

What distinguished them in 1982 – apart from their obvious ability – was their youth. Kenny and Pearce were 21, Sterling, Meninga and Grothe were 22. Yet even then, young as they were, they all looked the finished article. English fans watching these players did so enviously. Why was Australia producing young players of such quality and not Britain? That question was at the heart of the British problem.

Sterling and Kenny, Meninga and Grothe, were all to return to England in later seasons to play club football. Sterling is still revered at the Boulevard, as is Kenny at Central Park and this pair, colleagues at Parramatta, were on opposite sides in that highly entertaining 1985 Challenge Cup final at Wembley. Kenny won the Lance Todd Trophy that day as the game's outstanding player. If it had not gone to him it would have gone to Sterling, showing three years on all the tirelessness that had been one of his characteristics in 1982.

Meninga had a glorious season with St Helens in 1984–85, scoring 28 tries in 31 games; and Grothe, though his stay was comparatively brief, scored 14 tries in 16 appearances for Leeds the same season. Pearce, sadly, was not seen in England again. Injury kept him out of the 1986 tour and then put a premature end to his career with Balmain and Australia.

These were not the only ones to compel admiration. The wing play of Kerry Boustead, a tourist in 1978 but still only 23, was a delight: such balance, such speed, such alertness, the rapier on the right to Grothe's broadsword on the left. Craig Young was frequently compared with Wigan's Brian McTigue, one of the game's all-time great props. Les Boyd was prone to lapses of discipline but was a redoubtable competitor.

Ray Price, 29 now but still some way off the end of his career, was an inexhaustible, craggy, angular lock fired with the will to win. One could imagine him being a great success in the days of bare-knuckle fighting. He was the sort of man who would still have been coming at his opponent after 40 rounds. Indestructible.

Steve Rogers was a centre, we were to learn later, who needed constant reassurance. On the field, he was confidence personified. So much of his play was perfection. He looked as finely tuned as a Swiss watch. The mistakes he made tended to be in the less important games. In the Tests, he was invariably word perfect.

Another Steve, Ella, would have been an automatic choice for Great Britain if he had been eligible. But the closest he got to the Australian Test side was as a substitute (not used) in the first Test at Hull. He never failed to score tries in his 11 appearances in Britain and France, 22 in all. John Ribot, the winger who replaced Grothe in the third Test at Headingley, was an equally prolific try-scorer.

A comparative disappointment was Wally Lewis, the 22-year-old vice-captain to Max Krilich. Little more than a year later, when he signed to general astonishment for Wakefield Trinity, Lewis was regarded as the most complete Rugby League player in the world. He was a towering figure in the Ashes series of 1984, 1986, and 1988. In 1982, he gave only glimpses of his immense talent.

When he first arrived, Lewis was regarded as the first-choice five-eighth, with Steve Mortimer as his likely half-back partner. But when Stanton, whose mind was possibly made up even before the squad left home, decided that Kenny and Sterling would be his midfield partnership, Lewis started to sulk. He was a few pounds overweight and, according to Ray Price, was lax in training. 'By the time Wally stopped sulking and started to lift his game, it was too late.' Not quite, because Lewis's contribution to the last two Tests was considerable – even though he was a substitute. The monster of a pass that brought Meninga a try at Central Park is locked in the memory. So are the two long passes that were prominent features of the final try of the final Test – a marvellous move eventually completed by Brett Kenny.

The tourists did not make an entirely distinguished start to their tour. Rod Reddy and Les Boyd were sent off in a first half at Hull Kingston Rovers that reflected no credit on Australia, Hull KR, or the sport as a whole. Surprisingly, too, the Kangaroos were 5–8 down at the interval – a score which seems barely credible at this distance of time. It was perhaps the case that the Australians wanted to make a point as early in the tour as possible: that, if things became heated, they were well able to take care of themselves. But it made for unedifying watching.

When, however, they concentrated on their football, the quality was evident. Sterling and Kenny pressed their early claims to the half-back partnership; and in an awesome display of power, Mal Meninga gave notice of the remarkable phenomenon he was to become. An irresistible run of 65 metres brought him the final try in a 30–10 victory.

What followed was a remorseless and intimidating build-up to the first Test at Boothferry Park, Hull. Only 4 points separated Wigan and the Kangaroos in the second tour game, but it was not long before the points were flowing and a formidable force was taking shape, fearsome in attack, secure as an oak door in defence. In that first match at Craven Park, Steve Hartley and Gary Prohm scored tries against them. By the end of the tour, only five more opponents had managed to emulate them – Henderson Gill (Wigan), Brynmor Williams (Wales), Hussain M'Barki (Fulham), David Topliss (Hull), and Steve Evans (Great Britain). In France, two players managed it, Yvan Grésèque in the second Test and Alain Maury for France Under-24s.

Ray Price says that the players were never aware of history unfolding. Going through Britain unbeaten was never discussed, and did not become a conscious ambition until they were only one game away from achieving it. The public, says Price, were aware of the possibilities long before the players.

But the Kangaroos must have felt soon enough that it would take something exceptional to stop them. Barrow, after 40 indifferent minutes, were dismissed; a scandalously understrength St Helens were overwhelmed, but the performance which really confirmed the Kangaroos as something special came against Leeds, whom they beat 31–4. Their rugby under the floodlights was brilliant and produced one of the definitive moments of the tour, when John Holmes, the Leeds stand-off, sent downfield what he believed to be a relieving kick. But all it did was give Eric Grothe possession, and the hirsute winger powered his way back up the left flank. Defenders were bundled out of the way and, within seconds, he had touched down. Defence had been turned to devastating attack before Leeds had had time to draw breath. To British eyes, it was compelling – and chilling. It was that kind of wing play which was to earn Grothe his nickname of 'Rolling Thunder', one of the more evocative sporting soubriquets.

That game put the finishing touches to Stanton's preparations. The Kangaroos were ready, and the Tests proved to be as one-sided as the Rugby League public now suspected they would be. The inequality, to English eyes, was embarrassing. But this in no way devalued the play of the Australians.

The speed and dexterity of handling at Boothferry Park could scarcely have been improved upon. Great Britain were never sure where the next thrust would come from. The tourists were as likely to score on the third tackle as on the sixth. Tries came from long range and short, from backs and forwards. Grothe, on the wing, was fearsome; Kenny and Sterling full of flair and invention in midfield; Pearce fast and muscular in the second row; Meninga an irresistible force in the centre. Britain's worst fears had been realised. Australia were in a different league. The destination of the Ashes was a foregone conclusion.

Australia were reduced to 12 men for 45 minutes in the second Test at Central Park after the dismissal of the headstrong Les Boyd. But they still won with total assurance – and no little skill or style. One of the lasting memories of this 27–6 victory was a move in which the ball went through at least 11 pairs of hands. It did not bring a try but it did bring Central Park to its feet – and to generous and spontaneous applause.

The British game now had nowhere to turn, and the desperation was evident. A new cast of players was recruited for the final Test at Headingley and, in fairness, gave Great Britain's best performance of the three. Steve Evans, the Hull back, had the distinction of scoring his country's only try of the series, and there was a bit more pride and resolve in the British play. But it was disturbing that the home officials, grateful to cling to any straw, could take so much solace from such a comprehensive defeat, 8–32.

Most of Australia's points in this game came in the later stages. It was as if the Kangaroos were giving a resumé of all the good things they had displayed in the preceding weeks; a last chance for any late-comers to see how six-tackle football should be played. It was an intoxicating mix, and provided an appropriate finale to a dazzling campaign.

Not quite the finish, however. The Australians still had the French leg of their tour to complete, and Stanton was determined that his men would win all those games as well. The Australian coach still had two old scores to settle from 1978 when Australia lost both Tests – the result, the Kangaroos claimed, of atrocious refereeing. They did win, of course, but in losing 4–15 and 9–23 the French could take greater satisfaction from their performances in opposition than had the British.

Were the 1982 Kangaroos so good because their British opponents were so poor? There is probably some mileage in this theory, but not much. The Kangaroos, by any measurement, were exceptional. It is quite possible that the 1990 Great Britain side, or the current one, would not have capitulated anything like as abjectly as the 1982 side. But comparing teams from one era against another is a futile exercise. It must remain subjective; the arguments can never satisfactorily be resolved. All any team, or individual, in sport can do is to beat the best that is around. That is what the 1982 Kangaroos did, but they did it in inimitable fashion.

There would be no shortage of witnesses prepared to testify

that the 1982 Kangaroos were the best Rugby League side of all. It cannot be proved, of course, but the video evidence, even at this distance, still shows Stanton's men in a very favourable light. Telvista Television were a Leeds company with a brief existence but they did the game a service by producing a tape of the tour which included action from every game. Many good bits were left on the cutting-room floor – that remarkable sequence of passes in the second Test is sadly missing – but it was possible to watch the tape 12 years on and still be mightily impressed by a group of talented Australian players performing at the height of their powers.

In 1984, at home this time, the Australians again beat Great Britain 3–0. They were again vastly superior. But the magic that had touched Krilich's men was missing.

So many things about the 1982 Kangaroos were exemplary. Most of the time their discipline could not be faulted, although in that respect they did have their falls from grace: Les Boyd was sent off twice, and Reddy, Brown and Morris was also dismissed. But these lapses were rare and did no lasting damage to the squad's reputation.

So much of their work came straight from the textbook. Their tackles were low and hard. They gave and took passes at pace. An Australian rarely had to wait for, or look for, support. The Kangaroos played the ball with a speed and simplicity which constantly took their opponents by surprise. So many damaging moves stemmed from their sharpness at the rucks. Their defensive line moved backwards and forwards quickly and as a unit.

There is nothing mysterious about such skills, of course. They represent good, fundamental rugby. But, when so many skills and basics are performed well and, like a grooved golf swing, repeated time after time, the effect is compelling. So many of the basics in English football had, unnoticed, fallen into a shoddy state.

When Greg Brentnall, the full-back, kicked the ball into touch he might have been posing for a picture in a coaching manual. Everything was perfection: the stance, the balance, the right leg coming clean through the ball and finishing high. Brentnall was not one of the great players of the tour. But he still had something to teach his British counterparts. The mental image of his line-kicking is a lasting one – an example of excellence.

Only the really exceptional sides force opponents into a complete reassessment of their resources. In fact, the response to the thrashings of 1982 should have been more radical than it was. The least the British game deserved was a thorough, systematic investigation into all its aspects. But many of the changes that did take place were piecemeal, and were the result of the enlightenment of a few individuals rather than a concerted effort by the sport's governing body.

No plan, as such, was formulated. No precise long-term objectives were drawn up, as they should have been. Fortunately, one of the men most influenced by the Kangaroos was Phil Larder, the young, recently-appointed National Director of Coaching, and he set himself the task of overhauling a coaching scheme that had sunk into disrepair. New thinking was required. New avenues needed to be explored.

But it was a long haul back to credibility. The co-option of Rod McKenzie, a fitness expert from Carnegie College, Leeds, was a sign that things were moving in the right direction, but even his considerable presence on the 1984 tour could not prevent Great Britain losing all six Tests in Australia and New Zealand. They lost another series 0–3 in 1986, and it was not until the final Test of the 1988 tour, at Sydney, that Great Britain at last won – their first Test victory against Australia for ten years. Further victories came at Wembley in 1990 and at Melbourne in 1992. But it had taken Britain the best part of a decade to get anywhere near the standards the Kangaroos had set in 1982.

The improvements – slow though they were to arrive – that took place at club level could also be traced to the example set by Max Krilich's men. Players began to appreciate that the game offered big rewards but demanded personal sacrifices in return: that a lot of ingrained bad habits would have to be broken and much higher levels of fitness and commitment aspired to.

Wigan were the first club to grasp the full significance of the lessons of the 1982 tour. They signed two marvellous players from that tour in Brett Kenny and Steve Ella, as well as the remarkable John Ferguson. Perhaps most important of all, they engaged one of the world's outstanding coaches in Graham Lowe, who had guided the New Zealand national side to some fine performances against Australia in the early 1980s. And, when his contract ran out, they replaced him with the Australian John Monie, who was to achieve even greater success. These two men helped Wigan to dominate the game as no other club has ever done. They showed what could be achieved through top-class coaching – just as Frank Stanton did in 1982.

Unexpectedness is a quality which, by its very nature, does not have a long life. One of Thomas Love Peacock's characters, philosophising about the nature of a great garden, opines that such a garden is made by its 'unexpectedness'.

'And pray what do you call this quality on walking round the garden for a second time?' asks his companion.

It was for their unexpectedness that the 1982 Australians will be remembered. They arrived, and it was like a torch shone into a dark room. They departed, and it was like a light switched off. '. . . The unexpectedness of it all took our breath away,' wrote Geoffrey Green, *The Times* soccer correspondent, of the 1953 Hungarians at Wembley. That was how it was with the 1982 Kangaroos.

PAUL FITZPATRICK once wrote on football and cricket for *The Guardian*, before discovering the joys of Rugby League in the late 1970s. He is a man of varied sporting talents, but so dour as an opening batsman that he has been known to be sledged by his own team.

Blackpool Borough 1978–79: Borough Park, 'a highly effective antidote to the idea that there is necessarily any glamour in professional sport'
(Blackpool Gazette & Herald Ltd)

Blackpool Borough 1978–79: a team 'never quite as bad as Doncaster', including Bak Diabira, front row, second from right
(Blackpool Gazette & Herald Ltd)

Fulham 1985–86: the Chiswick Polytechnic Ground, 'a draughty relic of the days when ferro-concrete was considered aesthetically pleasing'

Australia 1982: (above) Kenny, Reddy, Sterling, Krilich, Grothe, Boyd and Pearce, 'so good they made you wonder what game you had been watching before'; (below) Frank Stanton, 'like an old-fashioned English schoolmaster', with Rogers, McCabe, Brown and Young
(Andrew Varley/Harry McGuire)

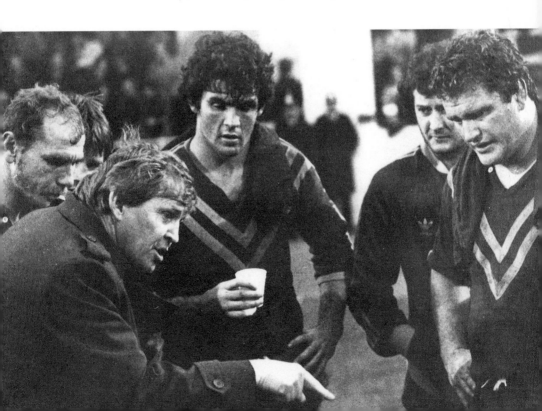

Wakefield Trinity 1978–79: (above) Keith Smith, 'not so much a golden boot, more feet of clay'; (below) left to right, Burke, Skerrett, Keith Rayne, Idle and McCurrie – 'a hybrid of youth and experience up front'
(Gerald Webster/Rugby Leaguer)

Featherstone Rovers 1987–88: Graham Steadman, 'a stereotypically smooth lounge lizard of a stand-off', loses his head against Widnes
(Andrew Varley)

Whitehaven 1962–63: 'a losing team, not a team of losers'

Wigan 1984–85: John Ferguson – 'watching him was more fun than Wigan supporters had been used to in years'
(Frank Orrell/Wigan Observer)

Hull 1975–76: Keith Boxall, who 'seemed to be everywhere on the pitch'
(Gerald Webster/Rugby Leaguer)

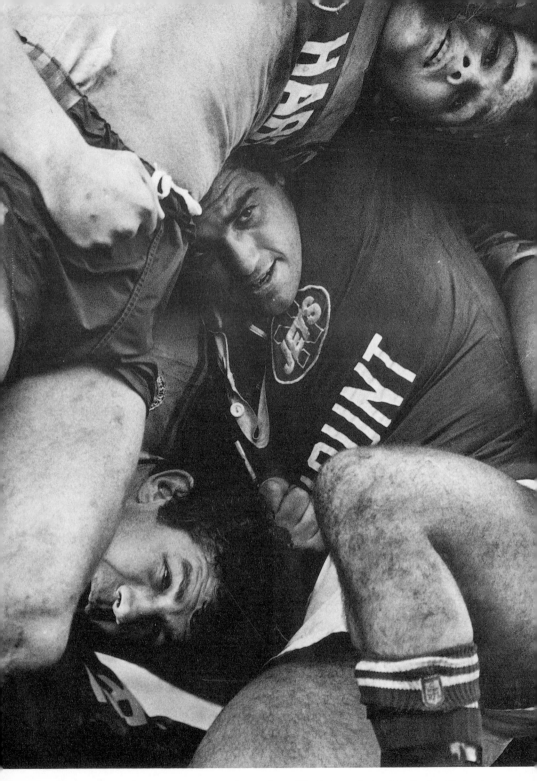

Newtown/Parramatta 1981: the Sydney Grand Final, 'an underdog-fight for the affections'
(Action Graphics)

WHERE WERE YOU WHEN THE LIGHTS WENT OUT?

Leeds 1990–91

Margaret Ratcliffe

This was going to be it. We'd been League runners-up the previous year, and the sensational, dramatic signing of the All Black, John Gallagher (even though I'd never heard of him), was to be the icing on the proverbial. 'The final piece in the jigsaw,' as Leeds's Chief Executive, Alf Davies, put it.

Sometimes I wonder if I am a true supporter. Okay, I arrange my whole life round the game, with everything else coming a poor second – but that's fine, because the whole family is involved. We don't like to miss a game: first team, A team, friendlies, internationals – but I'm rarely devastated when we lose. I enjoy every game, and a win is simply a bonus. I'm really more concerned that my current favourite player should have had a good game and, conversely (and I'm ashamed of this), I hope that the players I don't like will have stinkers.

I'd had a vacancy for a hero for a few years, ever since Cliff Lyons went home to Australia. I've always been one for heroes. Norman Field was the first. He played for Batley and gained county and international honours in the early 1960s. I used to walk up and down the touchline on his wing throughout the game. Then came Gary Sprake and he lasted a long time. I carried his photo with me everywhere, and my mum said, when I saw him unexpectedly one day in the centre of Leeds, I went all pale. I cried when he got married.

Running almost parallel with Sprake were Ken Thornett and Wilf Rosenberg and – difficult to credit now – Eric Ashton and Tommy Smales. Duncan McKenzie and Charlie Cooke followed Gary, and I seriously considered a formal return to Elland Road recently when Eric Cantona signed – but if Leeds United couldn't cope with his flair, then I'll stay at Headingley, thank you. It's Ryan Giggs now, anyway – I'm into the younger generation – and any day now I'm going to have a 'No. 6 Holroyd' stencilled on to the back of my Great Britain shirt (well, I would if I had one).

Eric Grothe and Gilles Dumas were others who sent tingles of anticipation through me, and Cliff had, of course, been wonderful. But now I had a vacancy and, heard of him or not, I was determined that John Gallagher was going to fill it.

The basic differences between a fan and a reporter are turnstiles, a cheque-book and a credit card. Between paying to watch and being paid. For years, the only items appearing regularly on my Access statement were Sainsburys, Kuwait Petroleum and Leeds RL. It would have been easier to hand the card over at the Souvenir Shop each August and simply say, 'Take what you need and I'll sign for it.' On the plane to watch Great Britain play in France each year, I scan all the faces, convinced I'm the only passenger who has paid by personal cheque rather than an expense account.

But all this was to change in 1990–91. Sure, I still had to pay to get in everywhere, but this season I was actually to be paid for setting down my opinions on the matches as words on paper – instead of just saying them to myself, as children do. Alf Davies had thrilled and flattered me beyond measure by commissioning me to contribute a regular piece to the official Leeds programme. Complete editorial licence. No strings.

What a responsibility! Deadlines at least once a fortnight, and more frequently for cup-ties and tour games, etc. I was determined, before the first scrum was formed, not to miss a single copy. But how was I going to cope when it takes me three weeks of concentrated endeavour to prepare one player interview each month for *Open Rugby*? Would I still be able to stay one ironed shirt away from divorce? Would my enjoyment of the game be adversely affected? Would I have to take notes and concentrate properly, instead of forgetting the score of each game immediately the final hooter blew? So many questions. So little time.

Apart from money, the only other factor that sets the journalist apart from the fan is access to the players. All my work for *Open Rugby* – planning, travelling, thinking, writing, worrying, typing, checking, faxing – is worthwhile to meet a hero every month. For, in truth, *all* players are heroes to me, even those I hate.

I boo them once a week and then I ring them up and make appointments to see them, tell them how wonderful they are, hang on their every word and report it verbatim, hope they maintain their form for a few weeks until the article appears so that I won't look an idiot for choosing them – and then forget about them (though not all of them). I can only liken this to a pop fan being granted an audience with a Beatle, a Simple Mind or a Take That. Or a film buff meeting Tom Cruise or the delicious Kevin Costner. That's how I regard all Rugby League players from any division in any country. (They won't read this, will they?) And, this season, I had been given a licence to interview whoever I wanted from my own team, as often as I wanted.

When I first started interviewing them, I was astounded at how well the players talk when you catch them in relaxed mode. I'm less surprised now because I know how articulate they all can be. They never know what I'm going to ask them; I never prepare them beforehand, but they are always really fluent. They don't say 'ye know' all the time; they're never short of an opinion; they're always polite and diplomatic, never slagging each other off (never on the record, anyway). I see them afterwards on TV with a microphone stuck up their nose after a game, mumbling incoherently, and I can hardly credit it's the same person to whom I've listened, spellbound.

John Gallagher, my new hero, didn't play in the pre-season Wigan Sevens, but Eddie Rombo did – so well, in fact, that Leeds didn't dare not sign him. Widnes expressed an interest, and Leeds moved quickly. I wonder if that Widnes interest was a bluff? If it was, it worked – as do most things which Widnes try – and Eddie never played as well again. Paul Harkin had also been signed from Bradford Northern, and we had four returning Aussie tourists: Schofield, Gibson, Dixon and Powell. Dear Roy. It was the last year of our traditional hooped home kit, and we sported a very dignified new away shirt. It was the first season for the new paddock seats, most of which are still unsullied by human bums, the price charged for them being so prohibitive.

Friendlies against Bramley and York were gentle warm-ups. Too gentle. We crashed out of the Yorkshire Cup at home against Bradford Northern 16–24. Paul Medley predictably rubbed it in with two tries for Northern.

Many Leeds players have come and gone in recent years. In fact, to be accurate, *every* player has come and gone from the team which played in that first game, with the sole exception of Garry Schofield. I look at the lists, and there are a few I miss, but many more I don't. In playing terms, very few have really shone elsewhere, but I always maintain that the combination of Paul Medley and Roy Powell in the second row could not be bettered. The contrast of styles should have been a winner.

This opening defeat against Northern was a crushing blow. Don't forget, this was the season in which we were going to win everything. Never mind, we'd just have to win the League. If the Yorkshire Cup-tie was a candle blown out, however, then losing the opening League game of the season at Oldham was the shattering of a crystal chandelier, followed by a whole Waterford factory-full in smithereens when we lost to Hull in the first home League game. A cup and the League gone already, and I had to write about it! Positively!

When you're contributing to the official club programme, you can't slate the club's own players, but what could I say? I opted for the neutral 'unmitigated disaster', and 'you were all quite dreadful'. That was very mild.

It's always nerve-racking for me to approach a player, but John Bentley had always seemed very human. We had set up a meet before the Yorkshire Cup game; 'I won't let you in if we lose,' he had warned me lightly. With fear and trepidation, therefore, I smiled weakly as I walked up his drive: 'I thought you weren't going to let me in,' I joked. 'You're not in yet,' he growled. He was disappointed but, as ever, tried to be helpful, and I got lots of material (and plenty I didn't dare use). John was a great favourite and, even now that he's at Halifax, I like to see him on his runs. He always frightens me when he's going forward, and even more when he's going back.

Hull were our *bête noire* in every sense of the words that year, which was destined to be their best season in ages. If Brian Smith had stayed as coach until May, I'm convinced they would have run Wigan very close indeed. They had arguably (a wonderful journalistic word meaning 'in my opinion') the best half-back partnership in the world. Definitely up there in the top three with Edwards and Gregory, and Kenny and Sterling. Definitely. That Mackey and Patrick Entat (who looks more like an urchin pushing cocaine in the back streets of Marseille than an international athlete) were so clever and nasty and evil, they terrified me. They certainly terrified the Leeds players. Perhaps good half-back duos have to be clever and nasty and evil – although Holroyd and whoever-we-eventually-decide-is-going-to-be-his-long-term-partner won't be evil, just clever and nasty. If I really concentrate, I'll remember Mackey's proper first name – but 'That' is better than saying it. He was wicked that year.

So, three played and three lost. Crisis time. Let's do the unexpected. Let's win away at Warrington. And buy two new props, Wane and Molloy. Mixed feelings.

We make a day trip of most away games – that way, a good result is simply a bonus – and Warrington is one of our favourite away days. We once started a barge holiday from Preston Brook on the Bridgewater Canal and were warned that there could be danger from hooligans on the stretch between Warrington and Manchester. Funny; I felt safe. Hard to define why, but I thought, 'We'll be all right; it's Rugby League country around here.'

Pizza Hut for lunch, then a visit to Ikea. Thousands of families just wandering aimlessly around, looking at the furniture displays. Very few buying. I looked at them and wanted desperately to go to the reception desk and commandeer the tannoy to tell everyone to get themselves down to Wilderspool for some real entertainment.

I never really trust a man who isn't into sport. I'll bet not many serial killers have been Rugby League fans.

After the three early defeats had left us all in utter despair, I'd written in the programme: 'The rest of the League is laughing at us, and it isn't funny.' But a graph of our progress that season would look like a cave full of stalagmites, because two more wonderful wins followed the Warrington one, and we moved to third place in the table. Hull were top.

So how was my hero John doing at this stage? About as well as the rest of them, though he was always prepared to back up and join the line at great pace. Poor John, he must have wondered what was going on. Presumably when he played for the all-conquering All Blacks he received protection from his forwards. (Then again, if you think about it, what is it that they have to conquer?) He took some fearful hammer throughout that season.

I hope you don't think I've forgotten the A team. Certainly not. If memorabilia is anything to go by, then the A team game on Friday 14 September at Goole was the highlight of the year. It was a special event, and I have a souvenir programme, autographed by Noel Cleal, a team sheet, and the ticket. We lost.

The A team sheets have developed rather better than the A team in recent times. In December 1988, they were hand-written on plain paper. By 1991, they were on a sponsors' letter-heading, and now the club has its own pre-set format advertising its commercial activities. Even dedicated collectors would struggle to keep Friday-night team sheets in pristine condition, however, and mine have done well to survive folded up like a church newsletter. How many others have been stuffed in coat pockets, washed, spun, shredded and subsequently cursed?

The 1990 Kangaroos were here by now, and Leeds prepared for their game with the tourists by losing at home to Featherstone. I have always pretended not to like Brendon Tuuta because I don't think you're supposed to unless you're a Fev fan. But that's not really true; I think he is pretty useful, but it seems disloyal to say so.

For Wigan and St Helens fans, club games are what matters, with everything and everybody else nowhere. I'm afraid for me it's quite the reverse – that's why I worry whether I'm a proper fan. For me, internationals against anybody are the *crème* of the game. And don't tell me that's the same for everybody, because it certainly isn't for Paul Newlove!

We were driving home through Manchester after a game when the 'Roos were announced on the radio. Definitely driving past Strangeways. I remember it clearly but, looking at the fixture list, I can't imagine where we'd been. That's a very funny way to come back from Warrington, and even funnier if it was Oldham. Anyway, I hung on to the announcement of the tour party with bated breath, knowing that ET would make it but less sure about Cliff Lyons and Mark McGaw.

I'd interviewed both in their earlier Leeds spells. I'd asked McGaw if his teeth were real. Christian had squirmed uncomfortably, embarrassed by mum showing him up, but Mark hadn't minded. He'd perched on our settee wearing his Cronulla socks, but he wasn't concentrating properly and he fell off the edge. Now it was my turn to be embarrassed because Christian couldn't help himself and sniggered. But Mark still didn't mind; he beamed, flashed those sparklers, picked himself up and went into the kitchen with his cup, insisting on washing it up.

Cliff hadn't been quite so relaxed; he'd left his girlfriend outside in the car, so I wasn't relaxed either. Cliff *is* my all-time favourite player, but I couldn't get him to say a word. Even when I fed him lines, he didn't say yes or no: he merely shrugged. Even when Christian fed him names, he was pretty neutral. Still, he *is* my hero, and he was coming back with those nasty Kangaroos and ET.

I'd always been so conscious of ET's looks that I'd deliberately not interviewed him in his earlier Leeds spells. Now my readers must not, under any circumstances, form the idea that I ever take into account a player's visual attractions when I'm assessing his playing ability. But . . . oh, what the hell! This time I decided to indulge myself for once. I'd look at that face and see if the skin really was as smooth and unmarked . . .

I hadn't been as nervous for years as when I went to keep our appointment. Tour hotels terrify me. I hid behind a palm where I could see the tourists straggle in after a training session, but where they wouldn't be able to see me.

ET was so cool, so composed, his face so clear, his hair . . . The cassette recording would make a radio programme in its own right, because I hardly say a word and the few I do say are so quiet and sensible – quite unlike my usual squealing, giggling and Mrs Thatcher-like painfulness. His teeth as well. He was so professional, and he said I was well prepared. Thank goodness I'd learned something in the years since I'd interviewed Howie Tamati at the Granby Hotel in Harrogate – but forgotten to take a pen.

No one ever invites me anywhere, so there was nothing else for it but to ask Bill Carter, the Leeds football secretary and my week-to-week contact at Headingley, if there was to be a reception after the Leeds game versus the tourists – and, if so, could I please have three tickets. I promised not to eat or drink anything – I just wanted to be there. Bless him, he sent me three of those prized passports, those badges which posers hang from their binoculars or lapels at the races and Test matches.

It was to be a marquee job on the cricket field. Couldn't wear the usual scruffy, comfortable, match gear. Had to make an effort. Wore the long, cream, wool coat and high-heeled boots, tottering carefully to my seat, terrified that I would fall and make a spectacle of myself or, worse, dirty my coat. It's not easy to keep a cream coat clean through a match, with people passing all the time and the seat mucky to start with. In those days, the season ticket-holders all had their names sign-written on their seats. Why they had to be blocked out later on I do not know; what harm were they doing? We were so proud of our seats. In the cricket season, when it threw down, we would retire to our named seats to check they were still there and watch the grass grow.

So, after the tour game, when we had performed very creditably – though not won, of course – we queued to enter the marquee. There was some hold-up – badges had to be handed in and, somehow, this caused a problem. Gary Belcher must have pinched one, because there's a photo of it in his miserable book *Kangaroo Confidential*.

We were in a long line just behind a group containing David Oxley and Arthur Clues. Arthur was holding court. No one else spoke; they were hanging on his every loudly-carrying word. He can tell a tale, can Arthur. Once in, it was decision time. To sit at a table, or stand and mingle. Not enough confidence to mingle properly – sit down and ogle.

The 'Roos who hadn't played were there first, looking smart in blazers. Cliff was there with Dale Shearer, but only for the briefest of moments before they both sneaked off, out of a back door. I did muster the courage to have a word with John, whom I'd met the previous week, and introduced him to my husband, Joe. It must have been one of John's best Rugby League moments (the game, not meeting Joe). He'd had a really good match and, when we worried about him in the months to come, I remembered that game and thought, if he could play so well against the mighty Kangaroos, why couldn't we build on that performance?

Then I pounced on Mark McGaw who, just for a moment, was alone. I don't think he remembered me, and I didn't remind him he'd fallen off our settee. But I did note that his teeth were as even as ever.

The 'Roos stuck together, the Leeds players of that day stuck together, and so did those from earlier eras: Dyl, Hynes, Ramsey, Holmes, Atkinson, Smith and, a little further away, Lewis Jones

with Arthur Clues. There were a few brief speeches and presenta-
tions, following which the 'Roos soon drifted away saying they had
a bus to catch.

Together with Eddie Rombo, Cavill Heugh and Mike Kuiti
were our overseas imports that season. I remember coming out of
the bank one dark, dreary, grey, wet, foggy morning in a corner of
Otley, where the stonework matched the day perfectly, and nearly
falling over with surprise when I saw Mike Kuiti across the road.
He shone like a beacon in a fabulous tracksuit, easily the brightest
object in Otley, with his magnificent physique looking like an
Eastern Island statue. I was so taken aback, I smiled before I
remembered I was shy. He smiled back, but I'd gone.

Everyone at Leeds liked Cavill Heugh, and the visit of the
tourists gave me an ideal excuse to go and see him. Twinkling eyes
and a lovely way of speaking. It made a brilliant article which was
blown completely when Bill Carter rather too sensibly showed it
to Cavill before it went to print. Naturally, he had second thoughts
and cut all the best bits out. Damn. And I'd left some of the even
better bits out anyway!

When Great Britain beat the 'Roos at Wembley the following
week, it was so unexpected, it was breathtaking. Cliff didn't play,
which cost the Aussies dearly – served 'em right.

Why does the world tolerate Bob Fulton? Complain, whinge,
moan, grumble, *ad nauseam*. We'd been to the tour game at
Wakefield Trinity, where the tourists' behaviour had been appalling
– but no, it was all the referee's fault. Now the Wembley defeat was
all the referee's fault as well. Pathetic. Offside is offside unless you're
an Aussie – in which case it's an umbrella defence. Sad.

We should have won that Test series, you know. We had the
better of the first two games. And the Leeds trio were well in there
– Schofield, Gibson and Dixon. (They say that the only reason
Leeds fans support internationals well is because that's the only
way they ever get to see a big match live.)

This should alienate most of Lancashire: for all their
undoubted talent, I can't help believing that even the best of the
Lancashire-born players think more of playing for their clubs than
they do for Great Britain. Perhaps Yorkshire-born players appreciate the call-up more because it's harder won (except Paul
Newlove). A Yorkshire-based player is, without question, less likely
to get the call-up than a Lancashire star. Of this, Neil Cowie and
Billy McGinty are the living proof, to mention but two.

It really irritates me that Wiganers don't flock to internationals. Remember, half their side is always in the Great Britain team and the other half are from St Helens – so where, when Great Britain played New Zealand at Central Park in November 1993, were the 29,000 who had watched Wigan versus St Helens the previous Boxing Day?

Let's alienate a few more people. All those ridiculous Featherstone and Bradford Northern supporters who clog up the Radio Leeds phone-in whining about the Leeds supporters whining are (a) totally wrong, and (b) missing the point. Leeds supporters don't, in fact, phone in all that much. I've taken a count, and by far the greatest number of callers to Radio *Leeds* are from Fev, Cas, Trinity and Northern. And anyway, we don't whine. We are stoical in the extreme. The reasons we don't phone are one, that we're out there on the terraces, supporting our team, home and away, win or lose; and two, we've more dignity than to blame the referee constantly for our players' shortcomings.

The point that Leeds supporters *do* occasionally try to make is that they think they have a right to expect their team to perform to their potential; at least to have an interest in the result; to try. Phone-in callers from other clubs frequently say, 'Leeds supporters think they've a God-given right to win everything.' What rubbish! We don't at all. There's a whole generation of fans on the terraces at Headingley who've only ever won the Yorkshire Cup.

There. That's off my chest. On the back of three defeats and a big win (against Rochdale, who had Neil Cowie and Martin Hall playing for them), my column in the programme for the Regal Trophy game versus Halifax in November focused heavily on the second Test at Old Trafford.

I was a bit like Paul Eastwood at Old Trafford: I think I was missing something. On the way home, Christian said, 'I talked to Johnny Raper before the game. He told me, "If ever you're down St George way, I'll give you a lift".'

'Where was I?' I asked.

'Wandering round outside, to see who you could spot.'

'Oh.'

'Have you seen all the Leeds United autographs I got on the programme?'

'No, when did you get those?'

'When you were wandering round outside, to see who you could spot.'

'Oh.'

Outside or in, I know I was absolutely drowned from having a seat on the front row in the pouring rain. For the Premiership final we're always on the very back row, which is binocular country at Old Trafford. Just who *does* get decent seats at these venues? Would American Express or Diners Card produce better results?

And so to my finest hour, my *pièce de résistance*, my moment of glory – though it wasn't planned as such. It was just a midweek League game against Castleford. I'd tried to get a little ahead of myself – to iron two shirts instead of one, to sew on a button or two – so I'd submitted three pieces at once, intending that they be used for the next three home matches. I couldn't believe it when I opened the programme and they were *all* there. I was everywhere. Tuesday, 27 November 1990. Crowd 11,221, so if one in just over two people bought a programme, at least 5,000 people read me, and probably as many as 10,000 – at one time. Most of them would have gone away happy because we thrashed Cas, 41–16. I didn't sleep that night.

I'd been able to be positive in all three pieces because we'd thrashed Halifax 58–6, scoring ten tries. I'd included two very different interviews, one of which was with Gordon Strachan – truly an adopted Loiner. Remember, he didn't start his career in Yorkshire. By no means. His best years were well behind him – in theory – long before he came to Leeds to play out his days quietly. Many, many times I'd wished that my forwards had half his determination to succeed. I'd seen him at Yorkshire cricket matches, and several times at our games, so I thought I'd give him a call for a celebrity interview. He could only say no or, even worse, ask for a fee.

He didn't do either. I left him a message at Leeds United, and he rang me back the same evening. (One day I'm going to do a real 'scoop' story, the 'Make Contact with a Wigan Player' exposé. That's not quite fair – but they don't half take some tracking down.) Gordon was mega. I usually prefer to do interviews face to face, to develop themes, to watch a player's expression, to try to judge whether he's being honest or simply feeding me the party line, the cliché. This phone-in would be a first. Gordon had no idea who I was, what I was going to ask, anything, but he was wonderful. There was nothing in it for him – he didn't need any publicity. He was so natural, and his wry, dry humour made it so easy over the phone. He laughed at the way Leeds United blame

Hunslet for the state of the Elland Road pitch. (They're still at it, by the way. Incidentally, I know why Hunslet win so few games: they play all over the country. Why, they were at Oxford in January 1994, churning up the pitch to stop Leeds United winning again!) Anyway, good old Gordon was man enough to dismiss this out of hand as footballers blaming anything or anybody rather than their own inadequacies. Bob Fulton could relate to that.

When I asked Gordon if he fancied a go at No. 7 for us, he nearly choked. 'Absolutely not, no way, never. Those guys are great athletes but if one of them got me, just once, I'd curl up and cry.' Bless 'im. Some time later, I saw Eric Cantona standing statuesquely on the cricket field after a night game, waiting for Gary McAllister. Soccer isn't all bad, you know.

Carl Gibson hasn't perhaps enjoyed quite the same publicity as Gordon Strachan, but he's been important to me. I didn't need directions to his house – I lived up the same street in Batley for almost 20 years, and he and I share a birthday. I was always so proud of Carl because he came from Batley. Funny: when I played the cassette back afterwards – alone, in private, as ever – I detected all my vowels in his voice. Not for the first time I wished I'd taken a camera. Carl with three children on his knee would have made a lovely study. He played so well in the Test series – not fancied at all against the much-vaunted Meninga who, without question, barged into Carl illegally to prevent him making that crucial last-minute, try-saving, match-saving tackle on Ricky Stuart at Old Trafford.

While we're dealing with Batley, it must be time to mention Roy Powell again, because he lived quite close to Carl (he had my vowels as well). Roy is so wonderful. How could Leeds let him go? I know they said that he wasn't damaging enough in the tackle – that the opposition would run at him all day. But he *was* always *there* in the tackle, not hiding, or resting, or losing heart. Every game, after 70, and 75, and 80 minutes, he was still always there – ready to take the ball up, ready to drop on any and every loose ball. When it was rumoured that he was on his way, I asked anyone who would listen (and a few who wouldn't), 'Who's going to tackle down the middle if Roy goes?' No one had an answer for me and, of course, the answer *was* 'no one' – at least until Ellery came.

Probably the most exciting game of that entire season was the next one, the evening Regal Trophy game against Hull KR. The full 80 minutes were breathtaking, and we sneaked it 26–22, but not before Dave Watson had given us a hard time.

We were snow-bound for the next Regal tie, at Widnes. Reduced to watching it on TV. Mortified when Paul Dixon was sent off – though that was inevitable because he'd been given a wonderful write-up in the programme. Poor performance, the sort that you hope no one was watching and you don't mention on a Monday morning at work.

When I grow up I'm going to be a proof-reader for programme editors. How can they all make the most blatant errors? Is it the printers, or is it carelessness by the clubs? Whoever it is, in the Sheffield programme for our first-ever game at Don Valley, only two of our forwards' names were correctly spelled. Still, I love the stadium. I don't like to see all those empty seats, of course, and the running track makes the play far away, but the architecture is exciting. We were making heavy weather of the game, and Sheff were beginning to look useful, coming into it. The ball was moved to the left, with Panapa, Gamson and Powell as a three-man overlap, clean through – and the lights went out. Since these lights had been billed as the best in Europe, there was a delicious irony here. When they came back on, Leeds had their act together and won comfortably.

And so to Wigan, two days before Christmas. The Wigan team photo that year included Kevin Iro, Andy Goodway, Shaun Wane, Bobby Goulding, Ellery Hanley and Andy Gregory. No prizes for making the connection. We didn't win, but then we don't really expect to at Central Park. Still, John scored two tries and was going well.

Schedules are tight and finely balanced at Christmas, what with family commitments, so I was devastated when the morning kick-off of the Boxing Day game against Bradford Northern was delayed to accommodate the large crowd. At the club office, they kindly let me use the phone to tell Joe's parents we would be late for lunch. I didn't want to get into trouble.

It was a good win, followed by another on New Year's Day against Oldham (John was man-of-the-match). My piece that day featured Shaun Wane, and I said, 'In every game he has performed as a top-class prop.' He'd been the players' player-of-the-match for three consecutive games. How quickly time passes! I can hardly remember him playing for Leeds at all now!

So we were on a mini-high before the away trip to Hull – Brian Smith's final game before returning Down Under. Hull were League leaders at the time, and so it was always going to be painful. But never let it be said we spoiled anyone's party. We lost convincingly, 14–34.

It was That Mackey again. I was so livid. Paul Dixon charged at one of his kicks, and he promptly went down pole-axed. To this day I don't believe he was touched, but Dixon was sent off, and that was that. (I wonder what they'll think if they read that – which one will be able to say truthfully, 'Stupid woman, she's completely wrong.' Perhaps both of them.)

By this stage, John had taken such a pounding throughout the season that it was beginning to tell. He was led off at Hull with yet another kick in the face. My season was now revolving round John Gallagher. He'd just moved into a house quite near me – well, near if I went out of my way, and I certainly could (and did) put it on my route to just about everywhere.

He was doing a college assignment when I called to see him. Looking back now, he was still full of enthusiasm, most pleasant, positive and co-operative. Where did it all go wrong? It's not difficult to find an answer: a fortnight later at St Helens, where he was spear-tackled and lost all semblance of confidence.

It wasn't one of our better days all round. Christian had a throat infection and became more weak at the knees with every try they scored. Eventually, like the Leeds defence, he buckled, and I took him back to the car before the final hooter.

Leeds then obligingly postponed a game for me when I went to the Great Britain international in France. We travelled with the team and could have stayed at their hotel but, on balance, decided not to in case too many dreams and ideals were shattered. Nice to be near, though, so that you might stroll past them in the street.

Perhaps it's busy in summer but, in late January, Perpignan is a bit dead. Avignon is nicer and Toulouse is a vibrant city, while Carcassonne is a bit twee for me. This is being picky, though; Rugby League anywhere in France is fine. Okay, if you travel with the team, a three-day trip costs the equivalent of a fortnight in Benidorm. But you pays your money, you takes your choice – and it did give me lots of material. I've kept the Monarch boarding cards, the special Great Britain RL luggage tags, the Avis Rent-A-Car invoice, receipts from both hotels (we were Chambre 39 in Carcassonne), the match previews from French and English newspapers, match reports, postcards, photographs, and even a Lion bar wrapper because it was in French.

Back home, Leeds's form continued to be up and down, and the Challenge Cup was our last chance of glory, a faint ray of hope still flickering – but not for long. After a terrible thrashing at the hands of Widnes at home in the League, we were never going to improve enough to go to Odsal and win a Cup-tie. At least the players tried and were respectable – but another light had gone out.

My poor dad, God rest his soul, had been acutely ill throughout the season – in and out of hospital. My attendance at every interview, every game, was subject to the state of his health. Many times I rushed straight from the ground to his bedside, gasping to arrive before visitors were thrown out. Parking spots at Rochdale and Hull were specially chosen for a quick get-away.

He was a great fan of Batley, York and Leeds and liked to hear how we'd got on. In fact, he usually knew because he listened to the radio and to our tales of woe. We always did match forecasts together on a Saturday afternoon. Mum took Nottingham City every week because she was convinced Brian Clough was their manager. She never took Batley who she said were a 'tuppence ha'penny' team – and she should know. She remembers the original Gallant Youths, and she still calls the game the Northern Union.

Even though he hadn't been to a match 'live' in 30 years, my dad consistently beat us all with his forecasts. There must be a moral there. One of his theories was, never take the away side unless you have to. On more than one occasion, Christian was mortified when Grandma beat him – Brian Clough and all.

However, as Dad's health deteriorated, I psychologically felt I must tone down the enthusiasm I displayed before him. It simply didn't seem fair. I gained so much joy, pleasure, stimulation from every game, win or lose, it just wasn't appropriate to walk into a sick room glowing, excited, full of it. I started to turn on and off. I'd visit on a Friday after work, but not mention that I was going to an Alliance game later that evening. Similarly, I'd not say I was going to the odd Batley game here and there, because it seemed so selfish that I should be so full of life when he was so desperately ill.

This guilt complex grew, and finally won over Easter. The combination of a public holiday, which would in the past have been a cheerful family event, and a particularly nasty, hospitalised bout of pneumonia, made me say, no, I won't go to Belle Vue, I'll go and visit my dad – see if I can get him to eat something. So I missed a match. He slept all afternoon, and I listened to the commentary through earphones, picturing the play and missing it dreadfully. Joe and Christian came after the game, and Dad woke up then, so I could have gone and still visited. And I did go in the weeks that followed, simply leaving the telephone number of the ground where I was with the hospital – but dreading that the next announcement over the tannoy would be, 'Will Margaret Ratcliffe of Leeds please return to the hospital immediately.'

We had a big win away at Featherstone, and then it was up to us to stop Wigan taking the title. Oh yeah. We never had a prayer. They set their stall out and took us apart, and it was only their fourth game that week.

But never mind: the dimmest of pencil-torch beams could still be made out. We were in the Premiership. The first-round game away at Cas was one of our best performances of the season and so, as a reward, we went to Hull for the final denouement.

We were still in with a real chance at the Boulevard when a towering bomb was launched into the night sky. John was underneath it. Oh please God, let him catch it! He did. I saw him. He did catch it. I sat down relieved. Why were all those Hull fans jumping around with joy? He'd dropped it. The lights were all out.

'Did That Mackey play that night?' I asked Christian recently.

'Course he did; he kicked the bomb.'

We went to the Premiership final anyway. As we were driving to Old Trafford, I opened the colour supplement in *The Mail on Sunday* (I'm not allowed to read broadsheets in the car because I obscure the wing mirrors). I'd only bought it because there was a colour feature on John, but it spoiled my day. John was described as 'the great mercenary – quitting the wonderful world of amateur, Corinthian Rugby Union for the grubby, commercial world of Rugby League'. I never bought *The Mail* again. Since then, I've also fallen out with *The Sunday Times* and, briefly, with *The Independent on Sunday*, one of whose numerous RU correspondents once described Warrington as 'dross' before the arrival of Jonathan Davies. That Mackey may be nasty, but he is certainly not dross.

It was difficult to decide who I wanted to lose the most, Hull or Widnes. But Mackey with a cup was the final straw.

It hadn't been a vintage season – just normal, really, a thoroughly bizarre, fulfilling, infuriating, enjoyable, wouldn't-have-missed-it-for-the-world sort of year. Still, everything would change in the new season, wouldn't it? Well, yes and no . . .

MARGARET RATCLIFFE is a fervent Batley and Leeds supporter. No life is entirely wasted, however, as she is also a wife, mother and property manager. She is a regular contributor to *Open Rugby*, one to whom players equally regularly make the most astounding confessions, and to the Leeds match programme.

MERELY FINE

Wakefield Trinity 1978–79

Neil Tunnicliffe

I remember once encountering Harold Box in the middle of Wakefield, shortly after he had signed for Trinity from Featherstone Rovers as a dashing, attacking full-back to replace the faithful old retainer, Les Sheard, in 1980. I was 16. Now, with all due respect, the only hint of star quality about Harold was the fact that – with the sun behind him, if you squinted through one eye – he bore a passing resemblance to Burt Reynolds. But there he stood, in polo shirt and Farahs, Clark Kent-like outside a phone box on the Bullring.

I was in awe. It was as if Achilles in full battle gear, or Captain Marvel in tights and cape, had suddenly jumped out in front of me. I must have been standing there like a goldfish, gob wide open, staring, for he turned and looked at me and, bless him, must have assumed he knew me from somewhere. He spoke, and immediately the spell was broken: 'Awreight,' he said. It had been going so well until that one word spilled out and revealed his mortality.

A part of me has always been slightly upset by Rugby League's proximity to the heart of its community: by the fact that you can work with, or drink with, or live next door to, or be related to the men you cheer on from the terraces every Sunday. Sure, it's the beating heart of the game, the source of its honesty and humility, its intimate and homely appeal, the quality which separates it from the brash commercialism and aloof, onanistic braggarts of soccer. But no man can be a true hero to his valet, let alone to his work-mate, his neighbour or his cousin. Take away your heroes, and you have nothing to aspire to; take away the ambition, and you belittle the man.

For me – and the pathos of the memories now drips like treacle – the Wakefield Trinity side of the late 1970s and early 1980s were gods, ones who materialised once a fortnight to gambol on their playground at Belle Vue – like the wraiths of the 1919 White Sox who come out of the corn to play baseball on Kevin Costner's home-built diamond in the excellent *Field of Dreams*. Okay, so they were gods with Homeric caprices and foibles, such as losing at Thrum Hall when no one else did. But gods they undoubtedly were, and I never wanted to learn that they spoke at 33 rpm in mile-wide accents, or that they plied the same plumber's or joiner's trade as the struggling masses among whom they walked.

Two or three years ago, the Australian journalist Neil Cadigan – who had come to Wakefield along with the legendary Parramatta lock Ray Price, in the inevitably futile hope of working a simultaneous miracle both on and off the field – sought to stimulate moribund local interest by running a competition in *The Wakefield Express* to establish the best XIII the club could ever have fielded. I listened to the line-up which the poll had produced with mounting astonishment: Round, Fred Smith, Skene, Neil Fox, Coetzer, Poynton, Holliday, Wilkinson, Marson, Turner, Exley, Vines, Haigh. How could they leave out Mike Lampkowski? And Alan McCurrie? Surely there were no better packmen than Trevor Skerrett and the Rayne twins? And what about Keith Smith, for goodness sake?

The accumulated wisdom of the years, and a proper sense of perspective, suggests that the Trinity sides of the 1960s, in which most of Cadigan's 'Golden Greats' appeared, were by far the best in the club's history. Two Championships, four Wembley visits, three Yorkshire Cups, two Yorkshire League titles, five players and the manager on the 1962 British Lions tour: not a bad decade's work. Contrast that with my lot – the seven full caps scraped by

Skerrett and David Topliss between them before they left the glorious technicolour red-white-and-blue for the monochrome black-and-white of Hull, and the single Challenge Cup final appearance in 1979 – and you end up agreeing with the last edition of the *Stones Bitter Rugby League Directory*, which obviously thought long and hard about the content, talent and impact of the ensemble before describing them as merely 'fine'.

Fine, my eye. It just goes to show that, just as some things in life are too valuable to be left to the experts, so the comparative assessment of rugby teams has nothing to do with the sober judgement of educated men, nor with statistical levels of achievement which, it is commonly known, are ever mendacious. No, this is a land where the long-haired and pimply enthusiasms of adolescence hold sway, where objectivity lies with the dodo at the bottom of the dark pit of extinction. After all, Keith Smith was capped once by England, you know.

So, if you asked any of us – me, Lanc, Wal, Burt, Kekhead, Ceuty, Borky, anyone – which was the real 'Golden Greats' XIII, then we'd answer with one voice that it was Trinity *circa* 1979. Not because it *was* the best – I don't think any of us in our heart of hearts truly believes that. But because it was an integral part of the best years of our lives, when we all went to the same parties, hung out with the same girls, started drinking at the same pubs, watched the same bands at Unity Hall (Stiff Little Fingers, Penetration, the Specials, an early and comparatively melodic persona of Iron Maiden, that kind of rubbish) and, on Sunday afternoons, gathered on the shallow, narrow terraced steps behind the posts at what used to be the Scoreboard End to natter and gossip, to josh and jape, and to support our team.

We sang rather more than Rugby League crowds did or do: the simple 'T-R-I-N-I-T-Y, Trinity, Trinity', the wonderful 'Chim-chiminey, chim-chiminey, chim-chim-cheroo/We are the nutters in red-white-and-blue', and the singularly inappropriate 'You are my sunshine'. If Wakefield were playing away from the Scoreboard End, we would duly troop back up the steps, round past the Supporters' Club kiosk, down through the tunnel under the old Double Two Stand (like the old scoreboard, no longer there; since I started visiting in 1975, Belle Vue has progressively weakened in the face of an incurable wasting disease which makes it look more like Milton Keynes every year) and into the paddock to stand by the far right-hand corner-flag, waiting for Zipper.

At a time when the nation's fashion sense was hauling itself back to respectability after suffering the indignities of the mid-1970s, Andrew 'Zipper' Fletcher was stoutly refusing to budge. Mexican moustache, sideburns, unkempt crinkly hair – Zipper would have looked more at home playing bass with the Eagles than right wing for Trinity. Yet, as he loitered there, hands on hips, head cowering into his shirt collar, and the play began to move across the field in his direction, your shoulders would tense and your fists would ball in your coat pockets, because you knew the scurrying pace he possessed within his spare, bony frame.

Zipper's acceleration off the mark didn't inspire many people to write home, and it was that more than anything which was to leave him with the goats when the game studied Trinity to sort out its sheep. Rather, his try-scoring tended to be from 20 metres-plus: give him the early ball on which he thrived and – inside? outside? – he would hand the dunce's cap to a distinguished cast of opposite numbers on his way past and towards our corner. Game as a hung pheasant in defence, it seemed a contradiction in terms a few years later when he was forced out of Rugby League temporarily by a dodgy heart; yet, true to the memory of those tightrope touch-line dashes, an electric hare heading the dogs by a nerveless few yards, he was back on the flank before we had had a chance to miss him and, in defiance of age, medical advice and – as always – fashion, he was still turning out for Barrow as recently as 1993.

Zipper was the crowd's sweetheart, the rapier point of a Trinity side which had been steadily evolving over the previous two seasons to the stage where, on Bill Kirkbride becoming coach in January 1979, it was just about the perfect beast – a swift and sturdy cross-breed incorporating several strains of Rugby Union *naïveté* and extravagance, a strong gene of youthful ambition, and an old head to walk it down the lushest tree-lined paths.

The pack was the crucible in which these last two ingredients blended most smoothly. Unusually shrewd transfer dealings had recently brought in the rehabilitated hatchet-man John Burke and the acclaimed ball-playing second row Bill Ashurst to add *savoir-faire* to the reliable grafting of Graham Idle and, although wonky knees meant that barely 20 games came out of Ashurst in three years, Burke hit such a rich streak of form that he went to Australia as a replacement on the Lions tour in the summer of 1979. Around these three, the sap rose in the form of Skerrett (whose whole style and demeanour was obviously determined by the fact that he was reared by a club called Bison), the Rayne twins (barnstorming second-rowers indistinguishable from the terraces, unless you could make out the slightly squarer jaw of Keith or the extra inch or two on Kevin's flowing mane), and the all-action, all-tackling, all-poaching and, sadly for him in the long term, all-too-light-weight loose forward, Paul McDermott.

It was the hooker, Alan McCurrie, an off-comer from Whitehaven, who embodied best of all this hybrid of youth and experience up front. He was in fact aged 25; but add an Arran sweater, and his outward appearance would have been that of one of the Spinners, 35 going on 40, with his grizzled beard and pre-maturely greying hair. However, he played his rugby with the zest of a teenager, always trying something – a grubber from dummy-half, a chip over the defensive line, a little flipped reverse pass into space – which made him alternately rooster when it came off, and feather-duster when it didn't. Since the success/failure balance tilted, percentage-wise, in favour of the latter, McCurrie was the butt of the crowd as much as Zipper was the bees' knees. But he was never less than watchable and, on the days when it all turned to gold for him, the bounce in his stride was irrepressible.

Behind the scrum, Zipper's supply-line relied for its steadi-ness on the expertise of Topliss at stand-off and, to a lesser extent, Les Sheard – for the twin challenges of the young Trevor Midgley, a highly capable footballer who was as good under the high ball as any, and the treatment room were beginning to strip the No. 1 shirt off Les's back with growing frequency. These apart, the rest were Rugby Union converts and, say what you like about that sort of cove infiltrating our game and hijacking the limelight, they were the ones who really lit the candle for me in those years.

Mike Lampkowski signed for Trinity in 1977 in the blaze of publicity which will always illuminate prominent Rugby Union signings. Prominence in this case meant four caps as a scrum-half for England, a brief international career remarkable only for the rumour associated with it which held that he had had to be taught how to spin-pass at the squad session which preceded his debut. True or not, Lampy appeared stung by this implied criticism throughout his time in Rugby League, to the extent that he seldom passed the ball in anger again.

Because of his sheer stockiness – 14 stone distributed evenly over his 5ft 8in frame – defending against him must have been like standing in a narrow street in Pamplona during the running of the bulls. Body low slung and cocked forward, a determined leer slicing his chubby, saturnine face in two, Lampy would set off always on a curving trajectory, heading for a gap which may or may not have existed two or three men further down the defensive line. Once there, the hand-off would come into play: leaning weightily on the shoulder of the crouching would-be tackler, he would lever himself onwards like a pole vaulter, simultaneously driving his hapless victim downwards, nose first into the turf. At a time when the typical scrum-half was more whippet than mastiff, Lampy initially proved unstoppable, and was Trinity's leading try-scorer in his first full season, 1977–78, before opponents started asking him to pick on people more his own size.

The legacy of Lampy's combative, confrontational style was twofold: one, a nose which looked more like the slalom course at Garmisch-Partenkirchen than any recognisable facial feature; and two, an eventual switch into the pack, to loose forward, to accommodate Allan Agar in the No. 7 shirt from 1980. The latter move did much to impress his handprints in the pavement on the personal Hollywood Boulevards of the Trinity supporters – one of the finest sights at Belle Vue that season was Lampy kick-starting his run from way out in the centres, looping fully 30 metres back infield to clatter on to a one-off close by the ruck. Unfortunately, however, it also foreshortened his career by a good five years, as a series of crippling injuries had effectively finished him by 1983.

If play was by the right-hand touchline, and you picked up movement from the left in your peripheral vision, and it wasn't Lampy winding up to charge, then a pound to a penny it was Brian Juliff coming over to sort out a member of the opposition for some imaginary transgression to which he had taken umbrage while fidgeting impatiently out on the far wing. Scrum brawls were a favourite for this particular brand of matesmanship: 'Mad Bri' thought little of a 50-yard journey to plant someone before being led away shouting 'hold me back, hold me back' over his shoulder to a perplexed prop forward roughly three times his size. This way, he probably notched up as many knockdowns as touchdowns after coming north from Wales in 1978. Still, despite lacking Zipper's Terpsichorean footwork and sustained sprinter's pace, Juliff complemented his oppo with a drag-racer's pick-up over the shorter distance and a robust, uncomplicated approach to the last-ditch custodians of the corner-flag. Neither of them boasted scoring rates in the Rosenfeld class; but their mutual average of one every two games meant that few weeks went by without one of them seeing his name in the Monday papers.

It is a little surprising now to look back through the programmes from the 1978–79 season and see that, for at least half the matches, the No. 2 shirt which I consider to have had Zipper's name permanently sewn inside the collar was in fact sported by the shorter, squatter figure of Adrian Barwood. Barwood emerged from the Principality at the same time as Juliff and Steve Diamond but, in unforgiving history as well as fray-edged nostalgia, never really made it. Diamond did, however: the occasional frailty of his centre play was successfully camouflaged by throwing the goal-kicker's cloak over him in autumn 1979, and he drew on this new string to the extent of putting over 100 goals in each of the next two seasons, topping the League's point-scoring charts in 1980–81. After joining Fulham for the following campaign, he promptly seized the opportunity to write his name in large letters and indelible ink all over the pristine pages of their brand-new record books. His passing from Belle Vue was not mourned with the same despair as signalled the departure of Topliss from this world at the same time, nor of Skerrett the year before; but when you spend three years playing straight man to a nutter like Juliff, you must expect there to be bushels all over your light at the final reckoning.

In all this gallery of character sketches, there was one name I would look for first of all in the team list, one player who offered the flirtatious promise of an everlasting moment of sublime, super-human skill, one man whom I would track from pit village to capital city in the hope that this would again be the day on which his fitful genius would discharge itself over a few square metres of humble turf. There are precious few players in any sport who can produce the paranormal on a regular basis, and these are the ones whom people will travel thousands of miles and pay out hundreds of pounds to see. Then there are players who have it in them, but need all the planets to be in delicate balance for it to come out. And there are players who do it perhaps just once in their careers and then retreat ever after to hide in the ranks of the mediocre, either terrified of their own potential or forgetful of the combination they had used to get the door to open.

Keith Smith most certainly belonged to that second group of players, although it often seemed more like Halley's Comet than the balance of the planets which served as his inspiration. For much of the time, he looked as though he would be happier among the third group; I was convinced, however, that his rightful place was among the first – if only he wasn't injured so much, if only he wasn't distracted by the burden of goalkicking, if only . . .

Like Lampy, Smithy was a former England Rugby Union international, capped four times by his country at centre between 1974 and 1975. These were the years when the England selectors picked their teams by the judicious means of a hatpin and a copy of *Rugby World & Post*, when Smithy was wantonly discarded and saw that even such a colossally talented fly-half as Alan Old was being overlooked in favour of the likes of Neil Bennett, Martin Cooper and Chris Williams (yes, exactly – who?), there was no just impediment to prevent his being joined in marriage to Trinity's cheque. He turned professional in 1977.

At 6ft 1in and pushing 14 stone, Smithy was perfectly equipped to handle the physical challenge of the new code, but he never produced much evidence to suggest that he relished that side of things. Instead, he played heavily on the souvenirs he had brought with him from Union: a ghostly glide to the outside of his marker, a seductive shift of the hips which both allured and dismissed the tackler, a pair of hands which passed with the sensitive timing of a Swiss watch. By virtue of his having been a part-time fly-half for Roundhay Rugby Union – and therefore able to kick, the reasoning ran – he was also employed as a goalkicker in his first two seasons with Trinity. In this, he showed not so much a golden boot, more feet of clay, and it must have been a huge relief for him to be able subsequently to pass the buck to Steve Diamond. It certainly was for the supporters.

There are two days which stand out in the memory, days when Smithy must have woken up, stretched long like a cat before a blazing fire, and thought, 'Yes – today we can turn it on.' Oddly, they fell within two months of each other, which for Smithy was reliability itself. And, equally oddly, they came only four or five months before, at the age of 29, he decided to quit, in what the *Rothmans Rugby League Yearbook* called a 'shock retirement'. Shock? You could have knocked me down with a feather. It had been no secret that Smithy was disillusioned (a) with his rather prominent nose being used for target practice by the League's flying elbows and swinging forearms, and (b) with a series of irritating, niggling injuries. But retire? It was heartbreaking: with Smithy went, for a time, a sizeable chunk of my enthusiasm for Rugby League.

Still, before he left, he was good enough to unearth two priceless gems as a legacy by which all of us could remember him. The first of these was remarkable for a number of reasons, not merely Smithy. It was February 1981, Fulham's debut season as a Rugby League club, and Trinity had been drawn against them, away, in the first round of what was then the Three Fives Challenge Cup. What an adventure: an early-morning drive the thousand miles to London, a whistle-stop gawp at the sights, a first taste of the almost-completely-unheard-of Big Mac, strawberry shake and large fries – what an exotic and wonderful treat! – and then strange streets, strange ground, strange accents on a strange terrace. And all of it laced with the adrenalin of risk, Indiana Jones-style, the danger that we would be ambushed by the hostile natives of this alien land, the first team ever to lose to Fulham in the Cup.

The upset was on the cards, too, as Reggie Bowden's Molotov cocktail of hardened north-western veterans and eclectic southern converts went up in the face of our boys and was still blazing merrily well into the second half. A cool head was required to douse the flames, and Smithy duly marched forward to man the pump from a set scrum 30 metres out. Receiving the ball from Topliss, he stepped smartly off his right foot and doubled back against the flow of the move, towards the breaking forwards. In quest of the narrow and now congested blind side, like a serpent through a colonnade, he disappeared momentarily from sight among the milling throng, and all you could see of him was his dark blond head carried high, noble, and bedrock-steady as he cruised unmolested through the choppy waters. Then, suddenly, he was out the other side and free, heading for the corner and into the pincer tackle of the covering full-back and the backtracking winger. From their respective angles of attack, they should have coincided around Smithy some five or six metres out from the line. But – a feint, an inclination of the shoulder, a barely perceptible change of pace, and our man was in.

I reckon Smithy must have beaten seven or eight men on the way to that try. It was nothing short of a miracle – like those soldiers in the First World War who are supposed to have gone over the top to certain death in a hail of enemy machine-gun fire, and yet reached the next trench without a scratch on them. Fulham were shattered by this phenomenon: Zipper added a characteristic second soon afterwards, and victory was ours, 9–5. The dreams on the way back up the M1 were sugar-sweet.

The 1981 Cup run didn't really develop further than a brisk walk but, come the season's end, Trinity were up with the leaders in the title race when Leeds came to Belle Vue. Leeds–Wakefield has the spice of a lively Madras curry for the Trinity fan, not least because the West Yorkshire rivals have traditionally mono-polised all the glory, prestige, money, players and – worst of all – arrogance that has been on offer in the county. There are few more belly-filling joys than to be an underdog who has knocked over a Chippendale table and bitten through a tweed-suited trouser leg.

The Leeds side who arrived that April afternoon contained a number of players who would only be understudies for walk-on parts in any of Ken Dalby's admirable club histories. Once again (ho ho), the Loiners had underachieved that year, and the presence of the unfamiliar likes of Massa, Lister, Mackintosh, Townend, Sykes and Miller in their line-up represented them marking time until the campaign was over and the annual rebuilding could begin afresh. But the threequarter line still included Atkinson, Dyl and Hague, and the pack was still mustered by the two Davids, Ward and Heron. So nothing should be allowed to detract from Smithy's achievement . . .

Quite simply, he was brilliant. They were the sort of condi-tions that centres and wide-running second rows would sell their grannies for: warm sunshine, a gentle, cooling breeze, and the ground firm for purchase underfoot. Despite the best attentions of the noisome Dyl, Smithy did much as he liked. Run after long, sweeping, graceful, arcing run slit the Leeds defence to ribbons, like an acutely-honed scimitar through a fine silk curtain. He scored a hat-trick himself, and the ruptures he opened down the right did much to earn a further three tries for the left-wing pairing of Steve Tinker and Juliff, as the cover scrambled across to stem his flow only to be swamped from the rear when the ball came back across field. Trinity romped home 43–10, nine tries in all, and we believed that we had been in the presence of great-ness.

We hadn't, of course. The only consistent thing about Smithy, after all, was his inconsistency and, in that, he had much in common with his contemporaries at Belle Vue – that was the real reason why they were merely fine instead of golden or great.

Everyone who followed Wakefield recognised that singular failing: when Trinity blew their Championship chance in 1981 by losing three of their last five matches, there was disappointment, yes, but not surprise. We had travelled similar roads for the past three seasons, where smooth stretches of freeway form had suddenly become pot-holed cart-tracks, and successive title challenges had trundled home in twelfth, tenth and tenth places. The only novel feature of 1981 was that it had taken so long for the team to hit the hard shoulder.

Nevertheless, there are scientifically viable theorems which unite the laws of physics and statistics that govern patterns of random activity and, when you apply these to the results of a Rugby League team who can beat anybody on their day, you get a Cup run. So it came to pass that Bill Kirkbride acceded to the dugout bench and – most certainly by accident rather than design – became the final and crucial variable in the equation, the one which bounced Trinity off down the road to Wembley in spring 1979.

Admittedly, in the early rounds, they were not called on to show that ability to beat anybody on their day. Instead, they beat nobody: Fev in the first round and Barrow in the third were both speed-skating down the slippery slope to relegation, while Oldham in the second round were a moderate side even by second division standards. But the true hallmark of every Trinity side I have known is their Samaritan generosity of spirit towards poor opposition, their willingness often to suffer tremendous personal humiliation in order not to kick a dog while he's down. Thus they gave Fev every chance to resurrect their ailing season before apologetically leaving their bedside, 10–7; thus Smithy sympathetically missed six or seven shots at goal to keep the Oldham score down to 19–7; thus Zipper left it as late as he possibly could before offering the humane killer to Barrow, 8–5. What great guys, eh?

And then, what d'you know, it was the semi-finals, and St Helens. The fact that the romance of the Cup had hitherto been little more than a grope behind the bike sheds meant that we – and, I suspect, the team – didn't quite realise exactly where we were, like Wily E. Coyote tracking Road Runner in the fog, only for it to clear and for him to find that he's walked off a cliff. So long as we were wrapped in the fog, and we couldn't look down, we were blissfully, innocently happy.

We had St Helens at home the week before the semi, in one of those cagey, close-to-the-chest dress rehearsals wherein neither side wants to open every drawer in case the trade secrets get pinched. The ground was packed, though: the part-timers realised better than the regulars what was around the corner, put down their pints and their pontificating in the pub, and returned to Belle Vue where they could be heard swearing that they'd always had faith in the team and, yes, of course, generally speaking, they never missed a match. Slightly miffed at having our prerogative, not to mention our patch behind the posts, purloined by these Johnny-come-lately pot-hunters, we none the less perched precariously on top of the terraces and lustily sang 'I'd rather be a Muppet than a Saint' for the whole 80 minutes. Trinity won, comfortably.

Buoyed by this, but increasingly disquieted by a dawning sense of history in the making, we went to Headingley the following Saturday in a mood of fettered optimism, one which dare not speak its name lest it put the Indian sign on the team. After 70 minutes, however, it was as if the very contemplation of the outcome had brought not just the sign, but the whole take-away down on our lads. It was tight – very tight. And, despite Lampy's taurean tendencies having been ignited throughout by the sight of the red V on the Saints' shirts, we were struggling, 6–7 down, pinned in our own 22 by Gorley, Nicholls, Chisnall and Co., and living in terror of Les Jones getting one more decent pass with only Diamond and Juliff to beat.

Creatures of habit, we were up the other end, close to ground level in Zipper's corner, craning to get a clear view of events, subdued now in anticipation of another let-down. Then it happened, and it is happening still in slow motion on dark, depressed, lonely nights in Trinity households where there seems little hope of them ever winning again. Somehow, Topliss wriggles free of the Saints front line and is away, up to the ten-metre line. There, outside him, is Smithy, elegantly moving through the gears, calling for the ball. He clasps it in those surgeon's hands, and now he's up to half-way, drawing the full-back. And Zipper's on the rails, messy perm streaming in the wind behind him, head bent forward as if sniffing the earth for the scent of the score. Smithy's done this, in training and matches, 100 times before: run at the full-back's inside shoulder, commit himself to yourself, release the pass. Perfect, like clockwork. Jones is corner-flagging desperately, but

Zipper has a good ten metres on him. He's hurtling towards us, straight as a crossbow bolt, and the only thing that separates us and him is an ever-diminishing volume of fresh air.

It was, as Cyril Briggs rather eccentrically explained in the Wembley programme, 'a really winning try'. When Zipper found sanctuary in front of us, we went up like a mistreated can of lager. All the photographers had gathered down the other end, waiting for Saints' *coup de grâce*, but we forgave them when we saw the fruits of their labours. Both *The Yorkshire Post* and *The Wakefield Express* carried panoramic shots of the whole of Zipper's corner – the man himself sprawling on all fours in the act of touching down, and you could pick out each one of us beyond him, arms aloft, faces contorted like gaping, gleeful gargoyles as we hollered our delight. Bloody hell, we were saying, now presuming to believe – we've done it.

Wakefield, nominally a city, but really a village, the smallest of worlds, went Wembley-loopy. The permanently-absents joined the part-timers on the terraces for the last few League matches, boosting the seasonal average crowd to over 4,000. The team, in strict observation of pre-Wembley ritual, lost those last few League matches and entered a number of players in the race to be fit for the final, with Ashurst (eventually placed) and McDermott (eventually nowhere) at the head of the field. Local bus companies called in every available chara and chartered out the lot at opportunistically-inflated prices for the Wembley weekend – with a fortnight still to go, there wasn't a seat empty to get out of town. Everyone you saw was wearing maroon, acrylic, V-necked 'Wembley 1979' pullovers, purchased from the lottery shop on Kirkgate, whose chief characteristic was that the seams went after a week, leaving you with huge ventilation holes under your armpits. *The Wakefield Express*, in accordance with regulations laid down by the watchdogs of the press for local newspapers whose teams come up trumps, published a 'Wembley Special' pull-out section featuring all the facts about Our Lads and their Cup run. Was the normally non-combatant Keith Smith really a debt-collector whose favourite film star was Clint Eastwood?

What happened at the Empire Stadium on Saturday 5 May 1979 has been well documented. As the coach took them up Wembley Way, the Trinity players saw the fog lift; they looked down, and there they were – off the end of the cliff. Folklore has it that their bottle went irretrievably at that moment, and the white-clad Widnes, sneeringly blasé on their fourth trip down south in five years, were the milkmen who duly collected it. The 12–3 scoreline represented neither real disgrace nor the actual gulf between the sides. Zipper – who else – got the try that ranked with Dusty Bin and the *Blankety Blank* cheque-book and pen among the great prizes of our time. And Topliss covered himself with what glory there had been allocated to Trinity by the Fates – about enough to knit a jockstrap – by claiming the Lance Todd Trophy. After you've said that, you've said it all.

I don't know to this day why I didn't go – why I never even seriously considered it. My best offering is that, somewhere inside, I knew they were going to lose, perhaps to be embarrassed; it takes an ego stronger than mine was then to stand idly by and watch those whom you have appointed as paragons of manly virtue allow themselves to be stripped, mocked and scourged in such a public arena. Instead, I made my excuses and went to watch Yorkshire play Nottinghamshire in the Benson & Hedges Cup at Bradford Park Avenue, a match which saw Geoffrey Boycott score 45 in as many overs, which was brought to an early close by sub-zero temperatures and a blizzard, and which was infinitely more fun than I would have had at Wembley. I didn't even ask the result when I got home – I only found it out later that evening by accident, although most of me already knew. Kekhead brought me a programme back, which I flicked disinterestedly through and then laid aside. I read no newspaper reports, watched no high-lights, and treated with incredulity all those insane rumours which dared to suggest that the Dreadnoughts had, in fact, dreaded everything. Getting to Wembley had been such a marvellous high, such a mountainous achievement by a wonderful team: let's leave it at that, shall we? Let's just say we were good enough to play there.

Two or three years ago, I met Les Sheard at a Student Rugby League conference in a hotel in Leeds. Gaunt and bespectacled, clad in brogues, cords, tweed jacket and cheesecloth shirt, he looked every inch the middle-aged, middle-of-the-road teacher he now is. Needless to say, I stared straight into his eyes and didn't recognise him. I had to be introduced, whereupon a *frisson* engaged the synapse of my brain which copes with teenage experiences. We chatted politely for a while over a coffee, and then I wandered off to talk to someone else. As I left him I thought,

'There's been some mistake. That's not Les Sheard. It might be *a* Les Sheard, but it's not *the* Les Sheard – *the* Les Sheard used to play for Trinity . . .'

NEIL TUNNICLIFFE works for the Rugby Football League, in a capacity which he finds difficult to put into words. He believes that seven years at Oxford University, a doctorate in ancient history, and two years as Dave Hadfield's publisher comprised the perfect vocational training for his current position.

'LIFT 'IM OWER, 'E'S ONLY LITTLE'

Featherstone Rovers 1987–88

Chris Westwood

Rugby League seasons, like all periods in history, don't exist in isolation, nor do they start and finish at specific times or dates, despite having defined portions of the calendar devoted to them. For instance, concepts such as 'The Sixties' and 'Victorian times' grate with me. Did the entire population of the Western World suddenly back-comb their hair, wear pink lipstick and 'piss-holes in the snow' eye make-up (*à la* Dusty Springfield), and start driving round in Mini-Mokes while doin' the hully-gully, the minute the chimes of Big Ben had ushered in the new decade? Of course not. If you take notice of the documentaries, though, everyone in Britain was either a mod, a rocker or, later on, a vacantly smirking flower child, yet my dad and uncles looked exactly the same as they had done since VE day. By the same token, people didn't start putting curtains round their piano legs, or sending urchins up chimneys, the minute Queen Victoria was crowned. You have to bear in mind that she was on the throne for over 60 years. Things can't have been as dour as the history books tell us for all that time, surely?

The reason I am telling you this is so that you won't be surprised, confused or, let's face it, downright incredulous when I inform you that 1987–88, the season I am going to recount, has echoes that go back as far as 1959 in its significance for me. For 1959 was the year that it got to me. It got to me in the way that Rugby League football has got into the blood of all those who stand with the sleet in their faces at the Watersheddings, Craven Park (Hull or Barrow, take your pick), or Post Office Road every winter weekend for the rest of their lives from that moment. I'm not parochial: I'm sure that the denizens of the ANZ Stadium in Brisbane, or North Sydney Oval, need the same weekly fix as the rest of us. I want the people of Soweto and the South of England to feel the same, for that matter. Because I have been going to Rugby League matches since the age of four – which is entirely typical of anyone who is brought up in my home town of Featherstone.

If you were around during the early 1960s you are supposed to remember where you were and what you were doing when Kennedy was shot – an overworked myth if ever there was one. But that was the impact that Rovers' against-all-odds victory in front of a club-record crowd against the mighty St Helens had on me. The Saints players – perhaps an optical illusion created by the red band across their gleaming white jerseys – looked huge. The crowd surged and heaved involuntarily, my calves throbbed with the soreness that the hem of my Jimmy Clitheroe-style gaberdine mac was inflicting on them. For a great proportion of this historic game, my main view was of the increasing amount of Woodbine ash which was accumulating on the Brylcreemed head of the bloke in front. Dads rolled up newspapers into cones for their kids to pee into. You wouldn't have wanted to leave the scene of the drama to go to the lav, even if you had been able to.

I was confirmed into the High Church of Rugby League from the day of that game with Saints. I was given a matching set of Samsonite emotional baggage which stayed with me into the period of my adulthood, when I had to decide if, when and how I was to introduce my own son to the inseparably intertwined pleasure and pain of being a Rugby League fan, together with the added responsibility of being a Featherstone Rovers supporter. Coming from Featherstone is not special: it is more than that. You are the result of a happenstance which is the genetic equivalent of the quest for the Dalai Lama, or Tony Hancock when he realised that he was in a rare blood group. 'Different from the rest of the herd', says it sweetly and unpretentiously.

The kid was five, and it was time. I'd thought about it a lot. There's nothing worse than foisting your dreams on your kids: the public parks are full of parents committing this sin every weekend; screaming at refs at junior matches, no matter what the sport; willing their children to achieve what they couldn't. It's the same with piano lessons as well, I expect. I was determined not to fall for that one. If he didn't like Rugby League, well, Okay. But who was I to deny him his birthright?

The 1987–88 season would have been a more poignant one in which to start us watching Rugby League together if Rovers weren't going to be spending it in the second division. An against-all-odds (that phrase again) victory at Wembley in 1983 against the mighty (that word again) Hull FC, in a final that could have been scripted by Captain W. E. Johns, was merely the prelude to two years of bitterness and poverty in the village, as first the local economy was wrecked by the miners' strike, and then its heart and soul seemed to be taken away when the pit was closed on the very day the miners marched back to work (they really did this time). This was closely followed by the Main Stand being pulled down at Post Office Road. Like most sports stadia in this country, the Main Stand housed the changing-rooms, gym, and administration of the club. Its destruction seemed to tear the heart out of the club as much as the closure of the pit had torn the heart out of the village.

Or had it? Well, no, actually. The village still exists, of course, making the best of unemployment figures well above the national average, and without the tinnitus hum of pit ventilation fans, and there are fewer blokes on the street with those tell-tale blue scars on their cheeks nowadays. And with much hard work, improvisation and vision, the Main Stand was replaced with state-of-the-art changing and fitness facilities and a superstructure cast in that 'mid-1980s, light industrial/commercial premises in an enterprise zone' mould. I'm not knocking it, just describing it. But I wouldn't want to be sat on the front row with the wind in the wrong direction.

Be that as it may, in the true spirit of the place and the time, the Rovers had gone down at the end of the 1986–87 season. Towards the end of that season we had a trial run, a night game with Wigan. I figured that, even if Martin (I can't just keep calling him 'the kid') didn't like Rugby League after all, then at least he would have seen the best. For Ellery Hanley was in his prime, probably the best Rugby League player in the world then.

The Rovers' floodlights at the time had been obtained second-hand from Elland Road greyhound stadium. The general consensus was that they wouldn't have done for a Subbuteo set. However, they still created the same effect that all floodlit sports events have: colours are heightened, the faces of the crowd seem to take on a certain glow, the stadium is an oasis of light and expectation isolated in its defiance of the surrounding darkness. Hanley and his team dismantled the Rovers defence like some of the more jerry-built sections of the Berlin Wall. Ellery seemed to be scoring arrogantly right in front of us every two minutes before disappearing into the semi-darkness, only to return.

I suspect that this, other than the fact that it *was* a massacre, isn't quite what it was like; but that is the impression I was left with. That and the effect of meeting my cousin, who played for the Rovers in the 1960s. The pound coin he pressed into Martin's hand was white-knuckle gripped for the duration of the match and, throughout this one-sided game and long after he had fallen asleep that night, my son's expression was like one of those pictures you see of open-mouthed kids at the circus. I knew then that, come August, we would be checking out some serious Rugby League together, even if it was in division two.

The Rovers had changed coaches during 1986–87 from Allan Agar, the local boy who took them to that comic-book Wembley victory, to George Pieniazek, who didn't stand a chance considering the turmoil, communal poverty and social unrest going on around him. Another local boy, the garrulous Paul Daley, came for a second spell, took the side into the second division, and went. Daley was followed for the 1987–88 season by another second coming, one that was to leave even the Jehovah's Witnesses impressed. Probably one of the most successful interludes in the Rovers' history had been between 1972 and 1974. Two Wembley appearances, one of them won with gusto, the second one lost through the team spending 80 minutes trying to wreak revenge on Alex Murphy instead of trying to win a game of Rugby League. The man with his hand on the tiller during this historic period was the legendary Peter Fox. Peter had been around a bit since then, of course. He'd coached Great Britain, for instance, and Bradford Northern during one of their intermittent golden ages. More recently, however, he'd been dismissed by Leeds at Christmas-time after being told that his job was safe. After this rather Dickensian episode in his career, it was somehow fitting that he should return to the village where he was given and took his first chance in coaching a pro club.

Although they had a spanking new set of facilities, Rovers were still skint. So Fox was going to have to steer the side back into the first division with one arm tied behind his back, and try to equip them to stay there on the income generated by the visits of such as Batley, Carlisle and Bramley – in other words, nothing. Still, if anybody could, he could.

Some of the players under his guidance for this season were to achieve unimaginable fame and riches within the next few years. Others . . . er, weren't. Graham Steadman, the club's record-signing stand-off, supplied that bit of dash; he was and is a stereotypically smooth lounge lizard of a stand-off (although he plays at full-back since joining Featherstone's deeply-respected and highly-esteemed neighbours Castleford – please read this bracket through gritted teeth for the desired effect). The Ronald Colman of Rugby League players, it was Steadman who made going to Whitehaven and Doncaster worthwhile during this less-than-glamorous season. Steadman's partner at No. 7 was Deryck Fox, signed just after the 1983 Wembley appearance, and the leading member of what was at the time a well-regarded cadre of promising young players – Paul 'Bosh' Lyman, Ian Smales and Chris Bibb being, alongside Fox, the best of the bunch. Lyman, an aggressive back-rower, was to move to Hull Kingston Rovers and obscurity the following year; Deryck Fox was to follow his name-sake and mentor to Bradford Northern for a large amount of money in 1992; and Smales, an international-class utility player, was to join Steadman at Castleford the following year (keep gritting those teeth), leaving the periodically-discontented Bibb now the final link with the period.

Elsewhere in the squad was the extremely local local hero Pete Smith, at the back end of a fine career and with the injury problems to prove it; and the well-thought-of-but-rarely-picked-for-representative-games, Steve Quinn, holder of several permutations of goal- and point-scoring records, whose recognition for all his achievements at Featherstone was a mere handful of Yorkshire caps. Meanwhile, prop forward, Karl Harrison, had been brought from Bramley by Pieniazek, and was to move around the same time as Steadman to find fame and probably fortune via first Hull

FC and then Halifax, while on the way taking part in Great Britain's historic 1990 defeat of the Kangaroos at Wembley.

The first nine games of season 1987–88 reside somewhere cowering at the back of my memory banks. There is a vague impression of games lost to people such as Barrow, and talk of Rovers' ascent back to division one not being as straightforward as a lot of people had predicted. I remember thinking that this might be a blessing in disguise, considering the threadbare nature of both the club's bank balance and the squad. But it is little things that I remember most. Little but significant in terms of the picture I had in my mind of how I wanted things to be for Martin in his first full season as a Rugby League fan. Things like the standard phrase, 'Lift 'im ower, old cock, 'e's only little', used by turnstile operators everywhere. The first tomato ketchup running down the jumper sleeve from the first hot dog (not my sleeve, I assure you), and the first 'I hope Graham Steadman's playing today', as we shuffled along in the queue outside the ground – an observation which assured me that we were getting somewhere. The first sputterings of the flames of hero worship (not my hero worship, I assure you . . . honest).

I had once seen a picture in an Australian Rugby League magazine of the Papua New Guinea centre Bal Numapo wearing full tribal regalia. This made a big impression. I thought it exotic, and telling, that a Rugby League player could look like that and not be kidding. It was as though Numapo had proved that Rugby League was part of the big wide world after all. In autumn 1987, the Kumuls, the Papua New Guinea touring side, were in Europe, and the first match of the British leg of their visit was to be against Featherstone Rovers. The idea was that the game would celebrate the official opening of Rovers' new facilities, but it was far more than that. Here was a group of people who lived in a country that consisted largely of tropical rain forest, a country that had been brutally occupied by the Japanese less than 50 years previously. This gave a poignancy, if you paused to think about it, to the plaque in the working men's club at the top end of the village, dedicated to a member who had died in a Japanese POW camp. Here was a group of people who didn't just come from the other side of the world, they actually looked as though they did. They spoke pidgin English, for God's sake. And Rugby League was their national sport.

It was a pleasant afternoon for mid-October. Some people

weren't even wearing coats, but it must have seemed like Siberia to the Kumuls. None of the side looked big, but they looked absolutely made for it. The game was full of skill and cut and thrust, and Papua New Guinea were the victors. This seemed almost irrelevant; what mattered most was that they were actually here. After the hooter, people – including the two of us – went on to the field to mingle with the Papuan players. Don't get me wrong, I'm not a pitch-invading sort of person; but nothing was going to stop me meeting Bal Numapo. 'Hi, Bal, great game,' was the furthest I could get from inadequate drivel. 'Yeah, great,' was his reply as he headed for the dressing-rooms. It was just starting to get dark as winter approached.

The Rovers started to pick up wins among the still worrying and uncharacteristic losses to clubs such as pre-Crusaders Fulham and pre-Border Raiders Carlisle. These games were usually away from home, though, and we hadn't started to go to away games just yet. So the Rovers were winning enough, and Graham Steadman was being flamboyant enough in the way he caused confusion and frustration in opposing defences, to maintain the interest in the heart of a six-year-old who, like all six-year-olds, feels the cold and has a yet-to-be-developed attention span. God help the parent who tries to initiate their child into the wonders of Rugby League via a team that loses regularly, or plays at a stadium where the climate and shelter dictate that the stewards are members of a mountain rescue team.

Perversely, I don't envy fans of the Winfield Cup clubs in Australia. I enjoy watching their matches on television, I like the way they stage the game, and I also like the little slices of real Australian life you see going on – the huge cargo ships that pass behind the popular side of the Steelers' Stadium at Wollongong, the gridlocked traffic in the background of games played at the Sydney Football Stadium, and the bloke in the vest who always leads the Balmain Tigers on to the field. But as my mother used to say when she plonked the suitcases down on the hall floor every summer, 'It's all right to go for your holidays, but I wouldn't want to live there.'

There's a lot wrong with standing (or sitting, for that matter) in freezing wet weather as darkness approaches, watching people crash into each other on a muddy field – but that's the whole point, isn't it? Why do you think all the best Christian and pagan festivals are in the depths of winter? The Christians usually hijacked the pagan ones and renamed them when they took over anyway; why do you think Christmas is on 25 December? As John Lennon once said: 'Whatever gets you through the night is all right.' And so it is with the British winter: whatever gets you through it is all right. And this is what Rugby League does. Would you rather be with the poor saps you see trailing round the local DIY Superstore, heads bowed with that defeated look, pushing a trolley full of chipboard that will either end up in the garage when second thoughts set in or be wasted on some botched shelving job? No, thank you very much.

Boxing Day brought the semi-traditional game against local rivals Wakefield Trinity. This fixture depends, of course, upon both teams being in the same division, and the fact that they were both in the second seemed to dull the piquancy of the occasion slightly – although the miniature of Bushmills Irish whiskey in my inside pocket ensured that I was at least able to extend a certain mellow bonhomie to those, even those from Wakefield, in my immediate vicinity. The miniature (or the hip flask, if you have pretensions) is a sure sign of the onset of the more reassuring aspects of middle age in the Rugby League fan – a kind of alcoholic cardigan.

The wins started to become more frequent after Christmas, and so did the dustings of snow which swept across the stadium like frozen acid. Enjoyable games were spent in the company of enthusiastic, uncritical Doncaster fans, whole families in matching home-made knitwear, devotees of a club which for many years was legendary for the wrong reasons. Another encounter with Fulham, in which one fan handed a huge bag of sweets round to the entire population of the stand. You'll recognise this man if ever you go to a London game: he's the little old guy with the hat covered in enamel badges. You get the impression that he was originally a Streatham and Mitcham fan, but he probably wasn't.

By March the climate was slowly, fitfully improving, and the enthusiasm of number one son hadn't just been maintained, it had blossomed. We were now deep into scrapbook and autograph territory, and being able to remember scores from games played seemingly ages ago, as well as slightly dangerous re-enactments of key moments of games on the kitchen floor, using a tea cosy for a ball.

We were now ready to go to an away game, and we picked a beauty. They don't come much more away than Whitehaven – unless you live in Workington, of course. Plenty of groundwork had to be done with the rest of the household, mainly on the 'it'll be a lovely day out for us all, it's near the Lake District, you know' theme. In the end, the time and expense of the trip were passed by the committee as justified, and we were away.

We nearly ended up watching Barrow versus Springfield Borough instead, after a wrong turning had us unwillingly exploring the Furness region. Grange-over-Sands looked okay and the Lakeside and Haverthwaite Railway was in full steam; it was all very tempting as we cruised tentatively past Craven Park and the steady ingress of Barrow fans dribbling through the turnstiles. Should we check out their game and put it down to experience? Should we hell! A quick look at a road atlas that should have been consulted more closely somewhere north of Skipton, and we were on the right road again and pretending we weren't too bothered about missing the kick-off. Soon we had Sellafield on our left looking like something out of *Quatermass* – you know, the one where those meteorites fall to earth and release a gas which gives people that peculiar mark on their face and they turn into zombies. I've often wondered, in idle moments, what happens when you ask an awkward question at the visitors' centre?

It would only have taken a downward slip of the cartographer's pencil for Whitehaven to have been a Scottish fishing town like, say, Arbroath or Stonehaven. The low-slung stone buildings had a red glow about them as they crouched in what was left of the day's sunshine; the country's last working steam-powered dredger drowsed in the harbour; all very untypical of a Rugby League town. There's plenty of cover at the Recreation Ground – there needs to be – but Rugby League is as much a part of the social fabric of Cumbria as it is of Papua New Guinea. When local amateur clubs such as Kells play pro sides in the knock-out competitions, their crowds are bigger and more passionate than those of Whitehaven, Workington, Carlisle or Barrow. Unfortunately for Whitehaven, however, people like Graham, Deryck and Bosh were now getting the heady aroma of the first division.

Rovers didn't finish up as second-division champions that year. They didn't deserve to. But they did get promotion, and they did round off their season in some semblance of a blaze of glory, and in surroundings which any team would be proud to play in, and in regard of which any fan would feel a glow when they spoke the oft-repeated phrase, 'I was there': the Premiership finals at Old Trafford. Chairman Mao said something like, 'The greatest journeys begin with a single step' – which just about gives you the flavour of the beginning of Rovers' quest for the grail of the second-division Premiership Trophy. (It also gives me the chance to look brainy, knowing some fancy quotations, but what the hell.) The first round was against Mansfield Marksman (see what I mean?), whom people used to call the Marksmen because the club hailed from Robin Hood country (*sic* – he was a Yorkshireman); but in fact they were called Marksman after a local brand of extremely insipid lager.

The semi-final was a home game against Wakefield, and the game went to the wire. What does this phrase really mean? What sort of wire is it? Is it a telephone wire upon which the result is gaspingly communicated to a panicky editor who has chanced his career by holding the front (or back) page? Is it a trip wire upon which the losers have stumbled in the dying seconds to be denied the spoils? Whatever, Trinity went down 16–20 courtesy of a Graham Steadman special, a kick from his own half which he chased and caught himself to score. You felt at times such as these that Steadman would be conjuring up this kind of alchemy for the Rovers for ever, but you knew different. There had already been rumours, and these rumours were to rumble on like the war clouds of the summer of 1939 into the summer of 1989 (do you see what I mean about Rugby League seasons not being governed by the calendar?). The rumours weren't just about him leaving, they were about him joining Castleford – a statement of similar moment to one that Ozzy Osbourne was going to join Black Lace, or that Picasso had been taking the mickey all along.

Let us return briefly to that moment of innocent bliss, when Rovers reached Old Trafford for the first time and the Wakefield fans didn't like it. They'd also been promoted, but only on the basis that three clubs were allowed up that year. And now they missed out on the glory and the necessary pay-day that an impoverished season in division two demands for a team who go up. But far be it from us to gloat . . .

So all our schlepping up the M6 to Carlisle, our searching for the Alfreton Stadium and the bleak afternoons at Mount Pleasant had been worthwhile. The seal was to be set on Martin's first season as a Rugby League fan in style. We joined the M62 behind a builders' van full of Rovers fans and beer crates. The banner tied to the back door said 'FEV ARE BACK', and these lads were going to make sure that everybody believed it. We lost them somewhere the other side of Oldham. Perhaps they have become a Rugby League equivalent of the Flying Dutchman, condemned forever to cruise some ghostly northern motorway, searching for a non-existent exit for Old Trafford. On the other hand, they probably went for a few beers.

Whenever you go to big Rugby League games, especially Cup finals and Test matches against the Australians, there is always an air of pilgrimage. The best example of this was at Leicester Forest East on the day of the 1992 World Cup final. People set up stalls to sell you things. People have a laugh with people whom they consider barely human on the day of a local derby. There is a cacophony of heraldry on the jumpers of clubs you have never even heard of. It was a bit like this at Old Trafford. Snapshots were taken under the plaque on the stadium wall which commemorates the Munich air disaster. Familiar faces, the faces of people you'd frozen with and grumbled with throughout the winter. People wearing a larger amount of home-made stuff in club colours than is the case these days (these were the early days of the replica strip).

It was a hot and dusty day. It was even hotter inside the stadium, and it was to become hotter still as a long, thrilling afternoon of Rugby League action unfolded. An afternoon which was to plumb the depths of despair as the Rovers players trudged from the field 0–22 down at half-time, and it looked like getting worse. But there was the messianic Steadman to apply cardiac massage to the fibrillating heart of Featherstone's hopes. Two typically flashy tries from him after the interval, one each from the long-disappeared Andy Bannister and David Sykes, five Steve Quinn goals, and we were ahead.

I don't think I have ever gone berserk in my life – although that is for others to say. If I have, then that afternoon is the only occasion on which I would freely admit to it. But then it was all snatched away from us when Des Foy scored for Oldham in the dying minutes, and Charlie McAlister potted the winning goal. Yet, there was no great sense of deflation. Perhaps being so far behind for so long gave no expectation of victory. Or perhaps it was like when you cut yourself badly, and it doesn't hurt for ages afterwards. I've never bothered to try to remember, because it was all subsequently overtaken by seeing Martin Offiah in the flesh for the first time in the first-division final. Offiah was considered a bit of a freak at the time – people weren't happy to call him a Rugby

League player, even. But that game, in which he didn't even score, was the only time I can think of when the crowd 'rose as one' – just like the papers used to say – whenever he looked like getting the ball.

Seven years' solid Fev-watching have now produced a 12-year-old Rugby League fanatic who can tell you results and scores leading on from that very first game under floodlights, when Ellery Hanley did whatever he liked right in front of our noses. That same person sleeps, plays and goes to weddings in a Penrith Panthers shirt and would welcome Graham Steadman back with open arms tomorrow. And so would I.

CHRIS WESTWOOD is Featherstone born and bred, and writes and takes photographs for the club's programme. Outside of that obsession, successfully passed on to his offspring, he teaches art in a secure unit for young offenders in Leeds.

KENNEDY DEAD, BUT WHITEHAVEN BEAT BATLEY

Whitehaven 1963–64

Harry Edgar

Laps, press-ups and touch-football. This was August, the month of optimism for every Rugby League supporter. The 1962–63 season had been hit by the big freeze and had run into June so, after the shortest close-season break you could imagine, pre-season training started in July. The game was on.

That 1962–63 season had been the one when I became a Whitehaven fanatic – didn't miss a single home game – after three previous years of steadily growing interest in Rugby League. But 1963–64 was to be the season when the doors of wider appreciation were opened to me and I started to see the big picture. And with that came the seeds of a frustration that has never left me, eventually for the game as a whole, but first fuelled by supporting a losing team. Note, *not* a team of losers: let's just say that you knew, when it came to the crunch, they were a team that didn't win. It has been a knowledge shared by other sports supporters all over the world, be they of the North Sydney Bears, Accrington Stanley, or even the Green Bay Packers in the post-Lombardi years. But, even if you wanted to, you cannot cut the ties that bind.

Whitehaven was my home town, and I was stuck with them. Forever.

Pre-season training in Whitehaven was a twice-weekly ritual, so eagerly anticipated by the most fanatical supporters, if not the players. It could make a 10-year-old leave the beach early on Tuesdays and Thursdays just to be at the Recreation Ground by 6 p.m., in time to see the first laps undertaken by panting, spitting, cussing, out-of-breath heroes.

I was never the first to arrive, though. Sam always got there before everybody. Sam Coulter had greeted players, visitors, directors, lords, ladies, mayors, anybody and everybody who had walked past the old black-and-white pavilion at the Recreation Ground since Whitehaven's very first game back in 1948. In the process, he had built up a collection of Rugby League jerseys and memorabilia that was – and still is – legendary. Sam was a walking hall of fame, with pen-pals and people prepared to send him souvenirs from what seemed like every corner of the globe. The ultimate was that, every year, he got a Christmas card from Reg Gasnier in Australia. We would gather round to gasp in awe at the genuine blue air-mail stickers and koala stamps on the envelope from Kogarah that Sam would proudly unfold from his coat pocket with a sense of timing and drama that was worthy of the Magic Circle. It was heady stuff: the world of Rugby League being revealed before my very eyes.

Standing majestically in the middle of all the training-ground activity was the coach, Jim Brough. Jim always, but always, wore his blue tracksuit with the words 'Great Britain' boldly emblazoned across the back above the Union Jack flag. It had been in his kitbag since 1958, when he had become the first man to accompany a British Lions touring team as their official coach.

Captain of the 1936 Lions, and the man at the centre of the storm in that most dramatic tour of all in 1958, Jim Brough was a living legend in our midst. He had been an accomplished journalist after his playing career finished at Leeds, before turning his hand to coaching with such positive effect with both Workington Town and Great Britain in the 1950s. He had been coaxed out of retirement for this spell in charge at Whitehaven, and his comeback was described as 'like an old war-horse unable to resist the scent of battle for one last time'. They don't write lines like that any more! Certainly, Jim had little to gain by coaching my team in 1963 except dents in his stately reputation, and he had by this time a world-weariness about him which told you immediately that he saw through all the banalities that would come to belittle many sports in this country.

Jim Brough had quality. He was my footballing guru, and even though I was just a kid I sensed he enjoyed our little conversations. They came as a tranquil respite for him from the bickering which surrounded the harsh realities of managing a struggling professional club. They gave him the chance to dip into a sepia-stained treasure chest of reminiscences, mostly of his tours as a Lion to Australia in 1928 and 1936 – not the one when he was coach in 1958, though; Jim never talked about that tour – when he was young, when they travelled down under by boat, wore plus-fours, the world was different, and he sat proudly as the captain in the middle of the Melba Studios photograph.

On those summer nights in early August 1963, I would sit on the grass with the Whitehaven players as they gratefully passed the water bottle during breaks in the pre-season trials. As they allowed their lungs to recuperate and wiped sweat from their brows, we would listen intently as the man in the blue Great Britain tracksuit quietly explained and cajoled, always returning to the key importance of operating an umbrella defence to force opponents to turn both the ball and their running patterns back infield. And you thought Warren Ryan first invented that a quarter of a century later.

For the fans, and the coach, the pre-season build-up is the best time of all. Optimism and anticipation are indeed the buzz words. Of course, all that will go out the window when your team plays its first competitive game and gets blitzed; but, as George Benson (the soul singer, not the excellent Hensingham prop forward of the time) once said: 'You can't take that away from me . . .'

Wrong, George! For Whitehaven fans in 1963–64, the wheels fell off even before the first ball was kicked, because the players went on strike. The anger, the shame, the sense of loss, was total. The opening weekend of Rugby League fixtures came, and we sat idle, not knowing what to do with the Saturday afternoon that had been circled in red on everybody's calendar for so long. The Recreation Ground terraces stood empty and silent; the chocolate-blue-and-gold jerseys stayed hanging on their pegs. We should have played Bradford Northern in that opening fixture, and its postponement eventually led to the game never being played at all, as Bradford disbanded after playing just 13 of their scheduled 26 second-division fixtures and their results were expunged from the League records.

It was like a nightmare to realise that money meant more to my heroes than the honour of the club – their club, my club, our club. Fortunately, the contract wrangle was sorted out speedily enough to bring the players' hold-out to an end in time for the second weekend of the season; but the nightmare would not go away. Bramley came to the Recreation Ground and turned our celebration of the new season into a 7–19 wake after one of their forwards had provoked our leader and inspiration, Bill Holliday, into a fist-fight and got him sent off. (When you're a fanatic, your team's player never starts any trouble – let that be clearly understood.) A week later, the first away game of the campaign resulted in a 0–35 débâcle at the hands of Batley at Mount Pleasant.

So, two weeks into the season, and even the bravest Cumbrian optimist had to accept that 1963–64 was not going to be a vintage year for Whitehaven. The League was in the second of a planned three-year experiment with two divisions, and we at Whitehaven, with quite blatant snobbery, had assumed that we were a better team than to lose to such as Bramley and Batley. But going down 35 to zip at Batley was the clearest signal anybody could have got that ours was not a happy camp, and my attentions were already starting to waver towards the more illustrious neighbouring team at Workington.

While I had pledged my undying home-town loyalty to Whitehaven, my father could not kick his habit – formed in his own youth by watching Gus Risman's Town and Willie Horne's Barrow – of seeking out quality Rugby League. That meant, on most Saturdays, he would jump on a train and head north for Workington or south to Barrow, towns built on steel, shipbuilding and Rugby League. Sometimes I would go with him – but only if Whitehaven were not playing at home. Workington's cavernous new stadium built of red-brick and concrete at Derwent Park was like stepping into another world compared to the cosy, compact Recreation Ground, with its ramshackle little wooden grandstand, old railway-sleeper terraces, and touchlines so close to the crowd you felt you could lean out over the fence and stiff-arm any visiting wingers who dared break away into the clear.

Workington Town were big-time, up there with the giants of Rugby League in 1963, like Wigan, St Helens and Swinton. Town eventually finished fourth in the first division in 1963–64, but they relinquished the Western Championship title they had won the previous season. The Western and Eastern Championships were supplementary competitions created to give clubs an extra eight fixtures to add to their first- or second-division campaigns. They were also deliberately structured to give clubs in division two matches against some of the more glamorous outfits.

Whitehaven, officially classed as minnows, drew Warrington, St Helens (the eventual winners), Swinton and Workington – thus providing a couple of local derby games after all, despite the two Cumbrian teams being in different divisions. Now 1963–64 was to be a Rugby League season full of dramatic tied games, most notably the Challenge Cup semi-final saga involving Oldham and Hull KR. We Cumbrians got in on the act too, drawing both October fixtures, nil-nil at Derwent Park – a result which was to be repeated in the League 30 years later – then 10-all at the Recreation Ground three weeks later.

Sitting on the perimeter wall at Workington provided the best seats in the house for kids. Every Saturday afternoon at around 4:15 p.m., the Bessemer Converter at the Moss Bay steelworks would tip its load of molten metal, and a pungent, sulphurous cloud would waft its way directly over Derwent Park. It was as regular as clockwork; the crowd knew that, when the smell came, there was less than ten minutes to go in the game, and the players would step up the pace, or start to relax, according to the circumstances. Or maybe it only seemed that way because we were all high on the fumes.

Gaining that draw at Workington was a big confidence-booster for Whitehaven and their fans because, even in the first division, precious few teams did not leave Derwent Park empty-handed and feeling sore. Town had a tough reputation. If being gang-tackled by the Martin brothers (the sporting equivalent of singing a simultaneous duet with both Bette Midler and Pavarotti) wasn't enough, Town also had Frank Foster standing guard and ready to sing an extra chorus. This was steeltown football like they've never seen it in Pittsburgh.

Local rivalry between Whitehaven and Workington, two towns separated by eight miles of coastline, was nothing like as bitter in 1963 as it became in the 1980s and 1990s, when changing social attitudes found a perfect vehicle in the tabloid mentality of British Rugby League. Instead, Whitehaven followers were in awe of Workington Town. We envied their success and their superb stadium, and respected their illustrious, if short, history. And we cheered the Town players like they were our own when they made up the bulk of the Cumberland county team.

The annual home game in the County Championship was a highlight of the season for Cumbrians, its traditions and legends having been handed down from older generations. Jim Brough, in particular, in his weekly column in the Saturday-night 'Buff' football final, would regale us with memories of great Cumberland county forwards from days gone by. Most notable among these names were Martin Hodgson, Douglas Clark and Miller Strong, who sounded like he should have featured in a song by Gram Parsons, or at least had a beer from Milwaukee named after him. And, in 1963, the county title was won for the eighth time.

The deciding game was against Lancashire at Whitehaven on Wednesday 2 October, kick-off 5:15 p.m., which gave just enough time to get home from school, have tea, and run to the Recre' where the smart boys, and the fat boys, were already in the pie queue. The majority of spectators hurried straight from work to the game, and it was one of those nail-biters which were always made better by the fact that the final quarter was played in near darkness, and the crowd urging on the local heroes were almost all clad in their work-clothes.

Cumberland county matches were the closest that the British game has ever got to the spirit of Australia's hugely successful State of Origin encounters. Just like the Queenslanders, we had a massive chip on our shoulders caused by the popular perception that 'Big Brother' Rugby League, controlled in Leeds by secretary-general Bill Fallowfield and dominated by the powerful 'southern' clubs of Lancashire and Yorkshire, didn't care about us. Or at least, when they did care about us, it was to come in and buy us.

Our outstanding players were consistently overlooked for international honours. Dick Huddart remains to this day the only Whitehaven player ever to have been selected for a Lions tour. And the dust hadn't even settled on the Sydney Cricket Ground, where Dick had ripped the Australian defence to shreds on the famous 1958 trip, before the ink was drying on his signature for a big-money transfer south to St Helens.

October 1963 saw Dick Huddart come home for his last appearance for his native county before he blazed another trail by signing for St George and emigrating to Sydney, where he went on to play in a Saints Grand Final-winning team towards the latter end of their amazing run of 11 straight. Dick was one of only three out-of-county players who joined forces with ten Workington and Whitehaven boys to defeat a star-studded Lancashire side captained by Vince Karalius. The other two returning heroes were prop, John Tembey, also of St Helens, and loose forward Derek Hurt, who played for Leigh. Huddart scored the decisive try as Cumberland won 13–8 to take the Championship.

Despite that achievement, only one Cumbrian (Tembey) was in the Great Britain team which lined up against Australia in the first Test at Wembley on 16 October. The Kangaroos had kicked off their tour as early as 14 September (the same day as Whitehaven provided Blackpool's opposition in only the second League match to be staged at their brand-new Borough Park stadium, my team losing 14–20 to a Boro' side which included American Chuck Wiseman on one wing and the ultimate icon, Brian Bevan, on the other) and played no less than ten fixtures before the first Test. The whole tour consisted of 36 games.

Taking the first encounter of the Ashes series to Wembley under floodlights on a Wednesday night in these pre-motorway days was an outlandishly revolutionary step. It proved to be too revolutionary for the League public in 1963, as a crowd of only 13,946 scattered forlornly across the open spaces of the Empire Stadium. There was no sight of any Southern Amateur Rugby League in those days and, although the staging of this Test at Wembley may have been one of the catalysts that got the game going again in the capital, the programme for the international revealed not a single word of any plans to promote Rugby League in London.

Bill Fallowfield always maintained that the Test was played there at the insistence of the Australians. Up north we joked about it being at Wembley to ensure that the chief guest, Prince Philip, had only a short bus ride from home to get there.

But it was in a deadly serious state of shock that we watched the television late that Wednesday night and saw the Aussies romp to a 28–2 win. Peter Dymock introduced *Sportsview*, and no sooner had the brief black-and-white highlights begun than Eddie Waring was describing, incredulously, Langlands and Gasnier skimming across the glistening Wembley turf for a succession of scores. It was one-way traffic. Clips of these tries were later used in the opening credits for an Australian television drama series about their involvement in the Vietnam War – something which, at that time, seemed so far away and irrelevant to a boy in the North of England but which was, later, to come much closer to home.

Only a year before, on the 1962 Lions tour, Great Britain had retained the Ashes so comprehensively that it seemed another era of Test domination lay ahead. And, before Arthur Summons and his 1963 Kangaroos arrived in this country, Australia had never, ever won the Ashes on British soil. Much more drama was to unfold in the second Test at Swinton.

The Test series was, of course, only accessible for Cumbrians via television, but I was not going to miss my chances to see the Aussies in the flesh when they came. The Kangaroos' one visit of the tour to Cumberland was on a Thursday afternoon and, while many bemoaned their inability to get off school or work to see the Australians play the county team at Workington, for the pupils of Monkwray Junior School there was no such problem. Our head-master, Lance Fitzsimmons, would rather have closed the school down for a day than risk us missing the Kangaroos.

With Lance at the helm, Rugby League was definitely a keynote subject on the curriculum at Monkwray Junior. After prayers it was the No. 1 topic when we discussed current affairs in assembly every morning. We learned geography from finding international League tour venues on the map, and history by bracketing famous 20th-century events with significant landmarks in the evolvement of the game we loved.

On Thursday 31 October, a dozen of the school's keenest rugby fans piled into Mr Fitzsimmons's Volkswagen minibus and headed for Workington to see the Kangaroos. Although it was only their midweek team, the Aussies strode to a 21–nil win. I sat on the Derwent Park wall, as always, and marvelled as a 21-year-old full-back with beach-blond hair called Les Johns cut the Cumbrian defence to ribbons.

The Kangaroos' scrum-half that day, wearing jumper No. 10, was a red-headed young fellow named Frank Stanton, described in the programme pen-pictures as 'Francis', and an accountant by trade. In later years, I met him when he returned to England to do a bit of coaching with a couple of not-bad teams in 1978 and 1982. Certainly, whoever advised young Francis not to give up his day job was way off the mark.

Two days after going with the school to see the Kangaroos' midweek team beat Cumberland, my father, maintaining his reputation for dealing strictly with the quality end of Rugby League, ensured that I went with him on his day-return to Barrow, where the full Australian Test team were to have their final rehearsal before the crucial second Test the following Saturday. He knew that the tourists' first-choice 13 were something very special, and he felt that I ought to take the chance to see them too, in the flesh. 'And you can get Reg Gasnier's autograph,' he threw in as the final tempting line of persuasion. Like Bart to Homer (Simpson, that is), I pondered this for a while, then fixed him with a pubescent 'okay'. Whitehaven were away at Rochdale that day, and I figured I could survive missing one A team game against Hornets if it meant seeing a real hero.

I had a new autograph book ready to be broken in as the Kangaroos hopped off their bus at Craven Park. The first name to be written in it was none other than Noel Kelly, and he was rapidly followed by equally illustrious signatures such as Ian Walsh, Dick Thornett, Kevin Ryan, Graeme Langlands, Peter Dimond, Ken Irvine, Johnny Raper, Jimmy Lisle and, yes, Reg Gasnier himself.

The Australians beat second-division Barrow 18–5 without giving too much away. The highlight by far was the sweeping running style of centre Gasnier, wearing jersey No. 7; even in Test matches then, the Kangaroos wore tour numbers. Yet little could anybody predict what was going to happen seven days later at Station Road, Swinton. Great Britain went into the second Test confident that they could square the series and prove that their Wembley defeat was just a temporary lapse caused by playing on a 'neutral' ground. Instead, they were hit by a green-and-gold blitz that saw Australia shake the game to its very foundations by running in no less than 50 points and securing the Ashes on British soil for the first time in history. We're now 31 years down the track, and no British audience has since seen a Kangaroo touring team relinquish their grip on the trophy.

That Station Road Test also played a key role in finally pushing the Rugby League authorities into accepting the use of substitutes, after Great Britain played most of the game with effectively only 11 players when early injuries to captain, Eric Ashton, and Frank Myler left them as passengers.

So the Ashes were on the way to Australia and, although the Kangaroo tour continued on its marathon way, thoughts returned to home base. Whitehaven's season in the second division was proving to be a real low-key, low-success, low-everything affair. But on Friday 22 November came some dramatic news that, with the passing of time, served to emphasise just how major world events come to be measured in the life of a Rugby League fanatic.

It started with a television news-flash in the early evening. John Roberts was the BBC news-reader who brought the first shocking words that President John F. Kennedy had been shot in Dallas, Texas. Later in the evening, programmes were interrupted again to confirm that the President was dead. The next day, as Whitehaven lined up against Batley, the players wore black arm-bands and stood for a minute's silence. From Dallas to Coach Road the sense of loss was being felt and, for me, that will always be one unimportant and highly forgettable match that will never be forgotten.

Kennedy murdered in Dallas, but Whitehaven beat Batley five-nil in the mud – try by Colloby, goal by Holliday. And, even now, without looking at any record book or old programme, I can recite the Whitehaven team who played that fateful day – Baker; Lowther, Shepherd, Cassie, Colloby; Hazeldon, McDowell; Evans, Moss, Moore, Williamson, Holliday and Lill. There, did it!

Like most Whitehaven teams before and since, the majority of those 13 players, the subjects of all these emotions throughout the 1963–64 season, were local boys. There were only three out-siders: Alex Cassie from Scotland, Ken Evans from Wales, and Harold Lill from Swinton, although both wingers – Les Lowther from Barrow and Tony Colloby from Kendal, neither of which were then in the county which came to be known as Cumbria – were almost outsiders in that they spoke with different accents and had to travel over a couple of hours each way every time they jour-neyed to Whitehaven.

Harold Lill was the one out-and-out import signing, in that he had been recruited from Swinton where he couldn't get a first-team place ahead of their Championship-winning captain, Albert Blan. Whitehaven had paid £1,000 for Lill, so the word on the terraces was that, no matter how good or bad he played, he'd never be dropped from the side. For the fans could see right into the psyche of the club directors, even back in those pre-imitation-sheepskin-coat-and-patronising-cliché days. The fans knew that, if the directors had gone on the line to pay a big fee for a player, there's no way they would allow their judgement to be questioned.

And, sure enough, Harold never missed a first-team game all season. He was a popular figure with the fans who, at every home game, would welcome him warmly by shepherding him through the crush at the main gates, affectionately banging on the roof of the Mr Bean Mini he had driven up from Manchester. It was, I'm pretty sure, a bit like Doctor Livingstone arriving in an African village with the excited locals gathering to welcome him. They had probably never seen a white man before – and we, most definitely, had never seen a bald-headed loose forward in a Mini before! Harold would smile and wave regally, obviously a little embarrassed, bemused and flushed by his sudden celebrity status. But, at the end of the season, he was gone – transferred to Rochdale Hornets, and a life of fewer miles on the Mini's clock.

The second-division title race had been given up by Whitehaven long before Christmas, leaving only the occasional Western Championship match against the 'big' clubs as the highlights. Predictably, our boys raised their game against better opposition. Warrington were beaten – another five-nil scoreline – on 4 January, and we dashed home to celebrate by watching the fourth episode of a new television series called *Doctor Who*. I was convinced it would never catch on; I mean, could you seriously believe anybody would get excited by a story about an eccentric old duffer who kept disappearing into a police phone box?

One day in January, Mr Fitzsimmons had an important announcement to make in school assembly. A very famous man had just died – had any of us heard of him? His name was Harry Sunderland, and mine was the first young hand to shoot up in acknowledgement. I knew only that Harry was an Australian and a journalist – it was only in later years that I came to understand fully and be inspired by the campaigning and pioneering he had done for Rugby League.

Headmaster Lance had already worked out another major adventure for his star pupils. At the end of the season, we were off to Wembley to see the Challenge Cup final. Lance had applied to Bill Fallowfield at Rugby League headquarters, and we were taking advantage of the League's special group scheme which afforded reduced prices to school parties. But still, each Wembley ticket was going to cost £1 (or 20 shillings, as it said on the ticket), which meant an awful lot of saving of pocket money and being nice to grannies for the next six months.

With the excitement of a first-ever visit to Wembley on the horizon, the arrival of the Challenge Cup competition put a new spring in the step of one group of young Whitehaven fans. Decked out with banners, rattles and scarves, we brought at least five square yards of frenzied cup-tie atmosphere to the Recreation Ground when our team entertained Hull in the first round. It was enough to get our picture in the local paper, but I couldn't understand why the headline writer, in stealing the slogan from my banner 'Whitehaven for the Cup!', had quite deliberately substituted a question mark for my bold exclamation mark. O ye of little faith!

For once, that faith of the fanatic was not misplaced. Hull were a first-division team, but were doing it tough and, although they had Johnny Whiteley back in their team after a long injury lay-off, Whitehaven beat them 7–4 to go into the second-round draw. A touchdown by centre, Jim Powe, and a last-minute disallowed 'try' denied to Hull's 'Flying Dentist' from South Africa, Wilf Rosenberg, were the two key moments which resulted in Whitehaven getting another home draw in round two, this time against Castleford.

Cas were the team everybody was talking about as favourites for Wembley. They had a great side, with Hardisty and Hepworth at half-back, Derek Edwards full-back, and a big pack of forwards that included Bill Bryant, Johnny Ward, John Sheridan, and a teenage second-rower who was going to take the Rugby League world by storm, called Doug Walton. Doug's star was to fade as fast as it had risen – but not before Cas wiped away Whitehaven 29–5 to go on to the quarter-finals on their seemingly inevitable march to Wembley.

Over 6,000 people were at the Recreation Ground that day, including a massive contingent of Castleford fans. We were baffled by their indecipherable accents, and they were positively gobstruck when a band (sorry, that should say group) rolled out to play rock music (or beat music, as it was called in 1964) to entertain them. At Whitehaven, we fans were pretty hip when it came to enjoying the latest hit records over the loudspeakers before kick-off and at half-time (in sharp contrast, I have to say, to our neighbours, Workington Town, who may have had a winning team, a brand-new concrete stadium, and massive grandstand with tip-up seats – but they were still playing Acker Bilk's 'Stranger on the Shore' before each and every game). At Whitehaven, the beat music craze had arrived and, although Beatlemania was in full flow, the record that always got the crowd jumping was the Dave Clark Five's 'Bits and Pieces'. Old Dave Clark may have been the world's most awful smiling drummer, apart from that girl in the Applejacks, but boy, did he liven up every half-time at the Recreation Ground that season. Cold weather, a hot pie, even hotter Oxo, and the Dave Clark drum-roll. It was half-time heaven, as the ties that bind with grassroots Rugby League were being unbreakably strengthened – musically, emotionally, and gastronomically.

You can see now that Whitehaven Rugby League club were way ahead of the New South Wales Rugby League and their Tina Turner performance at the 1993 Grand Final. A full 30 years earlier, we had Tina (and Ike) on the loudspeakers, but we were tapping our toes and drumming our rolled-up programmes (all frustrated Dave Clarks, no doubt) to the music of local group Rue and the Rockets. The good-time atmosphere created by live music most definitely softened the blow of seeing Castleford, in those distinctive yellow jerseys, rip our team apart. But, 31 years later, and the Whitehaven fans are still waiting for the experiment of putting on pre-match entertainment to be repeated, despite its resounding success the first time. They have no excuse: I was in the Kells ARLFC clubhouse in January 1994 and saw a poster advertising a New Year's dance – featuring none other than Rue and the Rockets. Those boys must have the same staying power as Tina Turner. And now, I understand, they sell out every venue they play with their repertoire of sixties music. Mind you, after 30 years of solid practice, they should be pretty good at it by now.

So, out of the Challenge Cup, battling to get away from the bottom of division two, this was the time to start wrapping up season 1963–64, file it away under 'F' for forgettable, and start looking ahead to the next season when hope would spring eternal once more. Bradford Northern had now dropped out of the League, and moves were under way to abandon the two-divisional system just two years into its initial three-year trial period.

None the less, I still had that trip to Wembley to look forward to, and Saturday 9 May was the date of destiny. Our big adventure started at first light the day before when, once again, we clambered aboard the Fitzsimmons VW and headed south on the old A6, picking up speed on the Preston bypass, the first stretch of six-lane motorway to be opened in Britain. It was gone 6 p.m. when we arrived in London, taking up residence in a YWCA hostel in Marylebone, feeling reassured after seeing a local thoroughfare aptly called Whitehaven Road. To think it stretched all the way from London to Cleator Moor! We were impressed.

The 1964 Challenge Cup final was the second to be played with the new roof on Wembley Stadium. Widnes and Hull Kingston Rovers were the finalists, after Widnes had knocked out favourites Castleford in a replay in the semi-final, and Hull KR had needed two replays, a referee without a light meter, and a steam train bellowing clouds of black smoke over Swinton's Station Road ground, before finally ending Oldham's Wembley dream.

Vince Karalius captained the Chemics to a 13–5 victory to take the Cup to Naughton Park. It wasn't that the game was unmemorable. It was just that our 20-shilling tickets provided seats on uncomfortable wooden benches so close to the front, the lack of elevation meant you hardly saw any of the action. Rugby League fans complaining about Wembley is one thing that has *not* changed much in 30 years.

Swinton won the Championship for the second successive year, finishing six points clear of Wigan, and Oldham finished top of division two, but that meant nothing as Rugby League prepared to go back to one division. Whitehaven were third from bottom, our worst-ever finishing position to date, only one point ahead of wooden-spoonists Doncaster. But we didn't have to wait until August to get our next dose of optimism: instead, it came in the last home game of the 1963–64 season. Leigh were overwhelmed 24–5, and coach, Jim Brough, welcomed three new players recruited from Workington in the swap deal that took our star threequarter, Tony Colloby, to Derwent Park. Whitehaven's new trio were centre Eddie Brennan, who was to re-emerge 30 years later with a splendid goatee beard, one less 'n' in his name, and in the position of club chairman; a giant second-rower called Hodgson, of whom nobody was quite sure whether his Christian name was Pat or Fred, so he answered to both; and a forward who became genuinely famous, Mattie McLeod.

On the Leigh side that day in April 1964 was a raw Rugby Union signing who was struggling to adjust to his new code. He was Bev Risman, and he went on to captain Great Britain, and Leeds in the 'watersplash' Cup final of 1968. In that very same Wembley game, Mattie McLeod was to be the Wakefield Trinity player who clasped a forgiving arm around the distraught shoulders of a weeping Don Fox just seconds after he missed that infamous conversion in front of the posts, and Eddie Waring summed up for the whole world the emotions of Mattie and every Rugby League lover with his two immortal words: 'Poor lad.'

It may have been a less-than-successful season in a quiet backwater of the game but, as the wider perspective of Rugby League unfolded before us, and world events ranging from Dallas to Doncaster were making their marks on our memories, we all – players and fans – were ourselves stitches in the tapestry of stories that would be told in the future.

As for Jim Brough, all his stories had already been told, many times over. All Jim had to look forward to were the laps, press-ups and touch-football that would mark the next round of pre-season training. He'd seen it all before – and now we all had – but he was still dusting down that old blue tracksuit again, because he knew optimism-time would soon be back.

HARRY EDGAR is the founder and publisher of *Open Rugby* and widely believed to be one of the most shadowy, sinister figures on the face of the earth. There is no element of revenge in the way all references to obscure West Coast (of the USA, not of Cumbria) bands have been ruthlessly excised from his contribution. He is now a smallholder in Wetherby.

THE SEASON OF THE WIN

Tameside Borough 1993–94

Peter Wilson

We knew we were in for a hard winter. And it was still only May.

The club's annual general meeting came only a couple of weeks after the coach's farewell speech. He was on his way to Australia for a holiday before moving on to another club that had been formed ten miles away. The message – delivered from a rickety chair in Cheers, the after-match pie-and-peas bar at the local sports centre – was plain enough. But then Trevor Howard, who had been with Tameside Borough through thick and thin, was a plain speaker.

Tameside had just lost the game which confirmed the fears that had first crept up on the club the previous August: relegation had become a reality. For the second year running. Trevor stood on his chair, waved his farewell gift – suitably a tankard – and smiled at his audience. 'I would like to thank all those players who have supported me over the season by turning up to training and to matches, whatever the opposition – thanks to all five of you! The rest are just a waste of time.'

For almost a second you could have heard a pin drop. Then somebody ordered a pint, and all was well with the world.

If that reaction suggests that amateur Rugby League players in general, and those at clubs like Tameside Borough of the lower reaches of the Pennine League in particular, don't give a hoot about their sport, nothing could be further from the truth. The hoot may not be very loud at times, but it *is* there.

Why else would they pay good beer money to play a game in which they can end up battered, bloodied and broken – for the fun of it? Why else would they turn out week after week for a regular hammering when they could be out shopping with the family? And why else would they turn up to the aforementioned annual general meeting to hear that they are a load of rubbish and that the club is deep in the how's-your-father? It may be significant that more members turned up to talk than to train, but amateur Rugby League is built on hopes and dreams, and Tameside Borough has always been full of both.

Tameside is a result of the boundary changes of the 1970s when they moved Hull to Humberside, Barrow to Cumbria, Wigan to Greater Manchester, and Lancastrians to tears. It (Tameside) consists of a clutch of towns on the fringe of Manchester, none of them having any connection with Rugby League except that they are not too far from Oldham. Ashton-under-Lyne, Stalybridge, Hyde, Denton, Audenshaw, Droylsden, Dukinfield and Hollingworth have a combined population of 250,000 – and a Rugby League club founded, as they nearly all are, in a pub.

It is hardly the land of legends but, over the years, the club has had its cult figures: the Reverend Roger, the Pioneer, Igor, Big Dog, Jay the Brick and Worm are all part of Tameside history. And cups, championships and medals have all passed through the club's hands since it was formed in 1982. But the mood at that May meeting was one of despair. The question – critical, if not serious – that faced players and members alike was: could we keep the club going?

Happily, the answer was yes, and the AGM resumed business as normal. As a certain player suggested a 'drink for the road' – meaning, in truth, the M1 – life, it was decided, would go on. While supporters and players at other clubs keenly look forward to an annual gathering of chat and argument about the Win of the Season, the followers of the game in Tameside have to settle for mulling over the Season of the Win.

The AGM may not have given out the most encouraging signals the club committee could have received on which to build a positive, dynamic future, but a quick thumbing through previous seasons' minutes revealed that doom, gloom and disaster cropped up with almost as much regularity as the item marked 'Any Other Business'.

Still, it was hardly expected that those who were planning and working on the game in Tameside would have so much to look forward to. Who could have possibly imagined:

* The Year of the Great Signing that never was;
* The Year that the worst bushfires in Australian memory would hit team selection;
* The Year of the Five Coaches;
* The Year Tameside won a trophy nobody knew anything about.

Life at the bottom of the world of Rugby League is like that. Its motto is, as a certain MP once had engraved on the back of a watch given to a certain businessman: 'Don't let the buggers get you down.'

So, although the coach had left, the chairman was about to leave, and two of the best players could hardly wait to follow them, life did indeed go on. A week after the annual meeting came the presentation of the trophies (even clubs who finish bottom of the League are entitled to their night out). And, although the long, hard winter was still four months away, in the meantime the club members braced themselves for a long, hard summer.

First, the local papers' revenue was boosted by a series of adverts as Tameside began their search for a new coach, and for players who had experience and were eager to offer it in this particular cause. For more than a month, not a dicky bird. Then, as the dozen players still at the club warmed up for their umpteenth midsummer game of touch-rugby, along came Mark Chiverall.

Mark confessed he was new to coaching, but he had seen the ad and was willing to have a go. The fact that he had got lost and had a puncture on the way to his first training session was not in the least off-putting – not to a team who thought they would never have a coach again. Assistant coach, Dave Marsh, who had agreed to stay on through all the upheaval, introduced the new player-coach to the players, and the Borough bandwagon was on the road again. We could hardly wait for the start of the 1993–94 season.

Gone was the doom of relegation. Behind us were only the scathing comments of a departed coach; ahead was a golden future of amateur Rugby League.

The club started the 1993–94 season with a cup final. Actually, it was a pre-season friendly. But nobody likes friendlies, so it was decided that the match against Bolton on 21 August 1993 would have as its prize the Sainte-Marie Trophy. Now that may not have the ring of the Silk Cut Challenge Cup, the Regal Trophy or the Stones Bitter Premiership – but the Sainte-Marie Trophy is a special ensemble of tinny plastic and gold-and-silver paint which had been inaugurated in a village outside Perpignan several months earlier, when it became one of the first trophies ever to be presented for losing. And Tameside, true to recent form, won it.

The occasion was one of those boozy trips to France for a Great Britain Test match. To make the weekend a bit more interesting than your average bar-to-bar stagger, followed by a visit to the Test for those who could still stand, the club decided to arrange a match. Contact was duly made by Jean-Claude somebody and it was established that Tameside Borough would meet a team called Palau on the Saturday afternoon. 'No problem, monsieur. Oui – le match will be arranged for you,' or words to that effect, came back from Jean-Claude.

But, we insisted, there was one proviso. The game must be played at 1 p.m. on the Saturday, thus giving players, officials and the supporter enough time to enjoy the real reason why the trip had been arranged in the first place. Again: 'No problem, monsieur.'

Barely a week before the game, there was a problem. The scheduled opponents, Palau, wondered if we would mind changing the kick-off time to 5 p.m. instead. The message went back: Yes, we would. Yet something was clearly lost in the translation because, on one side of *La Manche*, 'Yes, we would' meant yes, we would play at 5 p.m.; and, on the other side, it meant yes, we would mind . . .

The dutiful Tameside secretary, blissfully happy with his own interpretation of events, then contacted European Development Officer, John Maguire, to ask if he could arrange a replacement fixture at short notice. 'No problem,' he said, but at least this time it was said in Australian, a sort of English.

John explained that the opposition would be Sainte-Marie, a team from a village a few kilometres from Perpignan, and the kick-off would be 3 p.m. Still not ideal, but a lot better than 5 p.m. So, on the Thursday evening with the innocents aboard, the coach set off on its 26-hour voyage from pub to Perpignan. Meanwhile, the advance party – including, of course, the dutiful secretary – was flying out with the Great Britain party and staying at the best hotel in town, but would meet the incoming Tameside party on arrival to inform them of the match-day arrangements.

Yet again, however, there was a problem. The local paper in Perpignan carried a couple of items heralding the imminence of a team from the Manchester area and advertising the game. Or rather, *both* games. Palau versus Tameside, it said, would kick off at 5 p.m. And Sainte-Marie would play a team from Manchester, it announced further down the page (no name, but we put two and two together) and would kick off at 8.30 p.m. A lot of quick thinking led the advance guard to the conclusion that the best idea was to lie low and try to come up with a plausible tale for when the beer wagon arrived.

When Jean-Claude arrived at the Ibis Hotel the following morning to take the team to a reception, it thankfully took only a couple of pints of entente and lime cordiale, plus a couple of Ricards, to explain the situation. Anglo-French relations were intact, but then came the difficult part – restoring Anglo–Anglo relations. 'Blow that for a game of soldiers' was a mild version of the reaction when the news was conveyed to the team that, instead of playing Palau at the ridiculously unsuitable hour of 5 p.m., Tameside would now be playing Sainte-Marie at the far more acceptable time of 8:30-ish on a Saturday night. The players would, of course, be able to spend the day sightseeing (in Perpignan!) and have as much to drink as they liked – but only after the game. Wishful thinking at its stupidest.

It would be grossly unfair to infer that Tameside were not that keen on playing at all (except, of course, for the guest A. N. Others who had volunteered to make up the team). But then, it would be equally grossly unfair to ask a healthy rugby player who had travelled a thousand miles or more for a boozy weekend to lay off the booze. So, when it came to the time for the national anthems, it was utterly grossly unfair to expect the Borough to be in any condition to stand to attention. Nine o'clock on a Saturday night is not, it may now be safely assumed, the best time to play a tour match in France.

However, the game went ahead, even after the word had got round that Sainte-Marie were not exactly the most appropriately

Wigan 1966–67: 'the remnants of a good team', led out at Wembley in 1965 by 'Sir' Eric Ashton

(Andrew Varley)

Fulham 1985–86: Roy Lester – 'nobody since Michael Colin Cowdrey has been given more appropriate initials'

(Andrew Varley)

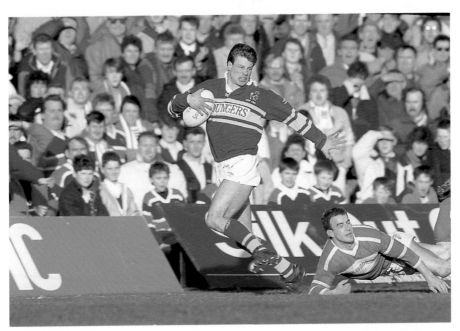

Leeds 1990–91: (above) Andrew Ettingshausen, 'so cool, so composed'; (below) Cliff Lyons
(Andrew Varley)

Leeds 1990–91: (opposite) John Gallagher, with fellow-Rugby Union signing David Young — 'he must have wondered what was going on'
(Andrew Varley)

Featherstone Rovers 1987–88: (above) Papua New Guinea prove that Rugby League is 'part of the big wide world after all'; (below) Post Office Road, a 'mid-1980s light industrial/commercial premises in an enterprise zone'

Wigan 1984–85: (above) Graeme West, 'a superb captain'; (below) Brett Kenny, 'cutting
a majestic swathe through the game'
(Andrew Varley)

Swinton 1985–86: (above) Danny Wilson – 'even if he was on the pitch, there was no guarantee that he would be playing'; (below) Gigg Lane – 'fine, but it's not Station Road'
(Andrew Varley)

Hull 1975–76: Mick Crane, who had 'the same gift with a rugby ball that George Best expressed with a soccer ball at his feet'
(Andrew Varley)

Australia 1982: Wayne Pearce, the 21-year-old loose forward 'sadly not seen in England again'
(Andrew Varley)

Parramatta 1981: Peter Sterling, who 'still had plenty to prove to a sceptical city'

titled team in the whole of French Rugby League. It was rumoured, though never proved, that such was their disciplinary record that they had not actually managed to finish a game all season. By the time this 'friendly' was 15 minutes old, the reason for this calumny became clear. When French rugby players decide to have a mêlée, punch-up or altercation, call it what you will, they try not to leave anybody out: players, subs, kitmen, sponge men, all are invited to attend.

It is only decent and wise to draw a veil over the contretemps and report instead that, with 15 minutes left, the teams were locked 18–18. Then Sainte-Marie pulled their master-stroke. While Tameside's tired and emotional players were taking a breather during one of the frequent stoppages for air, the foxy French made four substitutions: the referee, and three players who usually turn out for Avignon in the French first division. Needless to say, they all played a leading role in the eventual outcome, and Sainte-Marie went on to win the game 34–18. Then it was off to the village hall for drinks, eats, the swapping of ties and the presentation of the trophy – which, rather mysteriously, went to Tameside, presumably for turning up.

And so the Sainte-Marie Trophy came into being. The story of its subsequent journey from a French village hall to a sports centre in Droylsden is of little interest, save to the hard-working official who hid the prize under his coat, dodged into bus shelters to avoid shady-looking characters, spent two hours trying to find the right road back to his hotel, and eventually arrived only to find the bar closed.

Back at club HQ it was, as aforementioned, decided that the trophy would be the prize for the pre-season match between Tameside Borough and Bolton. It was also decided not to reveal the plan to Bolton just in case – and 'in case' turned out to be the appropriate phrase. Although Tameside were worthy winners of the match by 14–5, there was no presentation. Somebody had lost the key to the glass cabinet that had been the trophy's home since its arrival from France, and so the joy of winning it for the first time – the first cup win of any kind for seven years – was denied the players of Tameside. No 'over the moon' or 'sick as chips' quotes for the local press. Nobody knew about it.

Pre-season triumphs such as this one often encourage the average player with the average club to look forward to the new campaign with fresh hope and enthusiasm (especially after successive years of relegation). And an August win often prompts passive members to take a more active interest, to involve themselves in voluntary work such as ordering and collecting the pies, looking after the kit, selling the raffle tickets, collecting players left stranded outside the pub – all the mundane but necessary jobs which keep an amateur club afloat. But, however sweet the early victory, it can never be quite enough to provide a rush of volunteers to join the turd patrol.

Every club has one: the guy with the wellies and shovel who scours the council-owned ground for the left-overs from the neighbourhood mongrels (or pedigrees, as they must be if they are on leads). The poor chap isn't only looking for dog-droppings, though. If your ground happens to be situated between a housing estate and a pub, then he can usually find enough empties to pay the referee's fee. There was once even a case of a burnt-out car that had to be removed from the half-way line before a particularly important fifth-division game could go ahead.

Council officials and workers usually have no trouble in erecting soccer posts. They are simple enough: two uprights, and a crossbar across the top. But when it comes to rugby, the council have been known to make life so difficult that even Frano Botica would have trouble with his goalkicking. They may be a rare sight, but upside-down goalposts are not unique.

All these things are sent to try the amateur Rugby League man's enthusiasm to the limit but, by and large, he comes through unscathed. How else would BARLA be able to boast around 1,350 teams where there used to be 150? Tameside Borough probably rank about 1,000th of those 1,350 on current performances and so it was pretty tough on them to be pitted against a team from the top 50 in the first round of the Lancashire Cup a week after the memorable win over Bolton. When people talk about the luck of the draw they never seem to mean good luck.

It therefore came as no surprise to Borough's players and officials that the 1993–94 competitive season should start off with a quick exit from the county cup. Widnes St Maries (no relation to the cup donors of the previous week) won both the match, by 58–12, and the boat-race in the bar, by two legs to nil; and set in motion a run of 18 successive defeats for Tameside.

The trouncing by Widnes did not get much damaging publicity, so there was still no shortage of recruits during the early days of the new season. Would-be players who had always fancied having a go; others who doubted their own ability to make it into the local Rugby Union club's Extra 'B' XV; some soccer players; and even a few who had played Rugby League before – that was the mix Mark Chiverall had to work with.

Early-season results continued to be unpromising, though optimism remained high. 'That is just about the worst team we have ever played against,' said Jay the Brick after a match at Huddersfield, suggesting that there were indeed teams inferior to Tameside about. Alas, the view did not carry too much weight among his team-mates: they had just lost 14–51.

A week later, there appeared genuine grounds for the optimism. Five minutes before half-time, Tameside were leading 14–0. Five minutes before the end, Cook Street Rams ran in their seventh try, and it finished 14–42. Defeat No. 3 was less severe – only 24–26 – but by now the soccer players had drifted off, the line-outers, ruckers and maulers had gone back to their friends in the Extra 'B', and only the Faithful Few remained.

A week later there was a crisis in the Church – that is to say, the Church, a little pub in the Waterhead area of Oldham, which was the departure point for away games. Tameside were due at Peel Park, Bradford, to play Victoria Rangers. Before setting off, somebody decided to do a head-count. Panic set in. 'Where's Big Dog? And Jay? And Worm?' The whole front row was missing.

'I thought they were with you,' somebody said to somebody else.

'They'll be here,' suggested Ivan, helpfully. 'We'll wait.' We waited. They didn't come.

'I'll go past the Welly and see if they are outside there,' said the still helpful Ivan. And so the fleet of cars left the Church heading in various directions, completely unaware that the three front-row men thought it was a home game and were at that very moment on their way to Droylsden.

It was a makeshift team, then, with a winger hooking, a full-back and a centre propping, and a couple of novices dreading that they might be called off the substitutes' bench, which went into action. Under the circumstances, losing 24–34 wasn't too bad at all.

The following two weeks were relatively unimportant, since the defeats merely meant exits from cups which Tameside weren't going to win anyway.

Back in the League, the club learned to their distress that they would have to carry on without Jay the Brick for a while. He was off to Australia for a couple of months but promised he would come back. Thereafter, regular cryptic messages would filter through telling us that Jay was having a great time, keeping fit, and was eager to get back into the side on his return. Then, out of the blue, came a message that could only have been a secret code: 'Jay is staying on another couple of weeks to help fight the bushfires.'

Nods of appreciation all round, until somebody said: 'We haven't seen much about them on the TV lately.'

'Not surprising, really. They've been out a fortnight!' Somebody down the line must have told Jay that we'd rumbled him. He was back in the team within days.

Meanwhile, defeat had followed defeat, relegation loomed, and there were secret fears of a repeat of the club's record in their only season in division one two years earlier, when every match was lost. But then came the big day: the match between the bottom two. Shipley versus Tameside Borough, both teams winless. Something had to give. This was the chance for Tameside to put their first points on the League board. It will come as no surprise to learn that things did not work out quite as planned.

The match meant a return to Peel Park, scene of the defeat by Victoria Rangers and, this time, Tameside at least had the luxury of Big Dog and Co. being both in the same county and in the line-up. Unfortunately, although the players themselves were present, their boots weren't.

The problem was that, for once, the departure from the Church was not particularly well organised. Players threw their boots into the back of Bob's van and then travelled to the match with somebody else. And they didn't know that Bob was making a stop-off and wasn't quite sure of the whereabouts of Peel Park. So Tameside, with nearly a regiment to choose from, started the game with three subs on the field, and three first-choice players waiting for their boots to arrive. It was the sort of start that means disaster ahead.

Even after the boots arrived, nothing went right for Tameside. They had three claims for tries disallowed and eventually lost 6–10 – boots an' all. The first win was as far away as ever.

The following week brought the first round of the BARLA National Cup – the perfect stage to launch the New Image. Financial hardship and amateur Rugby League are no strangers to each other, and Tameside's hand-to-mouth existence meant that they had never had enough cash to enable them to discard their fading four-year-old kit in the local council colours of sky-blue-and-brown (nobody *ever* clashed with that combination), until help arrived from the Foundation for Sport and the Arts. The new blue-white-and-red kit duly made its first appearance now at Sowerby Spartans, and it was just the morale-booster the players needed. It even made skipper Becky's pre-match team talk a lot simpler and more encouraging than usual: 'Remember, lads, we have never lost in this kit!'

Eighty minutes later, when the jerseys were hidden under a thick caking of mud, the revised version was: 'Remember, lads, we have only ever lost once in this kit . . .'

Behind the scenes, things were taking a giant leap forward. Hush-hush talks, as they are called in the pop papers, were being conducted with a view to making the biggest signing in the club's history – a name that would put Rugby League on the map in all eight Tameside towns. Des Foy, a former Great Britain tourist, who had once faced the great Wally Lewis in a Test match, was on the brink of throwing in his lot with team No. 1,000 on the BARLA ladder. And, to prove it, the ex-Lion even turned up to train with the club.

The signing was rushed through, and it was too good to keep a secret. The story was clearly back-page headline stuff for the local press. Yet, unbelievably, another major sports story exploded in Tameside in the exact same week and pushed the Foy news off the back page. Which was fair enough, I suppose, since it was the news that Viv Richards and not Ian Botham would be turning out for local cricket club Denton in the coming summer. Even the Foy news couldn't match that for importance in Tameside.

So the story of the new signing went inside, but that did nothing to dampen the enthusiasm at the club. Until, that is, after two more training sessions, when the former Oldham and Huddersfield international reported that he was having trouble with an old knee injury and so would not, after all, be pulling on one of the new jerseys.

After all the hullabaloo and the big build-up, the club prepared for the climbdown. Perhaps a damage limitation exercise could keep this down to a couple of paragraphs at the bottom of a match report. But, just as with the good news, so it was with the bad: it turned out that Viv Richards would not be playing with Denton after all, and that once more gazumped the headlines, this time on the front page. There was only the briefest mention of Des Foy.

Life at Tameside got back to normal. Oh, except that the coach would have to take a month off because of work commitments. Not that he missed much during his enforced, and later voluntary, absence. Emley Moor and Victoria Rangers duly completed the double over the Borough and, by the time the club was due to meet championship favourites Deighton, relegation was a certainty.

None the less, it is a proud boast that, in the club's 12-year existence, they have only once failed to fulfil a fixture. Despite the doom and gloom, there was no question of pulling out against Deighton. So it was 11 good men and true who turned up on that February afternoon to face the visitors from Huddersfield, encouraged only by the reminder that somewhere in the dim and distant past – the mid-1980s, to be precise – Tameside had chalked up their biggest-ever win against the same club. That 100–4 victory is still in the record books.

It was clear enough, though, that there was going to be no repeat. Indeed, Deighton kindly loaned Tameside two of their best players, including former Oldham forward, Colin Hawkyard, who jointly won the man-of-the-match award! And, although Tameside finished the game with a flourish – a Chris Jinks drop-goal in the last minute – it served only to narrow the margin to 3–56.

February ended with a closer defeat, 12–20, but also with the loss of the last remaining member of the coaching team. Dave Marsh, who had been left carrying the can after Chiv's departure, finally called it a day. And, in doing so, he missed out on the golden moment of the season: the win!

Captain, Paul Cane, and former chairman, Dave Whitehead, now took charge of team affairs, and they could hardly have made a better start. It was a Cane drop-goal that gave Tameside an early lead in the return battle of the boys in the basement – Shipley hadn't improved any since they beat the Borough – and, before half-time, tries from Askew and Bryson had helped build up a healthy and, indeed, unprecedented 13–0 lead. Not that it was to be a cruise to victory: Shipley came back to 13–11, before a runaway try from Crowe took Tameside out of reach.

The 21–11 victory was greeted as the turning-point of the season – the day things started to go right. Even so, the local press headline was a bit over the top: 'Brilliant Boro', it told its readers, with scant regard for reality. But nobody was complaining. It was the first decent headline the club had had for years.

A week later, Tameside failed to score for only the second time that year, losing 0–14 in a local derby at Oldham, and that was followed by a couple of familiar scorelines (12–40 and 10–34) – plus the appearance of player No. 48. A season that had started with a trophy and high optimism was over, and the club about to die a premature death. At least, that was the way it looked to the outside world.

But the people who have struggled to establish Rugby League in an alien territory are made of sterner stuff than that. Far from being ready to throw in the towel, Tameside Borough have regrouped and are ready for a new challenge.

By the start of the game's centenary year, things will look a whole lot different. The club is expecting to move into a new stadium that will be the envy of every amateur club in the country. They hope to have attracted new players and sponsors, and a fresh audience for the game in Ashton-under-Lyne. They plan to develop a youth policy to secure the future of the club into the next century. They plan to have two open-age teams, a thriving support, and a healthy cash balance from fund-raising events, grants and membership subscriptions.

It is the sort of dreaming that keeps clubs such as Tameside – and most of the other 1,350 – going from season to season. And they have made a good start. Trevor Howard's farewell speech to the faithful five has had its effect.

There are now twice as many turning up to training.

PETER WILSON is a native of Barrow and remembers all too vividly the days when they built ships and great rugby teams. During a sojourn in Northamptonshire, he founded the Corby Pioneers. In recent years, he has divided his energies between Tameside Borough, which he also founded, and writing on Rugby League for *The Daily Star*.

DON'T EXPECT MIRACLES

Wigan 1984–85

Paul Wilson

Easy to say now, but had I known in advance about John Ferguson I would definitely have spent Saturday 1 September 1984 toiling up the M5 with all the other end-of-holiday traffic, instead of staying in Cornwall for an extra day's swimming and fooling about on the beach at Kynance Cove.

The first League match of the season always exerts a certain pull – but so does glorious sunshine at one of the unspoilt gems of the English coastline. This is not going to be one of those slightly unhinged accounts of devotion to a team above and beyond the call of duty. The pleasures of West Yorkshire being mostly winter ones, Wigan's visit to Castleford was all too easily resisted. Wheldon Road could wait. Reader, I gave it a miss.

Naturally, I now regret this. Kynance Cove is still there, at the tip of the Lizard, still unspoilt, and capable of being visited at any time; whereas the most astonishing rugby player I ever saw has retired, probably never to pull on a jersey in earnest again, and certainly not to add to his 25 appearances for Wigan in that never-to-be-forgotten 1984–85 season. I was lucky enough to attend most of those games and see something quite remarkable, all the more so for being unscripted, unforced and unhyped.

In the space of just over half a season, the quiet Australian became first a folk hero, then a local legend. It is no exaggeration to say that Ferguson is recalled with as much admiration and affection as any of the giants in the Central Park pantheon, even by old-timers. Certainly it was a treat for the club's younger supporters in the mid-1980s – brought up on the lean years of the 1970s and the subsequent indignity of the second division, and faintly brassed off with older fans constantly harking back to the good old days of 20 or 30 years ago – to witness undisputed greatness first hand.

There were many more treats to come that season, not least the equally undisputed greatness of Brett Kenny, but we didn't feel so proprietorial about him; we knew all about his awesome achievements long before he arrived. We knew he was brilliant, we knew what he had done for Australia and, in our heart of hearts, we were probably a bit worried that Wigan didn't deserve him. Central Park wasn't exactly chock-full of internationals to keep him company. For Great Britain's 1984 tour down under, Wigan had supplied just Brian Case.

We did have Graeme West as club captain, but no one was quite sure for how long. As sub-editor, occasional writer and general dogsbody at the sports desk of the old *Post and Chronicle* in Wigan, it was one of my duties to collect the Kiwi captain's column every Thursday, and organise his modest weekly fee of £15. One day earlier in the year, I had received a telephone call from Alex Murphy, the Wigan coach, who wanted to know whether we would let him pay West fifteen quid a week to keep his mouth shut.

Friction between coach and captain had been just one aspect of the previous season, an eventful one which had culminated in the heavy and not wholly unexpected defeat by Widnes at Wembley in the 1984 Challenge Cup final. A somewhat fortunate Cup run, fuelled by a kindly draw and the intermittent excellence of Australian stand-off Mark Cannon, had kept Murphy in a job when the board seemed poised to sack him. Had Wigan lost at lowly Bramley in the first round, instead of scraping a 10–10 draw and winning the replay, Murphy would not have survived. But, buoyed by breaking Wigan's 14-year Wembley duck, one of the game's great survivors lasted until a fortnight short of the following season, when a row after the annual summer sevens tournament finally gave the club a pretext for his dismissal. Mainly because of the inopportune timing, this was quite a shock even to those close to the club – though it came as a relief to West, who said he was ready for walking out himself had Murphy stayed any longer.

It was to this shambles, with coaching assistants Colin Clarke and Alan McInnes hurriedly promoted to take joint control of the first team in time for the new season, that the world's most elegant and excitingly talented stand-off had agreed to attach his name. The club's grandiose schemes seemed to be crashing about their ears. With the new season only days away, everything was up in the air. Good time for a quick holiday. Miss the Locker Cup – always a good plan – and possibly get back in time to catch this new geezer make his debut at Castleford.

Or possibly not. As I have said, just a bit of advance warning about Fergie would have made all the difference; but the whole point about Wigan's new winger was that no one had an inkling of what was about to unfold. Murphy, before his sudden departure, had just enough time to announce the player's capture, and to embellish the bald facts with the information that in his day job Ferguson was a truck driver, and from what he had heard this guy could really motor. Even the coach, you see, was relaying second-hand information – though this was fast becoming the norm at Wigan, where the board had been doing their own scouting and signing since stepping in to prevent Maurice Bamford wasting any more of their money a few years earlier.

But even seasoned Oz watchers knew little about the Aboriginal winger who had just transferred to Easts from the defunct Newtown club, and sources in Sydney confirmed only that Wigan were taking a chance on a somewhat erratic 30-year-old. The Wigan board revealed they had been tipped off by a business-man who had seen Ferguson play, and said they had acted on a hunch that they might have uncovered the new Des Drummond. The Wigan fans said nothing, but a few probably wondered what was wrong with travelling seven miles to Leigh and signing the old Des Drummond.

Driving into Rugby League airspace at around 4:30 p.m. on the first day of the season, we were informed by Radio Manchester that Wigan were down to 11 men at Castleford because West and John Pendlebury had been sent off for fighting. Then came the news that, despite this handicap, Wigan had won, scoring four tries in a second-half comeback and pinching the points with an unbelievable finish. And the new Des Drummond was on the score sheet, capping what Cliff Webb of *The Wigan Observer* called a 'most impressive' debut with a solo try, receiving possession at the play-the-ball and using his speed and strength to beat three men to the line. Later, we hacks would learn to preface mention of this sort of solo Ferguson score with the word 'characteristic'.

It is worth pausing here to mention that the Wigan team that day had Edwards at full-back, Ferguson and Ramsdale on the wings, Stephenson and Whitfield in the centre, and Cannon and Fairhurst at half-back. Courtney, Paul O'Neill and Case formed the front row, with a back three of Potter, West and Pendlebury, and Dunn and Juliff both got an outing from the substitutes' bench. Not a bad team, by contemporary standards, but not one to set the world on fire either; anyone carried away by the Castleford result was swiftly brought down to earth in the first home match of the season, when the Bradford pack did a familiar demolition job in a 2–9 defeat, the outstanding Ellery Hanley scoring the only try of the game for the visitors.

Wigan could accept this sort of up-and-down form cheerfully enough. The present levels of consistency would have been dismissed as Orwellian fiction at Central Park in 1984 when, with no particular expectation of winning anything at the end of the season, crowds were less inclined to greet home defeats with boos and catcalls. After what Wigan supporters had witnessed in the not-too-distant past, it was enough to know that crowds were on the up again and that entertainment was making a comeback.

So the season progressed. There were notable home victories over Widnes and Leeds, with Cannon scoring two tries in the latter game to underline his value at stand-off, but these giddy heights were put in perspective by utterly predictable defeats at Leigh and Featherstone. Still, this was par for the course. Post Office Road was a notorious graveyard for Wigan hopes while, at Hilton Park at least, Leigh seemed to exercise an inviolable annual right to put one over their wealthier, more famous neighbours. The previous season, Wigan had unveiled hairy Kerry Hemsley at Hilton Park, to no avail. This time Leigh were without Drummond, busy doing *Superstars* for the BBC, but it made no difference: Woods and Donlan had more than enough class to do us on their own.

Meanwhile, it was becoming increasingly obvious that the Fairhurst-Cannon half-back partnership had severe limitations. Both players were capable of individual virtuosity, but rarely meshed well with each other or the rest of the team, and the paucity of attacking ideas meant that Wigan were easily dominated by sides which displayed any degree of organisation. These criticisms surfaced again after the 10–20 defeat at Featherstone: 'We are going to have a hard look at team selection,' Colin Clarke said. 'Wigan can do a lot better than this.'

Ostensibly, Wigan did do better in their next couple of matches, a win at Salford in a Lancashire Cup semi-final and a 40–24 success against struggling Barrow. But the statistics do not show that the home side were jeered by the crowd at half-time in the League match, when they were trailing 16–18 to the Cumbrians. Fairhurst in particular took some stick from the terraces in that match and, though Cannon finished with a hat-trick, it was the non-scoring Ferguson who earned all the plaudits for setting up three second-half tries in the space of 11 minutes.

By this time, Ferguson had five tries to his credit from Wigan's first nine games, a useful if unremarkable contribution, but he had already been involved in several notable assists. Word was beginning to spread that Wigan had a very watchable player. It wasn't that he had scored spectacular tries, and it wasn't that he dashed down the wing with great speed or unstoppable strength. It was just that some of the tries he did score were improbable, in that it was difficult to imagine anyone else scoring them; and that, every time Ferguson received the ball, you could put money on him beating the first man. He seemed to have a precious gift for going past people. It was not easy to work out how or why, since he was not endowed with exceptional power or pace. But as well as the mesmeric shimmy which left defenders clutching empty space, Fergie also seemed to possess some form of spring-loaded, self-righting suspension which gave him the ability to ride the heaviest challenges. You could never tell, no matter how many tacklers ganged up on him, whether Fergie would beat half of them or all of them, and watching him was more fun than Wigan supporters had been used to in years.

The match that let everyone else in on the secret was at Hull Kingston Rovers towards the end of October, just before the Lancashire Cup final against St Helens. Rovers were the defending League champions, they were on their way to retaining the title, and they had so far not lost a match all season. Fortress Craven Park was pretty well impregnable, and few Robins supporters would have been expecting Wigan to ruffle any feathers. The first defeat of the season had to come some time, of course, but 10–30 at home to Wigan was not on anyone's agenda. Especially as Rovers barely got a look-in, spending most of a long afternoon chasing the shadows of the visiting wingers.

Henderson Gill scored a hat-trick, while Ferguson contented himself with a single touchdown – but it was Fergie's match. Rovers just couldn't get near him, and his part in the final try was simply sensational. Running from his own line, he drifted around Prohm, accelerated past Laws, and dummied the by now exasperated Fairbairn. Just short of the Rovers try-line he was stopped by Garry Clark, who had crossed from the opposite wing – but so had Gill and, when Edwards continued the move, there was literally nothing left of the home defence to keep the winger out. 'We have been telling people all the time that Fergie is a world-beater,' Colin Clarke said. 'Perhaps now they will start to believe us.'

They did, but Wigan had the misfortune of running up against a more recognisable world-beater in their very next match, in the form of Mal Meninga, of Queensland, Australia and St Helens. Every club had been out signing Australians in the summer of 1984, and Saints were convinced they had captured the best of the lot. After the Lancashire Cup final, Wigan could see what they meant. Mighty Mal scored two tries, made two tries and walked off with the man-of-the-match award – and that was before half-time. A fairly creditable second-half fightback from Wigan, which narrowed the final margin of defeat to 18–26, could not disguise the harsh reality: in front of 26,074, on our own ground (Wigan having won the toss for venue), we had been stuffed by our arch-enemies. And, while their Australian had done as he pleased, ours had scarcely figured in the game. It was difficult to see how life could be lived again after such an embarrassment. What was the point of Brett Kenny arriving in December now? The damage had been done.

Having had their illusions crushed almost as comprehensively as at Wembley the previous May, Wigan set about ringing the changes. None of the umpteen Australians on Halifax's roster happened to be called Meninga, so a young scrum-half called Mike Ford, one of a couple of promising teenage half-backs at the club, was given a run against them in place of Fairhurst. The other, Keith Holden, was given his chance a week later at Workington, where he earned rave notices in what looked like a winning partnership with the equally youthful Shaun Edwards. But it was

Holden and Cannon in the next game, a big win over Huddersfield in the first round of the John Player Special Trophy – a match which saw the debut, on the right wing, of Nick du Toit, an enormous South African who had made his own way to Wigan and asked for a trial, and had been terrorising opponents in a handful of A team games.

But Holden and Cannon did not quite hit it off against Leeds in the JPS second round and despite having their chances, Wigan slid out of the competition in a 4–10 defeat. I watched this game glumly on the television in my brother's bedsit in Chelsea, noting only that Ferguson scored another memorable try which the BBC, with a camera virtually over the winger's head, miserably failed to show to its best advantage. Still, Brett Kenny was waiting in Wigan when I got back. 'Don't expect miracles,' he told the local papers. As if we would.

Nevertheless, miracles were what we got. Kenny made a quiet debut at Warrington, where he was noticed more for his tackling than his running, with most of the credit for a 22–8 victory going to his half-back partner, Holden. But after that game Wigan simply kept winning, with Kenny coming more and more to the fore, and the wingers in particular enjoying a succession of field days. Kenny's long pass to the wing was something to behold. From almost anywhere on the field, often without warning, the stand-off would suddenly hurl toward either touchline a pass which appeared destined only for the crowd until Ferguson or Gill – especially Gill – arrived on cue at the last moment, and some unsuspecting defence would realise there was little point even starting the chase.

All through December Wigan kept winning, with Gill scoring three against Leigh and Kenny scoring four against Hunslet. The sequence was not even interrupted by the Boxing Day visit to Knowsley Road, where Kenny and Holden and a superb pack performance helped atone for the Lancashire Cup final defeat with a welcome 30–22 victory. All through January Wigan kept winning – though this was a less impressive boast because only two matches were possible that month due to three weeks of freezing weather.

This was the last thing Wigan supporters wanted: Ferguson was due back in Australia on 24 February and, as he neared the end of his stay, every week without a game was considered wasted. But, when the weather relented, he gave us double value to make up for what we had been missing: four tries against Castleford, in what was arguably his most famous individual performance. Central Park was blissfully stunned. I still have several photographs, and indeed a specially commissioned painting, of the various trails of destruction Fergie left that day. But the overriding mental impression is of a cartoon strip in the *Beano* style, with our hero scooting effortlessly all over the pitch, little puffs of air illustrating every acceleration, while in the background a series of hapless opponents crash into each other, give futile chase, or lie helplessly prostrate.

This is not quite how I described it at the time for, due to the sad demise of *The Wigan Post and Chronicle* and its replacement by an extension of *The Lancashire Evening Post*, I was now covering Wigan games for a living. Suddenly it was quite a challenge. Some of the things we were starting to experience on Sunday afternoons had to be seen to be believed. Of all the clubs to cover, and all the times to be covering them, things could hardly have fallen into place better. It seemed to me at the time, and I am even more convinced of it now, that I had been incredibly lucky.

In light of my new capacity as Central Park newshound, I ought to fill you in on some of the off-field developments which took place while we were freezing in our homes in January. Edwards, Kiss, Gill and Wane are called into the Great Britain squad, while the more senior but still devastating Case and Potter are considered unlucky to miss out. Colin Clarke starts a column in *The Wigan Observer* (now the opposition, we stuck with Graeme West) by remarking that Wigan have high hopes for 1985. John Pendlebury is sold to Salford for £16,000 in a move which surprises some fans. 'Our players' panel is now so big, we are getting lots of enquiries from other clubs,' chairman Jack Hilton explains. 'But we are not prepared to part with top-class players, just those on the fringe.' Wigan bid £60,000 for Andy Gregory, transfer-listed at Widnes but, for reasons best known to themselves, the Cheshire club will not sanction the great home-coming, deciding instead to spite Central Park by fixing up a last-minute deal with Warrington. Disappointed not to get the player they have been angling for all season, Wigan sign Leigh's Steve Donlan on the eve of the Challenge Cup deadline, and identify Warrington's Phil Ford as a possible replacement for Ferguson. Donlan is getting on a bit at 30, but is still a class act, as anyone familiar with his displays for Leigh against Wigan will be aware. He makes his debut in the 28–12 victory over Widnes at the end of January, a match which also sees Mike Ford deputise ably for the injured Holden. Wigan's crowd average is now almost 9,000, second only to Hull's, and still rising. And, in the way that newspapers do when not much else is happening, a meeting is fixed up between Billy Boston and John Ferguson in the former's pub, mine host offering the opinion that the lad is fabulous.

Ferguson's four tries against Castleford having proved that beyond any lingering doubt, it was off to Burnden Park, Bolton, in mid-February after another unwanted delay, the Wanderers' heated ground ensuring that Wigan's 'home' Challenge Cup first-round tie against Batley could go ahead despite the wintry weather. Win number eight in a row was followed six days later by win number nine, also in the Challenge Cup, the fixture chaos having telescoped the first two rounds of the competition to within a week of each other. This was Fergie's farewell match, and boy was it memorable. Warrington, now including a peeved-looking Andy Gregory in their ranks, could only stand and watch as tries by Kenny, Gill and, most unforgettably, Ferguson, plus six goals from new kicker Stephenson, swept Wigan into the quarter-finals.

Fergie's farewell try is indelibly imprinted on the mind. When Kenny received the ball in his own half and looked up, most of the Wigan contingent knew what was about to happen. The ball was duly swung out to the right to Stephenson, then on to Ferguson, and the winger's gallop to the line from beyond half-way out, with Kenny in perfect step, pointing and shouting encouragement, was captured brilliantly by television and still photographers alike.

But this was not just a leaving party: Warrington were a good side who had been confidently beaten. After this win, it dawned on Wigan fans perhaps for the first time that they now had a side capable not only of reaching Wembley, but of putting up a decent performance when they got there. Amid the disappointment of the previous year's Wembley let-down, the Wigan directors, notably the vice-Chairman, Maurice Lindsay, had promised that the club would be back. It had not seemed a likely prospect, but their wishful thinking now seemed to be taking shape and, this time, it was due less to luck than good judgement. Ferguson in particular, Jack Hilton confirmed, had been one of Wigan's best-ever signings. 'How he missed out on tour selection I'll never know. Surely the Aussies can't have *four* wingers better than him!'

Leaving Wilderspool after the game in the general direction of Bank Quay station, with every intention of taking in the odd pub or two on the way, our little party bumped into Maurice Bamford, who was walking along deep in thought, raincoat slung over his shoulder, looking like a Great Britain coach with a lot on his mind. To a man, we all wanted to know how much longer he intended to ignore the claims of Ian Potter. Surely it was time for an international call-up? 'I think you might be right,' Bamford agreed. 'Sometimes you need someone to carry the piano as well as someone to play it.' We all looked at each other, wondering if there was still time to find the pub where Bamford had been drinking. But, sure enough, Potter received his invitation before the end of the season.

Following the Warrington game, Wigan completed the signing of Phil Ford, who was called on to spend the rest of the season pretending he was Fergie. In fairness, he didn't do a bad job. The little fella he wasn't, of course; but there was no denying that he was an extremely useful winger, even if Wigan had been forced to stump up £40,000 for a player who was ineligible for Challenge Cup games. The club put a brave face on the business, saying it was now their policy to sign only the best players around. They had in fact been saying this for a while, but now there was reason to believe them.

Ford had only had time to prove his worth on his home debut – two tries to complete the double over Hull KR, including a last-minute dash to touch down Kenny's kick which preserved Wigan's winning sequence – before he had to take a back seat for the Cup quarter-final against Bradford at Odsal. This was a daunting prospect. Considerably bucked by their best League attendance of the season (14,510) for the Hull KR game, Wigan had appealed for travelling support, mentioning that it would be nice for the players to see a sea of cherry-and-white when they ran out of the tunnel at Bradford. Tunnel? Ran? In those days, teams took the field at Odsal by means of a walkway through the crowd, descending some considerable distance from changing-rooms to pitch level – but Wigan did see a sea of cherry-and-white. Unfortunately, Odsal – never exactly a show ground at the best of times – was in the throes of major redevelopment, and 15,000 people turned up to what was basically a building site. If Odsal couldn't cope, neither could the M606 which, at 3:30 p.m. on 10 March, resembled a linear car park. Fans simply left their cars on the hard shoulder, or on some portion of the plentiful waste ground thoughtfully provided by the side of the motorway, and went to watch the game.

The Cup-tie was almost unbearably exciting. Every time Hanley got the ball, Wigan were in danger of conceding yards if not points; therefore Bradford's understandable plan was to give him the ball at every possible opportunity. This was the season in which Hanley became the first player in 23 years to score 50 tries in a season, and it was easy to see how. He was not a natural stand-off, but in that position he saw a great deal of the ball, and he certainly knew how to run with it. Even with half the Wigan team hanging off him, Hanley still seemed capable of scoring at any moment and, in a torrid, physical encounter fought out at close quarters, the Bradford man was more of a threat than Kenny. The contest bore no resemblance to the open, running games Wigan had been dominating, and only the visitors' collective determination enabled them to defend a one-point lead in the second half, when Bradford threw everything bar the bulldozers at their line.

A drop-goal from Mike Ford provided the slender margin of victory, though arguably the scores might have been a little wider apart than 7–6 had Gill been able to get nearer the posts after crossing in the corner for his try. Instead, he was mobbed by his own fans as soon as he crossed the whitewash. This sounds ludicrous, and indeed it was; but so was the sight of several rows of Wigan spectators watching the game from portable seats within the Bradford in-goal area. When Henderson scored, what did anyone expect they would do? Applaud politely? Beam with satisfaction? With hindsight, it was blessed good fortune that no one at Odsal was hurt or injured that day. It would be impossible to play such a game in similar circumstances now; the authorities would rightly and properly refuse to sanction it. A sobering reflection is that, when the work at Odsal was finished and the 'new' ground opened, the safe working capacity was approximately the same as the number of spectators allowed in for that quarter-final.

Theoretically, Wigan now had a squad large enough and capable enough to take all League and Cup obstacles in its stride, but a little momentum was lost when they could only draw their next League match at Halifax, the end of an 11-match winning run dating back to Kenny's arrival. That lapse was understandable, only a couple of days after the most demanding game of the season, but there was still the fixture backlog occasioned by the winter postponements to contend with. Equally theoretically, Wigan were in a position to attempt a League and Cup double, but this had never been achieved in the modern era and was still considered improbable. This, in any case, was a bad season for any team to try for it, so it was perhaps as well that the Wigan fans, and eventually the team, trained their sights exclusively on Wembley.

Still, the League had its diversions. A feature of the home match against Workington, when Wigan rested half their side and still won 52–6, was the try scored by du Toit, who came on as substitute for Stephenson. Bearing down on a line protected only by a trembling Geoff Rae, the burly South African launched himself upwards and over the full-back, grid-iron-style. The crowd loved it. Life without Ferguson was proving bearable after all.

To reach Wembley, Wigan simply needed to beat Hull KR for a third time. They had every right to be confident, after disposing of Warrington and Bradford away from home *en route* to the semi-final, and with the League double under their belt. But meeting Hull KR then was a bit like being drawn against Wigan now. They were the big cheeses, the established power. For all their new-found entertainment value, Wigan were still upstarts. Humberside was where it was all happening in Rugby League, and people were starting to talk about an all-Humberside final. I knew that few members of the Rugby League press rated Wigan's chances very highly because, in the week prior to the game, I finally got to go on one of the game's most jealously-guarded junkets, a gin-soaked freebie on a canal barge, at which the last thing everyone said before passing into oblivion was that Hull KR would be at Wembley.

To be fair, the press view only just missed the mark. Hull KR gave Wigan a run for their money in an Elland Road semi-final which was closer than the 18–11 scoreline suggests, and the Robins did make it to Wembley the year after. But, once again, Wigan were fuelled by an extraordinary desire. In the end, will to win was all that separated the sides. Like the Blues Brothers, Wigan appeared to be on a mission, never more so than when West came striding massively out of defence in the second half to beat Fairbairn on a 50-yard run and sent Stephenson cantering to the posts. Juliff, a surprise choice on the right wing, had opened Wigan's account with a try in the right corner, brilliantly engineered by Wane but at the expense of a knee injury which eventually ruled the prop out of the final. Wane could only watch as Miller and Clark scored the tries which kept Rovers in with a shout at 12–11, before West finally used his height to settle matters, popping a basketball pass out of a tackle for Gill to score. Kenny was relatively quiet apart from his usual defensive stint, while Mike Ford played well enough to secure a Wembley shirt at the end of his first season. Other unsung heroes included Courtney, who clung on to Broadhurst for a solid 80 minutes, and Mick Scott, who just managed to grab Clark's waistband to prevent a try which could have changed things dramatically.

The big question, as Wigan embarked on a suicidal pre-Easter programme of four League games in eight days, beating Oldham comfortably enough before seeing dreams of the title and a record unbeaten run evaporate with three consecutive defeats in Yorkshire, was whether Ferguson would be flown back for Wembley.

The big answer was yes. Armed with this comforting knowledge, plus the fact that we were going to Wembley and they weren't, the Wigan supporters in a huge Good Friday crowd of 19,768 were able to smile indulgently as St Helens picked up their second win of the season at Central Park.

Away wins at Oldham and Widnes proved Kenny and Co. could still do it when they wanted to, although there was no escaping the fact that a home defeat by already-relegated Hunslet was worrying. Three straight wins against Hull, Featherstone and Barrow rounded off the League season, Wigan finishing in third place, five points behind Hull KR and two behind St Helens.

Hull awaited Wigan at Wembley, by virtue of beating Castleford in an epic semi-final, but first there was a less-than-epic encounter between the two finalists in the first round of the Premiership at Central Park. Phil Ford, who wouldn't be playing at Wembley, scored four tries in a 46–12 victory which proved little, Hull also having selected several players who would not be featuring in the Challenge Cup final.

The 1985 Silk Cut Challenge Cup final, Rugby League's 50th Wembley occasion, was instantly and universally hailed as the best of all time, certainly of the television era, and has been extensively documented elsewhere. You probably don't need me to tell you what happened. You can probably still see Fergie dashing in for his couple of tries; Brett Kenny slouching insolently during the presentation ceremony, then cutting a majestic swathe through the game to win the Lance Todd trophy; Henderson Gill grinning from ear to ear after his barnstorming run down the left; and the terribly unlucky Peter Sterling shedding a tear or two on the pitch at the end. I know I can. And, like a thousand other

Wigan supporters, I can still recite chunks of Alex Murphy's idiotic commentary for the BBC, especially the bits about Fergie's allegedly bad leg and West taking several minutes to get up off the floor. I can still see Arthur Bunting eating his cigar, and I still get a bit tense when Hull mount their second-half fightback – and this is without the video.

In researching this piece, I stumbled on a remarkable piece of foresight from Reg Bowden, who seems to have forecast most of these things. Asked for a Wembley prediction, the Warrington coach said he was backing Wigan. 'I've fancied Wigan all along, even before they beat us. West is a superb captain who has brought necessary discipline back to the side. Kenny and Sterling are both brilliant, but Wigan have the ace up their sleeve in Ferguson.' Which was not a bad summary of the final, in advance.

That should have been the end of the season really, with Fergie and Kenny and Wigan all bowing out together in glorious technicolour. But, as the season was a Rugby League production, not a Hollywood one, it had to end in a grotesque shambles. The Premiership competition was a piece of unfinished business the League wanted over with and, in order that the Elland Road final could be played on the Saturday after Wembley, Wigan were asked to play their semi-final at St Helens two days after the Challenge Cup final. On appeal, the League relented and made it three days. Wigan were torn. The competition was plainly half-baked and completely unimportant but, on the other hand, if the opponents were St Helens, there was pride at stake and an obligation to the fans.

In the event, a tired Wigan sort of half-played at Knowsley Road on the Tuesday after Wembley. Kenny's thoughts were clearly on the next flight out of Manchester, and it was no great surprise to Wigan followers when he subsequently admitted not trying terribly hard, in an interview back home in Australia. Ferguson had already flown home – straight after Wembley, without even picking up his winning money – but the annoying thing about the late collapse which allowed Saints a 37–14 victory, apart from the fact that it gave Meninga and his side a chance to shine against a demoralised Hull KR in the final, was that not all the Wigan players were willing to throw in the towel. Phil Ford, who had missed Wembley through no fault of his own and was desperate to bask in a little bit of glory, tried his heart out all night, to no avail. The following season, Ford was sold to Bradford as a makeweight in the deal which brought Hanley to Central Park. I felt even more sorry for him then.

In a short while, Wigan would add players such as Goodway, Gregory and Lydon, and corner the market in domestic glory. The 1984–85 season was the start of an incredible era at Central Park, but it was also the end of something intangible. The element of surprise, perhaps. Success came in spadefuls, though it was never quite the same when the possibility of losing was all but removed from the equation. There was only a short time during which Wigan were good enough to beat the best without automatically being expected to. That time has long gone, but what a time it was.

PAUL WILSON was formerly a Rugby League writer for *The Wigan Evening Post* and for *The Independent*. Now with *The Observer*, he has the opportunity to look completely brassed-off at a wider variety of sporting events.

PASSED DOWN FROM FATHER TO SON

Swinton 1985–86

Martin and Simon Kelner

MARTIN:

The A1 may be the Great North Road but, at the junction of Holloway Road and Drayton Park in London N5, the heartland of the great northern game might as well be a million miles away. This is inner-city London – Arsenal country – and Bert's Cafe, a greasy spoon in no imminent danger of making it into the Egon Ronay *Just a Bite* guide, is the kind of place the lads like to drop into for a cup of tea and a fag on the way to Highbury. For two Sunday-morning regulars, though, Bert's was truly the gateway to the North, and starting-point of a Rugby League odyssey that, over the course of the 1985–86 season, was to clock up more than 10,000 miles.

Heaven knows what the other customers made of it, overhearing talk of Danny Wilson's knee injury, whether the stand at Station Road would get a safety certificate, or how the suspension of Joe Grima would weaken the team. We were oblivious, eager to turn our backs on the attractions of the capital in favour of a bacon sandwich and a battle with the roadworks on the M1.

It was the winter when every fixture was an away game as far as we were concerned, but distance lent enchantment to a lifetime's love affair. There was something special about this season: a season which found my brother and me both working in London, and our team newly promoted to the first division; a season which started rich in hope but ended, like all the others in living memory, in disappointment; and a season which saw the passing of the man who had bred and fostered this ridiculous obsession.

Dad died in October, after the Widnes match and before the game at Bradford Northern. Excellent timing, as I remarked to my brother at the time, since it meant we could travel up for the funeral and take in the match at Odsal on the same trip.

This was the kind of smiling-through-the-tears, laugh-or-you'll-cry humour which the old man appreciated and indulged in himself constantly. Thirty years as a Swinton supporter tends to encourage graveyard humour, some of it quite literal in Dad's case. He frequently said he wished to be buried at Rainsough, a cemetery midway between our home and Station Road, so we could chalk the Swinton scores on his headstone on our way back. He used this gag regularly for at least ten years before his death, during most of which time he enjoyed perfectly robust health. It was the decline of his beloved Swinton through these years that was more likely to be described as terminal than his own.

As it turned out, Rainsough was full, so the lifelong Swinton fan was laid to rest alongside Manchester United people and other infidels in Whitefield cemetery, a greener, more modern site – a sort of overspill estate for the dead – and inconveniently north-east of Station Road. The punch-line, though, is one Dad would have relished. A few years after his death, Swinton moved grounds to Bury, which means his resting-place is now, as he wished, almost exactly half-way between the family home and that of the team. The only thing that stops us chalking up the scores as we pass is the thought that he's suffered enough.

Perhaps he liked to suffer. On the way back to Mum's house after the funeral, the talk turned inevitably to Swinton and the central part the team played in his life and ours. Only then did we raise the question. Why Swinton?

I knew why I supported Swinton. It was because he did. Not that I slavishly followed all the old man's dictates in the area of leisure-time activities. I probably first attended under protest so that Mum could have some peace at home to cook and clear up (we're talking northern marriage in the early 1960s) but, once I discovered that the chap who operated the PA at Swinton and I had a shared interest in the music of Del Shannon, the die was cast.

I remember particularly one brilliantly sunny day walking from the car to the ground – it must have been a big game as we had parked half a mile away in Bolton Road – and hearing the B-side of 'Two Kinds of Teardrops' blasting out at fairground levels. Strangely, the sunshine and Del Shannon (of whose fan club I was a member) are all I remember of the day out but, according to the *Guinness Book of Hit Singles*, 'Two Kinds of Teardrops' entered the charts in April 1963, so the match must have been part of the glorious charge on the 1963 Championship by the team of Gowers, Buckley and Stopford. What is more, my friend on the PA seemed to have not only the Del Shannon singles collection but also the 'Hats Off to Del Shannon' album, which he featured regularly – hideously distorted, of course, in the way that Del's music was best appreciated. Clearly, I didn't stand a chance.

My younger brother was an even softer target. With two male members of the family already stricken, and with Billy 'Daz' Davies, Graham Williams and Dave Robinson having joined Swinton's stellar squad by the time he entered the fellowship, he was soon hooked. The growing-up, the bonding, the music were all part of it. Before the 1969 Lancashire Cup final, we went up to my bedroom and listened to side two of the Beatles' new album 'Abbey Road'. After Swinton's demolition of Alex Murphy's Leigh side, the LP became something of a talisman, and the playing of side two was a ritual indulged in before every match.

But Dad had no adolescent, rock 'n' roll-related excuses. He was a fully-grown, responsible adult by the time he started following Swinton. What is more, it was the 1950s, and the great Championship-winning side was still in the future. We had moved from Salford to Prestwich, which was a rock-solid Manchester United constituency. Why would he deliberately choose to mark himself out as an outsider and, having made his inexplicable choice, why stick with it? As far as I know, he had never lived in Swinton in his life; it would have been no treachery for him to switch his allegiance to Salford when Swinton's decline in the 1970s coincided with the golden years of Watkins, Coulman, Fielding and Richards at the Willows.

By then, though, he had lost two sons to Swinton so maybe he stuck with the Lions for our sake. Maybe, we concluded, he was a closet optimist. Despite all evidence to the contrary, perhaps he had managed to persuade himself the good times at Station Road really were just around the corner. On the surface, at least, his view of life – and certainly family life – appeared to veer towards the bleak, his personal philosophy falling somewhere between the less cheerful films of Ingmar Bergman and the work of Woody Allen.

He ran a small clothing business, which didn't help. In the 1950s, he had produced items called windcheetahs or jerkins, which people packed in their baskets with a thermos and a grease-proof-paper pack of white-bread sandwiches before boarding the train for a day trip to Blackpool. But, in the 1960s and '70s, Dad became increasingly bewildered by the speed at which fashions changed. It was a fairly safe bet that, if he got his production line working on big corduroy jackets with four-inch wide lapels, the hot new pop group of the moment would turn up the next day on *Top of the Pops* wearing pencil-thin Italian mohair suits.

His sense of frustration received little in the way of ameliora-tion from his soul-mate. Bizarrely for a man who loved wisecracks, especially cynical one-liners, he had chosen as a life partner a woman who did not, and does not, bless her, understand jokes. So his outlet – and where better for gallows humour – was Swinton. It used to be sheer joy, when I was little, to be with him in the stand at Station Road with an audience who actually appreciated his gags.

There was once an article in *The Manchester Evening News* in which Swinton forward Ken Roberts, a robust player with a quick temper, expressed a desire to go to Australia with the Great Britain touring party. During the match the following day, Roberts got involved in a heated dispute with an opposing forward, which resulted in his rival being laid out by a right hook in full view of the referee. 'Sure he'll go to Australia,' shouted Dad. 'If they bring back the convict ships.' Mum would never have understood. When my sister passed her language exams, he told one of his mates in the stand: 'She's thinking of teaching English as a Foreign Language.' A pause. 'To Eddie Waring.'

So this was how we remembered him when we put him in the ground on that Wednesday before the Bradford match – as a funny man, who taught us that having a laugh can be as important as winning. As it happens, this has turned out to be a particularly useless life lesson, as winning is invariably more satisfying than having a laugh. But we were grateful to him for it none the less.

Perhaps a more important lesson he taught us was the role sport – and, in particular, blind illogical loyalty to one side – could play in wilfully arresting development. After an away match at Featherstone in the 1962–63 season, when a Gowers drop-goal had given Swinton the narrowest of victories, Dad and his friend Dennis Wilson rolled down the car windows as we drove through the town and taunted the Rovers fans as they queued for their chips. It was the first time I had ever seen adults behave like children. These days, of course, there are all sorts of opportunities for 45-year-olds to let their remaining hair down – Bruce Springsteen gigs and so on – but it was something of an eye-opener in the back of the car on that Saturday afternoon, and made me view the old man – thwarted and frustrated at work and at home – in a new and softer light.

As we sat in that stand at Odsal four days after the funeral – my brother, myself, and our wives – the last thing we wanted to do was grow up. A father's death, possibly even more than the birth of our children, brings home to you the fact that the game is entering the end-zone, and it might be time to start behaving like a proper grown-up person. Happily, Swinton allowed us to live in unreality a little longer.

SIMON:

Odsal Stadium, that vast, decaying bowl in which any crowd under 50,000 looks sparse, is unreal at the best of times and, with the sun streaming down mockingly on that afternoon and only 3,500 present, it seemed particularly soulless. Yet this relatively meaningless match was not lacking in meaning for myself and my brother.

Nevertheless, it was memorable for reasons other than being the first Swinton match in an age when we could be *sure* that Dad was not going to see them play at Wembley. We had secretly hoped that the significance of the occasion would be transmitted by osmosis to the team; and perhaps it was, because they turned in exactly the sort of half-hearted and exasperating performance that sent Dad to the grave an unfulfilled man.

Bradford won 48–20. The Northern stand-off John Woods broke the club record for points in a match with five tries and eight goals and, adapting the cliché, Swinton were lucky to get 20. It was also the match in which we saw the last – until the final three fixtures of the season – of Danny Wilson, the one man who kept the anticipation level high on all those trips up the M1. Danny limped off the field after a dozen minutes and, with him down the tunnel, went Swinton's already slim hopes of survival in the first division.

How different it had all been only a week earlier. The visit of a star-spangled Widnes team to Station Road did not, on the face of it, offer much prospect of success for a side who had only won once (at Oldham) so far this season. We wanted to see Dad in hospital before going to the game, so we left Bert's especially early that morning.

Dad was in particularly chirpy mood, and was eager to tell us that, in between getting nurses to put his bets on, he had adapted and refined an old party game. Soup charades, it was called. Sadly, after he had gone through energetic mimes for green pea (easy), mulligatawny (difficult) and minestrone (well nigh impossible), we left for the game.

The day was irredeemably grey, the drizzle was unremitting, and our hearts were full of foreboding, and not only because Widnes were then in their pomp. Almost the last thing Dad said to us was: 'Is Danny playing?' We nodded reassurance to the old man yet, even if Danny was on the pitch, there was no guarantee that he would be playing.

Danny Wilson had joined Swinton from Cardiff Rugby Union club in 1979 for what was then a club record fee of £15,000. Danny had not come from the Welsh fly-half factory. He wasn't your clean-living Phil Bennett or Barry John, although there are some who say that, had he not been black and had a reputation for, shall we say, unconventional behaviour, he would have come close to representative honours. He arrived at Station Road, and immediately a host of dark, and probably apocryphal, tales of his past did the rounds. Whenever he was written about, his name was usually preceded by one of that famous trinity of euphemisms: 'unpredictable', 'enigmatic' or 'wayward'.

But what did we care? Unreliable he most certainly was, but here was the purest talent that had been seen at Station Road since Daz Davies. A side-step that would make David Watkins look clumsy, blistering acceleration off the mark, and an ability to wind up the opposition that ensured he was a favourite with the Swinton faithful.

At that time, an attractive young blonde lady took to sitting in front of us in the Main Stand. We subsequently discovered that she was Danny's wife. Invariably, she was accompanied by a well-behaved little toddler. A decade later, this little boy was to become one of the most prodigious talents in British football. Ryan Giggs took his mother's name after Danny was estranged from the family but, when Giggs turns defenders inside-out with the skill that is only God-given, it is difficult not to believe in heredity. Danny may not have conferred his surname on young Ryan, but he gave him something altogether more valuable.

For, on his day, Danny had it all. I have long been convinced that you can tell whether a rugby player –and especially a stand-off – has got something special by the way he runs on the pitch. Danny, seemingly on tiptoes, almost prancing, light on his feet and with perfect poise, was clearly a cut above.

He was certainly too much for Widnes to handle on that damp October day. He scored three drop-goals (echoes of the great Peter Kenny's performance in the Lancashire Cup final of 1969–70 against Leigh, when he played Alex Murphy off the park to score four two-point drop-goals) but, more important, manufactured a magnificent pass for Mark Viller to score the only try of the match. Swinton won 17–6 in the upset of the season and, even though we had an horrendous journey back to London in the wet, we were secure in the knowledge that, in a hospital bed in Manchester, an old man was smiling to himself. Danny had indeed been playing.

But that was as good as it got in the 1985–86 season. Three days later, Dad died in the operating theatre. He left behind a betting bill of £43 and, we're sure, an implicit wish that we keep the faith. Not that our fidelity was in doubt: we drove up in the fog to see them beaten 16–30 at Widnes; I got a speeding fine on the way to a 2–36 defeat at York; I interrupted a holiday in Wales to see them lose at Dewsbury in surely one of the worst first-division matches on record.

Not that there wasn't the odd high spot. Probably the most bizarre game of that season was on 8 December when, in the return of that Odsal fixture, Bradford were the visitors to Station Road. The crowd was 5,257 (four times the season's average), the press box was overflowing, the TV cameras were there, and there was an explosion of flash bulbs as the teams took the field. Not your average Swinton game, you might say. Playing his first game for the visitors was Terry Holmes, the great Welsh scrum-half, and the most significant convert to League since Watkins joined Salford.

Holmes lasted just 13 minutes, his professional career irretrievably damaged in one bone-crunching but fair tackle from John Allen. With Holmes out of the way, Swinton seized on a rare moment in the public gaze and, remarkably, won 8–0, winger Ken Jones scoring all the points. The season yielded only another three victories, against Featherstone, Hull and Castleford – how we wish that we could even compete with their like today – and a return from whence we came became increasingly inevitable.

And here we are today, still in the second division (although we have twice had a similar, one-season spell in the first), but it is not how we remember it. The loss of Station Road was the most grievous blow; it was as much our home as any house we ever lived in, and the day the bulldozers moved in something irreplaceable went from our lives. Gigg Lane is fine, but it's not Station Road. Now they're playing in blue-and-white stripes, and I can't recognise more than two players on the team photograph.

But we still go along, and maybe in time we'll get used to it. And, maybe in time, our children will curse us, and yet be unutterably grateful, that a father's mad obsession has been passed on.

MARTIN AND SIMON KELNER are media heavyweights. Martin is a BBC Radio presenter who now lives in Leeds and whose dulcet tones make the small hours bearable for the nation's insomniacs. His younger brother, Simon, has been everything from a cub reporter on *The Neath Guardian* to editor of *The Observer Magazine*, and is now sports editor of *The Independent on Sunday*.

ALF, GEORGE, MICK AND KEITH

Hull FC 1975–76

Trevor Gibbons

There is an added spice to life in a two-team town. Not only can your team do badly, but *they* can do better. Failure can be tolerated as long as it is not relative. As Mr Micawber would have put it had he been born in West Hull, 'Hull FC above Rovers, result happiness. Rovers above Hull FC, result misery.' It was a blessing that the decision of which team to support was not a choice, more an accident of birth and family history. This meant that, when results didn't go for your team, you couldn't be tempted to transfer allegiance to the other shower.

There was no doubt who had been top dogs in recent seasons, with Rovers having finished above the FC nine times out of the last ten years. I had been lucky enough to avoid much of the pain associated with this by conveniently living in Essex. However, we had then moved back to Hull, and 1975–76 was the fourth season in a row that I was to be found in the Threepenny Stand, ever-expectant of a success-filled season, and ever-envious of the Rovers a division above us.

My chosen winter is by now so deep in the mists of time that there was even a Labour Government. I suppose that, had I been remotely interested, I should have known that tremendous changes were afoot as, earlier in 1975, Margaret Thatcher had been elected leader of the Tory Party. It didn't exactly strike me as this then but, in that summer of 1975, the great post-war political consensus began to break up and, as recession set in, there was the worst unemployment since the Second World War. Although the actual totals are almost laughable in the light of what we have now become used to, then the concept of even one million out of work seemed fantastical.

I had yet to begin my economics O level and, to that end, hadn't persuaded the family to take *The Daily Telegraph* so that I could read a 'serious' newspaper for my education. But what did I care? I had discovered Dr Feelgood. There I was one day watching *Magpie*, and it happened. (Now I know that, in those days, Mick Robertson and Jenny Hanley were considered very second-rate to Auntie's established *Blue Peter*, but I was always a risk-taker.) Suddenly Feelgood were on and, as 'Back in the Night' blasted out, I was gobsmacked. These guys were the original Essex men. I was smitten: here was noisy, good-time, loud music played by people in suits with attitude. You could have knocked me down with a 20-inch loon-pant bottom.

The River Hull might not have a name like the Rio Grande as a legendary border, but it splits the city in two and no twain e'er meets. Now I was West Hull born and bred, and black-and-white all the way through. This now presented me with a problem because there was only one place in Cottingham, where I lived, to buy records – and the map, as well as my sense of direction, said Cottingham was safely to the west of the river. But the fine emporium in question was called *East* Hull Radio and Records. This caused me great consternation: could I possibly patronise a shop with that title? What was it doing over our side anyway? What if my hard-earned money was being secretly channelled into the red-and-white slush fund? I never did get over the uncomfortable suspicion that the establishment was a secret front for Rovers.

Little did I know it, but the 1975–76 season was to run concurrent with the birth of punk rock. One thing you could be sure of, though, was that you wouldn't have noticed anything down the Boulevard as the Faithful lined up for the first League game of the season, at home to Workington. The loudest sound as people entered the ground was the swish of flares around thousands of pairs of ankles – or, if you considered yourself slightly more hip, your brown, high-waisted, many-pleated baggies which were designed complete with patch pocket on the knee (an ideal sanctuary for the programme). Hull FC kicked off with a 21–21 draw against the Cumbrians.

I considered this state of affairs during August from deep in the recesses of East Hull R and R. Hopelessly old-fashioned then, a symbol of another time in what was then called hi-fi. Here I had secured the Feelgoods' first single, 'Roxette', in a plain white sleeve with a black label which proclaimed 'MONO'. Record shops still mended things then and the owner, Mr Sugarman, would shamble out of the back office with his hearing aid discreetly feeding back, mumbling incomprehensible things – about what? The cast of our jibs? The records he was selling us? I also bought their first album, 'Down by the Jetty', there. A moody foursome stared out at me from the sleeve, again in black and white. In truth, they looked not unlike the Hull team pictures of the time, all Zapata moustaches and unruly hair competing for attention with sideburns that had a life of their own.

Nobody, but nobody in that Hull team, though, looked like the Feelgoods' Wilko Johnson: black suit, scuffed boots, and a barely-contained lunatic grin. Rugby League may have had a few homicidal maniacs of its own over the years, but none of them showed in their team pictures the menace that Wilko managed from that album sleeve. It was not to be displayed better until Jack Nicholson conjured it up for the publicity pictures for *The Shining*.

Meanwhile, back on the pitch, Hull's first test was coming in a season which was to be dominated by cup games. The Yorkshire Cup seems a quaint idea nowadays, but then it provided us second-division sides with a chance to see some glamour. And when, like Hull, you had finished below Huyton last season, almost anything seemed glamorous. This time it fell to Castleford to enliven our poor diet. Clad in duster-yellow with the merest hint of black on the collars and cuffs, they still appeared incredibly aristocratic, and were already coached by one Malcolm Reilly. Get this: we drew. Boy, were we going to go somewhere this season.

Strange forces were definitely abroad that August, although in spheres other than Rugby League their influence would take some time to reach the banks of the Humber Estuary. The pub rock revival – then in full swing and headed by the Feelgoods and their mates – was soon to throw up its bastard offspring. Bromley, Kent has yet to feature on the Rugby League map, but there a revolution was under way. It was in this month that the band destined to become the Sex Pistols had their first rehearsal, but all I was looking forward to was the replay at Castleford. That duly arrived, and the true order of things was restored with Castleford winning – but only by one point. Hull's hairy collection had done the business.

It was another cup competition, the Player's No. 6 Trophy, that was forever to become, for me, the motif of success for a bunch of second-division upstarts. In late September, we were drawn to play the perennial strugglers, Doncaster, whose home ground, Tattersfield, has always been cruelly seen as aptly named. I was going to go there in some style, bearing as I did a letter asking me to join the Doncaster directors in the board-room before the game. How was I moving in such rarefied circles? Well, the season before, when the Dons had come to the Boulevard, they were beaten by some 40 points, which passed as a walloping in the days when the gap between poor and adequate was not so large. I had taken pity on their efforts. I don't know what use it was supposed to be, but I wrote and sent a letter to the club urging them to keep fighting the Rugby League fight. They had replied with their offer of hospitality, and now I had the chance to take it up.

Cruel the jokes at Tattersfield might have been but, as we pulled off the Bentley Road, our only worry about leaving the car on the piece of wasteland that passed for a car park in front of the ground was, would we find it again through the head-high grass? As we made our way to the turnstile, through the jungle, I also noticed that the more intrepid spectators crossing the beck that winds along the side of the ground, were doing so by walking along a rounded pipe spanning the water – presumably because it was a longer trip to go over the bridge proper. All this excitement, and the match yet to kick off. I headed for the back of the Main Stand and the board-room, grubby letter clutched in my hand. Would it be exposed as a fake? No, the rather disappointing piece of paper worked, and I was through.

There, under the stand, in a small room with rather restricted headroom and a roof reflecting the shape of the terraces above, I received two bottles of slightly warm beer. As all beer does when you're under-age, it tasted like prize-winning brew. I kindly refused the offer of watching the game from a seat. What would I do with a seat? True fans stood, I knew that, and so I made my excuses and dashed round to the popular side of the ground.

Popular was somewhat of a misnomer, and there was no problem spotting my father as the only thing that was thick on the terraces was grass. One of the advantages of such a sparse crowd is that you can feel a personal affinity with the players, and this was definitely helped for the Hull fans by Alf Macklin keeping up a running conversation with us from his position on the wing. From this distance in time I don't have a photographic memory of tries scored that season, but one still stands out from that day – stand-off Brian Hancock, who seemed to run as though in slow motion, slicing through the line. Truth to tell, I can't remember much else: the scoring order has faded, leaving only a vignette of Hancock looking like a thoroughbred as he glided about the pitch.

And so, back to Hull in the Mark III Cortina, with the black-and-white scarf trailing out of the window in a victory salute. I was always paranoid that the whole scarf would be ripped out of the car by the slipstream and would go cascading down the road to be squashed under the wheels of a following juggernaut.

On match-days, when you travelled the same route as a team with a good away support, you could mark their progress by counting the sorry woollen objects, like so many roadkills by the side of American freeways. Therefore care had to be taken: the scarf was knotted firmly to the passenger hand rail above the window, and then a further knot put in so that it could not slip through. Then, and only then, the few inches of scarf that remained were fed out. Sometimes, so little scarf was let out that it did not even have the length to flap with that satisfying crack against the car roof. As you became more confident of your tying technique, though, greater lengths would be let out to ensure that this crack would happen and, indeed, another scarf would become necessary for the opposite window. The trip back could then be spent with your head resting back on the parcel shelf, looking up through the rear window to study the Cortina's complicated air flow over the roof and marvelling at how filthy the scarf could get.

All this could have been different, though, had I not snapped my guitar in two sometime before. There it was leaning against the wall when, as a result of some pre-WWF wrestling, I fell against it. My backside on the strings produced a sickening crunch, almost completely separating the neck from the body. Although this did allow for interesting effects with string-bending undreamt of even by Jimi Hendrix, it did render the instrument useless in the conventional sense. I was therefore unable to answer the advert placed in *The Melody Maker* the same week as the Doncaster game, which read:

WANTED, WHIZZ-KID GUITARIST
Not older than 20. Not worse looking than Johnny Thunders.

I knew I was just what the Pistols wanted and, as an added bonus, I couldn't even play. Malcolm McLaren had just put up £1,000 to guarantee them rehearsal space, and they needed another guitarist, and I'd smashed mine. On such slender thread is history hung.

October brought that other reminder of a bygone age, the Floodlit Trophy. The Tuesday-night coverage on BBC2 proved that I was a very sad case. Just when every other boy in my class was busting a gut to watch Frank Finlay as Casanova on the other channel to see if they could pick up any clues about this sex thing, I was happy with Uncle Eddie Waring and the delights of Rugby League. Hull disposed of Bramley in the first round of the competition but, before we could go any further, we had the tie we wanted: Leeds in the Player's No. 6 Trophy.

This was it. The big-city brethren were coming to town. Hull–Leeds games have always had a spark which they retain to this day, and this second round set up the needle match. Sure, the Hull–Rovers derby is important, but that is a family affair. When we play Leeds, it is our chance to put the rich boys in their places. Back then, the Yorkshire Cup final was even played at Headingley when Leeds had got there – the Loiners seemed to think that the county cup was their own property. So Hull and their fans went into the game with a well-balanced attitude: we had a chip on each shoulder.

The first thing that struck me on the way down the Boulevard – after which the ground was named – was that there were other people going that way too. There had yet to be any sort of boom in attendances within Rugby League after the decline of the late 1960s, but that day there was a stream of people heading for the game.

My father and I always went through the turnstiles at the top end of the car park in Airlie Street that led round to the Threepenny Stand. Well before kick-off there was a queue. Our well-worn ritual meant getting there in plenty of time to claim our favourite spot on the terraces and join in the gossip. The infamous

Threepenny Stand may only have been some 75 yards long, and it was only 11 wooden terraces, but it meant far more than the ramshackle structure it was in reality – I had my own personal bar mitzvah when I was considered old enough to join my father within it. Here we had stood since the opening of the Boulevard, three generations of Gibbonses each home game on that small area, almost as carefully guarded as a cat's or dog's territory: on the 25-yard line, opposite the best stand where the players came out. Our spot was also marked by the first of the metal roof supports which joined the terraces about four steps up in a small wooden groyne-like structure. If you stood right at the junction of this with the step, it provided you with a platform on which you could edge precariously forward to crane your neck whenever play went into the blind spot near the corner-flag at the Gordon Street End. Just what is so important about getting the exact same spot every week? All regular fans will know the feeling. It does act as a great calmer and provides a welcome familiarity.

Against Leeds that day, the stand was so full that we had to turn sideways just to fit extra bodies in. At kick-off, 6,000 people were there – an unimaginable number now – and they provided support for their team of an almost primeval intensity. In the second half Hull, urged on by the wall of sound, saw that a drop-goal from Chris Davidson was enough to catch a 9–9 draw. Of course we wouldn't win the replay, but honour was satisfied. We had caused the Loiners the embarrassment of having to play us again to swat us out of the way.

In the way the team played I was beginning to see what was possible – and that next week's *New Musical Express* showed me what was possible in other ways. 'Are you alive to the jive of . . . THE SOUND OF '75?' asked Charles Shaar Murray, writing about C.B.G.B.'s, a music club in New York featuring a madcap bunch called the Ramones. 1–2–3–4 . . .

Later that week there was the agony of a game that I couldn't attend, the more so because it was the replay against Leeds. For the news from far-away Headingley I was forced to rely on that miracle of 1970s kitsch, the music centre. This beast stood in the front room (which was only used on special occasions), a riot of smoked plastic and teak-effect surround. There, lying snug on top of the Mantovani and Batchelors records, in the centre's integral record stand, were your genuine 'cans', a set of earphones bigger than the handles on the Challenge Cup. With these in place, the ordeal began. At first, I could hardly listen for more than a few minutes at a time because we were going to get beaten, so I would pace between the front room and the kitchen, constantly knotting and then loosening the scarf which I just had to wear to show I was with the lads.

Then it started. Hull were outplaying the home side. Now I couldn't listen in case my intense hope communicated itself through the ether to Headingley and upset the apple-cart. Expectations of the tie had not been high, and such was the umbrage of the Leeds fans at having to go to all this trouble that a mere 2,880 filled the spaces at Headingley. Oh, those lucky few who had journeyed from 'Fish Town', what a tale they would have to tell if they could find anybody who was interested. Leeds beaten . . . forward to the next round.

It was time for the standby cliché of the cup draw: 'We don't mind who we get, as long as we are at home.' Well, that was the theory. We were indeed drawn at home, but it was against St Helens. So it was official: the week commencing Monday 17 November was declared 'Saints Week', with the dress rehearsal for the cup-tie coming in the Floodlit Trophy on the Tuesday when, at Knowsley Road, we received our expected mauling 13–36 before a national television audience. Still, there were encouraging bits of news for me from this defeat – like we did actually score, *and* we had the best kit.

On to the main event four days later on the Saturday, the third round of the Player's No. 6. Back at the Boulevard we did it again, winning 9–8. First Leeds, now St Helens: this was getting serious. These heartstopping margins were becoming bad for the health. It helps to understand the depth of the shock to my system when you consider that St Helens went on to play 52 games that season, winning the Challenge Cup and Premiership, and jetting off around the world to play Eastern Suburbs in the inaugural World Club Championship. Hull were getting a taste for this . . . next, please.

These shocks on northern Rugby League grounds were nothing compared to what some innocent concert-goers were discovering at colleges around the London area. November marked the first live appearance by the lovable Sex Pistols. Over the next couple of months they were to play some 15 dates, several of them obtained by the simple expedient of turning up and then convincing the promoters that they were the support band. (Honest.)

December in League-land, and it was the most nerve-racking time of any cup run, the semi-final. Years before Coronation Street found its place among the heritage trails, we were off to play the nearest professional Rugby League team to the Rovers' Return in Weatherfield, the mighty Salford, who were destined to achieve their second Championship in three seasons that time round – but we weren't overawed. Off on the bus I went with my Uncle Billy and the hordes of Hull fans, to take our places in the middle of the popular stand right behind a fan in a painstakingly-created papier-mâché Hull FC stove-pipe hat. There was a real carnival atmosphere.

This was Keith Boxall's game, as the blond forward tore the Red Devils apart for two tries and we blasted through to the final. It was an early Christmas present for us all: victorious by 22–14, Hull had breached 'Fortress Willows', joining Wigan, Australia, Wakefield and St Helens as only the fifth team to win on the ground that season. There were perhaps about 700 Hull fans there to see it, but the Red Army Choir could not have produced a more emotional rendering of 'Old Faithful' – even if they sang in English, which they didn't (the Red Army Choir, that is, not the Hull fans).

For the moment, however, none of that mattered as we played the traditional game for away supporters of finding your coach. To make it more interesting, the driver never picks you up at the same place that he drops you off. And loudspeaker announcements add to the fun by directing you to a street which you have never heard of. Somehow, though, you always manage to win, the prize being the return trip home.

January and 1976 began with Hull in a final for the first time since 1969 (when they beat Featherstone in the Yorkshire Cup, and my family made the trek from Essex to Headingley especially for the game). Now we were returning to Leeds to play Widnes for the Player's No. 6 Trophy, and we climbed aboard the East Yorkshire Motor Services coach to take us to our date with destiny (although first stop was the transport caff at Boothferry Bridge across the River Ouse). January 24th was a bitterly cold day, with flurries of snow falling as our coach eventually wound its way through the streets of Headingley. As I eagerly wiped the condensation from the window to look out, I had my first shock of the day. The coach was stationary in traffic, and through the cleared window I saw a knot of black-and-white clad fans, including one brave soul in his shirt-sleeves wearing a large decorated bow tie. My heart was filling with pride at this vast army of Hull fans ready to urge the side on to victory, when it suddenly missed a beat. These were Widnes fans. Of course – Widnes played in the same colours as us; my black-and-white scarf would not stand out. People watching on telly might even mistake us for them. We would have to let our support sing for itself.

Sport teaches you about life. Life is cruel, and life has decided that Hull are to be a team that often gloriously fail. Hull are the so-near-but-yet-so-far team; perhaps it is that very trait which is behind the special fanaticism of support that the team's fans are capable of. We revel in glorious failure (you have to when it seems that is all you get – the hiccups of success in cups and League in 1982 and 1983 apart). So we weren't surprised that day when, within eight minutes, we had gone eight points down. Following that season's script, though, we fought back to 8–8 and, with 20 minutes remaining, there was only one point in it as Widnes led 14–13. It was agonising. If support from a crowd could win a game, Hull were home already: it was magnificent. But, with two minutes to go, the dream was extinguished as Widnes's man-of-the-match, Reggie Bowden, scored to put the final nail in the coffin.

All that was left to us was the gesture of a benign pitch invasion to cheer the underdogs off. As we all converged on the corner of the ground where the Hull players were, I felt a tap on my shoulder and turned to see the sun – if there had been any that day – blocked out by the imposing presence of Big Jim Mills. He politely said 'excuse me' as he made his way through the throng. And everybody did excuse him. How could such a nice man – a very, very nice man – have been sent off 21 times in a career?

So ended January. February crept in, noted for two things which I did not think were connected: Hull FC signed Jimmy Crampton from New Hunslet for their then record fee of £8,000; and the Sex Pistols achieved their first national review after a gig at the Marquee. In the music papers there was no mention of headliners Eddie and the Hot Rods, simply a stunned amazement at the antics of Malcolm McLaren's protégés.

It would have been remiss of such a David-and-Goliath season to end without us playing St Helens again, at the Boulevard again, in the Challenge Cup. Heroics again, but not enough: we were just edged out 3–5 by the eventual competition winners.

And so it came to pass that there were only two months of the season left, and so far it had been dominated by tremendous battles in the cup. Suddenly I woke up to the fact that promotion from division two was also on the cards. It became a dogfight with Leigh for the fourth remaining place, and the battleground was Easter. On 28 March, when Barrow visited the Boulevard, there were three League games remaining. Barrow had already won the second-division Championship, but Hull still needed all the points they could get. Hull and Leigh were level on points, but the Lancastrians had the advantage through scoring difference. There was a holiday atmosphere as Barrow, who had done a pre-game lap of honour round the ground, were demolished 46–15. We were ecstatic: that showed them all – at least it did until the score came in from Leigh, who had been playing Doncaster. They had won 75–3 against the League's basement club. (Must have been lucky.)

So, 4 April, and Hull again visited Tattersfield, this time with a grim determination to beat their hosts in a similar fashion to Leigh. Havoc was duly wreaked (38–0). After the game we fiddled with car radios yet to have the magic of push-button tuning, to learn that Leigh had thumped New Hunslet 41–2. Curses. Leigh's season was then wrapped up on 16 April by beating Batley 30–5, whilst we awaited the visit of Whitehaven, sacrificial lambs to the slaughter, three days later. This gap left ample time to do the mathematics of promotion: all Hull had to do was win the game. Oh, and by a margin of at least 93 points. Nothing to it.

The showdown began with the team throwing specially-created black-and-white-striped rock to the crowd. Hull FC was written all the way through it like, er, Blackpool through rock. I kept my carefully captured stick for years on a shelf in my bedroom until it was thrown out as a health hazard by my zealous mother. Success it was not to be, however: normality was resumed. We fans knew the score by now: a gallant effort to win 47–10, but it was not good enough. Once again, a glorious failure, Hull destined forever to be on the wrong side of the dotted line which signified the four promoted teams. We had blown it right back at the beginning, remember? On the first day of the season, dropping one home point to Workington.

The only consolation to be gained in the month of April was the arrival of the brilliant minimalist thrash of the Ramones' first album. At least I managed to get that record. 1–2–3–4, indeed.

So why does a team that failed still resonate down the years for me? Actual concrete achievements were nil, yet that Hull team rates as one of the finest I ever supported. Because, when you get down to it, they were *Hull's Team*. They had used 14 players in the Player's No. 6 final against Widnes, ten of whom were born in the City of Hull, and even the most parochial would allow Brian Hancock to join that list, seeing as his passport showed him to be a native of Beverley just up the road. And, of the nine players who played more than 30 games that season and formed the nucleus of the team, only Kenny Foulkes and George Clark were not from Hull.

It may seem hard to accept now that the team did not have a weirdly-named antipodean to disrupt the list of Mike, Alf, George, Steve, Paul, Brian, Kenny, Bill, Peter, Alan, Keith, Mally and Mick. Just what heights could Hull have reached with a name like Tawera, Frano or Esene in their ranks? Still, we were in the dark age about such things then: we were a long way distant from tackle counts, blood-bins and Tina Turner.

But there must have been more to it than the fact that the players could all understand each other, and there was. The Stooges, Degrees and Men in a Boat may have come in threes; Dave Clark and the Gold Rings plumped for five. We had the fab four – Alf Macklin, Mick Crane, George Clark and Keith Boxall.

Alf Macklin: There have been better wingers and, if we were selecting an all-time Hull FC XIII, Alf would not be knocking on the selectors' door. But there has never been another one like Alfie. Whenever the team ran out that season, I would always agonise whether Macklin would actually be on the field for the kick-off. It was far more likely that he would be propping up the fence on the Threepenny side, in animated conversation with someone he had spotted in the crowd. Alf actually delivered a stick of that celebration rock by hand to someone in the stand, tearing off his tracksuit as he vaulted back over the fence into the field of play with seconds to spare before kick-off.

Alf was one of that breed of sportsmen who reached the top in two disciplines. Darts was his other love and, if he threw his arrows with the force he displayed when heading for the white-wash, there must have been many a landlord shoring up the wall on which the dartboard was secured.

He was the living personification of cartoon hero Alf 'Tough of the Track' Tupper. Macklin achieved his own feats on the field by will-power, sheer brute strength, and possibly a diet of chip butties too. He may have had more skill than I credit him with, but I could not see it for his sideburns. Alf was definitely the tonsorial star of a fashionably hirsute team. I would watch in amazement as his sideburns flapped in the wind and his hair spread out in his slip-stream as he ran straight towards the nearest defender. When some wingers score nowadays, the moonwalks and celebrations would shame Michael Jackson. When Alf scored, as he did 18 times that season, the most you could expect was a gap-toothed smile and a profane comment as he jogged (slowly) back, and we chorused 'Super Alf, Super Alf, Super Alf . . .'

Mick Crane: Of the four heroes, Mick Crane was the natural genius. He had the same gift with a rugby ball that George Best expressed with a soccer ball at his feet. That rugby ball seemed glued to Mick: just when it appeared he must drop it, he would come up with the pill, overstretching himself but always recovering the situation to leave you gasping. All of this was done with the cheekiest, most lop-sided grin you could see. Mick relished every minute.

What would he have been like if he had trained? It was always rumoured that the skills Mick showed on the field were as nothing to the excuses he could discover for him not to train; but who cared? We loved him, even if he would not have fitted into the 'my body is a temple' approach.

Hull didn't actually have any Australians in the team, but Mick would fill in some of the missing gaps by (allegedly) going walkabout in the way of Aboriginal warriors. It was said that he would disappear from the club for days on end, only to return mysteriously and pick up the threads as though nothing had happened. As with all true warriors, nobody asked him where he'd been and Mick, we can assume, volunteered no information. He let his talking be done out on the pitch, walking in for 19 tries that season, and none better than the one right between the posts in the Player's final at Headingley, the great grin lighting up the day as he put the ball down (one-handed) over the line. Mick Crane's approach to Rugby League may well have brought shrugs from his coaches, but he played the game as though he was born to it.

George Clark: Now we come to one of the imports. George came all the way from New Hunslet. He was a slight bloke, with a mean moustache, but his frame belied his impact on the pitch. He was the finisher of the team, with fast acceleration and a particularly wicked step. Capable of making defenders look foolish as they were left grasping thin air, Hull's Exocet missile found the target that season for 23 tries to make him our top scorer. It was one of those bolt-out-of-the-blue, nothing-can-go-wrong streaks. In his eight appearances the previous season there had been little to prepare you for this spectacular strike rate.

We have become used recently to players lifting more than their own body weight in the gym: who knows what George might have done with this sort of upper-body strength? When this hero soared into my sporting heaven he looked like he might have difficulty raising his voice, never mind a dumb-bell. Watching him made me feel like a helpless spectator to a car crash; just as you see that the collision is inevitable, you close your eyes and wait for the bang. When George had the ball and was heading towards the opposition's man-mountain, I would close my eyes waiting for the crunch. When it didn't come, I would open one eye cautiously to see the forward flat on his face with nothing in his hands but dirt, and George placing the ball over the try-line. The only clue to the route he had taken to get there would be two or three other confused opponents in a heap on the ground. George was a thoroughbred.

Keith Boxall: For me that year, if one man was to epitomise Hull FC it was Keith Boxall. He seemed to be everywhere on the pitch because his shock of blond hair was always so visible. Boxall was awesome, the hardest-running forward you could want, but without the edge that took other forwards into the thuggish tendency. If Hull scored a point that winter it would be a good bet that Keith had been involved somehow, because he not only scored 21 tries but also topped this off with 58 goals to be the club's top kicker. No wonder my memory replays a series of shots of Keith converting his own tries.

He was also special because he was the only one of my fab four that I met. The magic moment was some 12 years later, in the unlikely setting of a shipboard disco in the middle of the North Sea. I was going to Holland to oversee a couple of games of Rugby League in that country; the boat sailed from Hull, and among the passengers was Keith Boxall. I could have bored him for hours after we were introduced but couldn't get past a few mumbled clichés about that season. Hero and worshipper chatted a few minutes, and my last glimpse of Keith was as he crossed the dance floor. It was a strange picture: the disco floor pitching up and down and the dancers swaying precariously from side to side, clinging to each other for support. As Keith moved through the throng, they parted before him like the Red Sea before staggering back. He was gone. I closed my eyes and was there again on that day at Salford.

Funny thing, memory. You can dream, but you can't go back. Things were never the same again. In the real world in 1976, a heatwave broke out and lasted all summer. By July, the Sex Pistols had actually made their first recordings. Down in Oxford, as the sun shone, something stirred: *Open Rugby*, initially a humble four-page fanzine, was born and I was one of the people who sent off their ten pence to get issue No. 1. It fitted in nicely with my prized copy of the punk bible, *Sniffing Glue*. Ahead of me stretched my 16th birthday, my first trip overseas, O levels and, last but not least, 'Anarchy in the UK'. You remember the world when you are 16 in such vivid colours but, back then, there were two colours that stuck out a mile . . . black-and-white.

TREVOR GIBBONS is 34 and now lives in Leeds. He still follows the Airlie Birds and that other lost cause, the return of a Labour Government. His interest lies in real ale and, in the real world, he is promotions manager for *Open Rugby*.

WASHED UP WITH THE BLUEBAGS

Newtown and Parramatta 1981

Dave Hadfield

I was at one with most of Australia, I suppose, when I stood in the steaming rain at Henson Park and blamed it on the flamin' orientals. Slant-eyes, a proper Aussie would have called them, but I hadn't been there very long. Long enough to know, though, that they were responsible for the shortcomings of the economy and the weather, and for the way my fast-disintegrating, unsuitable shoes and sodden corduroy jacket – well, it never rains in Sydney, does it? – were welcoming in the water.

I had realised that Hong Kong was getting to me when, after almost two years of having to wait for a gap in the crowd before I could step out into the street from my flat above a bookie's and a Filipino night-club in Wanchai, I banjoed a frail-looking youth who was trying to push into my bus queue. He was slightly less surprised than I was at the way I sandwiched him between my shoulder and the No. 67 to Shek O beach. Thereafter, it was necessary to get away before the throngs, the noise, the lack of privacy had me lashing out in all directions.

A friend's Japanese girlfriend – too nice for him by a long way

178

– was an air hostess with Cathay Pacific, flying, among other destinations, to Sydney. When she came back from trips there, she brought not only the usual barely-nibbled whole Stilton cheeses and hardly-sipped bottles of wine from first-class, but also copies of *Rugby League Week*. Over the cheese and wine, the idea was planted that maybe I should go to Sydney and try to work for this paper. Certainly, I was going to start throwing the computer terminals around *The South China Morning Post* if I stayed with them much longer. And that was how I came to be contracting pneumonia at Henson Park, Newtown. 'Bloody slant-eyes,' I thought, with apologies to the delightful Sajiko; but then either John Ferguson or Ray Blacklock, or possibly both, came side-stepping through the mists, and it seemed that it wasn't such a bad place to be after all.

If geography had anything to do with it, I should have developed an affinity for Eastern Suburbs because, like countless visitors before me, I gravitated automatically to Bondi. That caused an interesting reaction in a society that likes to think of itself as classless. In a polite gathering in England, the subject of where you live might produce a response such as: 'Moss Side . . . That must be [miniscule pause] interesting.' The Australian equivalent, I learned, was: 'Bondi? Whaddya want to live in a shit-heap like that for? Only Jews and Maoris live in Bondi.' It could have made me very defensive about the place and its Rugby League club, based just up the road at Bondi Junction. I could have said that living on one of the world's most renowned beaches a couple of miles from the city centre didn't seem all that bad a deal to me. But that would only have started a tirade about Bondi's infamous sewage; and, admittedly, there was a conspicuous waste outlet on the north headland of the beach, which ensured that its water was not Sydney's purest. But I had come to Bondi via Blackpool and Hong Kong; after those places, my only complaint about the Bondi surf was that the relative shortage of any obvious detritus made for lonely swimming.

So I became stubbornly attached to the place, to its out-of-season atmosphere and even to its cavernous pubs, where it was possible to spend the occasional unforgettable night of gloating bliss as Botham belted Australia all round Headingley. There wasn't too much wrong with the local team, either. They had players such as Kerry Boustead, Noel Cleal (still officially a centre), Kevin Hastings – arguably the best scrum-half never to play for Australia – and just about the best second row around in Paul

McCabe. They finished on top of the Championship table and were most critics' tip to go on and take out the Grand Final but, somehow, I never took to them. There was something just a little too self-satisfied about them. They had all the swagger of their great days in the mid-1970s, but not quite the substance to back it up. I was happy enough to survive on schooners of Tooheys and subsidised baked lunches at their leagues club but, as a team, I never quite trusted them.

Newtown were something else again. They were what Australians call battlers – which doesn't mean that they were scrapping all the time, although they did have something of a tendency in that direction. History is vague on this point, but they may have been the first Rugby League club in Australia, and much of the time since 1908 had been spent struggling against the economic decline of their area and the dispersal of the Anglo-Irish working class that had formed their playing strength. By 1981, they were widely regarded as doomed – a prediction which turned out, all too soon, to be perfectly correct and which added poignancy to their efforts that season.

It was a club without pretensions, but with a good-hearted flavour all its own. Henson Park was a dump, with one small, rickety stand, and neighbours with back yards adjoining the oval would stand on stepladders to watch the game for free. On one particularly wet afternoon, one of them took pity and passed down a three-foot square of lino which I held above my head for the rest of the match. Compared to palaces such as Easts and St George, Newtown Leagues Club resembled a mission hut; but when my long-time drinking companion Dave Part and I decided to make our mark on history by having a beer in every leagues club in Sydney on the same day, Newtown was the one that rolled out the red carpet, with their secretary Frank Farrington grinning like the battered old fighter he was as he lined up a couple of schooners on the house.

One subtlety I missed at the time, but which the club's recently-published history notes with glee, was that Paul Hogan's prototypal Ocker character on TV wore Newtown socks! That surely clinches it: Crocodile Dundee barracks for the Bluebags. And note the nickname. Whilst other teams were styling themselves the Tigers, the Panthers or the Bulldogs, Newtown were called after the little sacks of washing soda that were lobbed in the laundry to stop their jerseys fading; the blue in Newtown was dolly blue, something calculated to strike fear into any opposition. Nor did a late attempt to redesign themselves as the Jets carry much conviction; to the blokes up their ladders, to Hoags and to me, they were the Bluebags. They were so hopelessly out of step that it was impossible not to fall equally hopelessly in love with them.

The affair might not have been consummated with such haste if my first job for *Rugby League Week* had not consisted of going to a Newtown versus Western Suburbs match at Henson Park in order to write a compare-and-contrast piece about the differences between this experience and what I was used to in Britain. Contrast I had promised them and, when I turned in my copy, any other Australian newspaperman I've ever met would have told me to fuck off back to a deserted Henson on the Monday morning and damn well find some contrast. Not so the saintly Ian Heads, the then editor of *RLW*. If I couldn't find much to distinguish Henson from Halifax, but could explain that failure in English, double-spaced, that was fine by him. Still, it was a genuine confession: it wasn't as far removed from what I knew as I had expected. Any image of sun-baked ovals with families lounging on blankets con-suming picnics and six-packs soon went down the gurgler, washed away by the incessant rain. Gloomy groups of men huddled under umbrellas, peering towards a dark rectangle of mud. Even the pies had a familiar taste.

I spent a lot of wet Saturdays and Sundays at Henson – often Saturdays, because Newtown, enjoying their unscheduled success that year, were a regular choice as the second-best match of the round, the one televised nationwide by the Australian Broadcasting Corporation on Saturday afternoon. To begin with, their modest little run of victories was treated indulgently but not seriously. A washed-up club was having a last fling, nothing more than that. Even when they beat Manly, Penrith, Canterbury, South Sydney and Cronulla in rapid succession, still no one fancied them to make the five for the play-offs. They were far too irretrievably unfashionable for that.

Newtown, though, had players who were a joy to watch, even at Henson, and Ferguson and Blacklock were the star turns. Both had joined the club that season – Blacklock from Penrith and Ferguson, at the fantastically advanced age for starting a Sydney career of 27 (although some said older) from Glen Innes in north-ern New South Wales – and, after a few early experiments with the shape of the back-line, settled down on opposite wings. 'Chicka'

Ferguson later played an unforgettable season – and Challenge Cup final – with Wigan, won Grand Finals with Canberra and, eventually, after a scandalous delay during which the selectors were determined to show preference to any centre, full-back or passing stranger, was chosen on the wing for Australia. His side-step and acceleration made him one of the most dazzling of players to watch, but Blacklock – also an Aboriginal and therefore equally unreliable and likely to go walkabout, according to the conventional wisdom of the time – was just as accomplished a footballer.

I look back a couple of sentences now and realise that my phrase about them settling down on their respective wings misses its mark by as wide a margin as many of the attempts to tackle them during that Sydney winter of 1981. Settling in their ordained roles was the last thing they did. Instead, they would do the unthinkable by cropping up in support on each other's wings. Or you might find the pair of them jinking through the middle, swapping passes and knowing grins. And, of course, it was all considered to be hopeless. They were leaving the Newtown flanks exposed to the counter-attack. They were another reason why the side's early, illusory promise was inevitably destined to fall away.

There were other individuals to relish, like the wonderfully stylish and dashing full-back, Phil Sigsworth; the gnarled old battler himself, Tommy Raudonikis, in his second season at Henson after 11 years at Wests; and Ken Wilson, an even more venerable scrum-half with a sedate kicking and passing game, who sometimes kept Raudonikis out of the starting line-up. The forwards were big and rough, apart from Phil Gould, who was on the small side and as smooth as satin. Gould, who went on to become far more celebrated as a coach with Penrith and New South Wales than he had ever been as a player, was often described as an 'English-style' forward – which meant, in the shorthand of the day, that he did unimaginably daring and risky things like passing the ball.

The coach was Warren Ryan, in his first senior job and less abrasive, less dedicated to falling out with anyone whose personality might counterbalance his own in the running battles of club politics, than he was to become in later life. He was still a pretty hard-boiled character, though, which was probably what Newtown needed after three consecutive wooden spoons between 1976 and 1978, with a grand total of seven wins over the three years.

There was a slight improvement in Ryan's first season and a marked one in 1980, but nobody had spotted the semi-final run of 1981 on the horizon.

As a new choom (translation: recent arrival from Britain), I wasn't saddled with any of the prejudices about the essential uselessness of Newtown. I could simply enjoy them for what they were, which was bloody good. The way that the Sydney press – which I realised, as soon as the thrill of finding page after page of Rugby League in every paper wore off, was 90 per cent bollocks – kept knocking them only deepened my affection for them. They became a personal cause. I might not be prepared to prolong tedious debates by defending Bondi, with its vast pubs full of Kiwis and its occasional floating turds, but I could go out on a limb with pleasure for the Jets, if I really had to call them that. New choom and Newtown were made for each other, and the bond was tied.

* * *

Besotted as I was with the Bluebags, even I had to concede that there was another team in town. Looking now at the side they fielded that season, it might seem incomprehensible that Parramatta were not short-priced favourites to win the Premiership, but they weren't. They had players such as Mick Cronin and Ray Price, who were recognised as being as good as any in their positions, but others – like Eric Grothe, Steve Ella, Brett Kenny and Peter Sterling – were just starting out and still had plenty to prove to a sceptical city. Worse than that, Parramatta had some very dodgy veteran forwards who were not fancied to stay the pace. There was Bob 'The Bear' O'Reilly, who looked just about knackered, and there was 'Stumpy' Stevens, who sounded to me like one of the dwarves who missed the cut when Snow White picked her sevens team. ('Shall we give Stumpy a run in the forwards? Nah, better stick with Grumpy and Dopey.') One colleague on *RLW* was so confident that these two would conk out that he vowed, in print, to walk from one end of the vast sprawl that is Sydney to the other wearing thongs (translation: flip-flops) if Parramatta reached the Grand Final with Stumpy and The Bear in their side. He had to go through with it as well, and it made his most memorable story of the year. Hope the blisters are better, Zorba.

Parramatta also had an unenviable reputation as chokers (translation: teams or individuals who crack under pressure within sight of the prize). They had reached Grand Finals in 1975 and 1977 and the play-off series in 1978 and 1979, before choking more comprehensively than ever and missing the finals altogether in 1980. What was different a year later?

Well, just about everything, as it happened. Ella and Grothe defied medical opinion by staying healthy and fulfilling their potential. Stumpy and The Bear – appropriately, in what turned out to be a fairy-tale season – lasted the course. Kenny and Sterling gelled together in one of the great half-back partnerships of all time. And brooding over it all was the dark, heavy presence of Jack Gibson.

Since that season in Sydney, I have looked into the cold fire of Malcolm Reilly's eyes when he thought I was accusing his Great Britain side of lacking pride and self-respect. I have walked unsuspecting and whistling a happy tune into both barrels from Peter Fox, and I have got Maurice Bamford out of a hot bath only to tell him that I'd forgotten why I'd phoned him. On a scale of one to ten, however, these are Unnerving Encounters with the Great Coaches that barely register, compared with asking Jack Gibson the time of day. Asking him any question, in fact, was like throwing a pebble down a well of unknown depth, waiting for what seemed like several minutes for a distant 'plop', and then trying to deduce something from that sound. If he was feeling particularly communicative, he might fix you with a baleful gaze that made you wonder whether he was going to invite you to dinner or have you shot. I found him completely unfathomable and I wasn't alone, although it was obligatory higher up the media tree to pretend that you could make him out.

The initial impression Gibson conveyed was one of toughness, even ruthlessness. But, paradoxically, his Parramatta sides must have been some of the most principled to play the game. That is using principled to mean having an identifiable set of principles and sticking to them – things like honesty in pursuit of personal excellence, discipline, simplicity and a focused concentration on the basics of the game. Players will tell you that he changed not just their careers, but their lives by instilling this sort of stuff. You would never have guessed that the stoop-shouldered, rumbling, mumbling figure in the winning dressing-room could do any such thing, but he could and did. Parramatta were a great rugby team – still the best club side I've seen – and being able to watch Kenny and Sterling in tandem week after week was like a continuous 30th birthday present.

Like Newtown, Parramatta has a reputation as one of the more rugged parts of town. Most places west of City Hall are spoken of in the seaside, eastern suburbs – yea, even upon the Beach that is Bondi – as lying somewhere within the Seven Circles of Hell. It's all about concentric degrees of westernness: the inner western suburbs like Newtown; the western suburbs proper, original home -- surprisingly enough – of Western Suburbs; the outer west, like Parramatta; and the outer, outer west of Penrith, before the Blue Mountains and the Black Stump. It's a matter of opinion in the Sydney that is within sight and sound of the ocean as to which west is worst; but it's a well-known fact that it's all bad, however habitable and inviting it might look to the residents of any other city.

Elsewhere in the metropolis, Westies – especially outer Westies – are renowned for their fibreboard houses and their boorishness. I was sceptical about this latter charge until one evening at Parramatta Leagues Club. My partner at the time has been a silent presence so far in this narrative for the simple reason that she could barely get a word in edgeways through the racket that Rugby League was making in our lives. It wasn't a case of her not liking the game. She'd tried her best in that department and had even experienced her own moment of glory when roped in as a late stand-in at a quiz evening. Asked for the nickname of Huddersfield, she had scrolled her memory back to a crib sheet of essential information which I'd scribbled down for her to study. 'I know it! I know it!' she screamed: 'The Fart Owners!' Neither ignorant nor squeamish, as you can see, but she was always a bit wary of the way the game was swallowing me whole and gulping her down as dessert.

As she went to the bar for the après-match beers at Parramatta, she was revoltingly groped by leering drunks, whilst I was no doubt gossiping happily about the game elsewhere in the club. She never felt quite comfortable in the ambience of Australian Rugby League after that. It wasn't that she expected to be set upon whenever she entered a room on her own. But the realisation had dawned that, if she wanted to spend time with me, it would be in places where her chances of being treated as a respected equal – like the sunstroke patient in the XXXX advert decides he wants – were rather less than those of her being selected to play second row in the Under-23s.

Newtown and Parramatta, my loyalties increasingly divided

between the two of them, finished second and third respectively at the end of the regular season, between the leaders, Easts, and the team most widely regarded as being capable of upsetting them, Manly, in fourth place. From the point of view of earning a crust, there was no longer any reason for me to be in Sydney. With only one match taking place at a time during the finals series, there was no work for back-ups and out-of-towners, so it was obviously time to see the rest of Australia. You can't spend six months in the country and see only football grounds and leagues clubs – well, you can, but in my experience it puts a strain on relationships built on respect, equality and all that bullshit.

Thus it came to pass – Greyhound bus pass, to be precise – that I watched the next, most crucial phase of my two teams' season from a pub in Adelaide. Lovely place, Adelaide, but not the least bit interested in Rugby League in 1981, so we had the bar pretty much to ourselves as the Eels played the Bluebags in the opening match of the play-off series. Newtown should have won it as well, because they caught Parramatta on one of their less sparkling days and scored two spectacular tries through Blacklock and Mick Ryan. But Parra hung in to win 10–8, Newtown losing their chance to make it a draw when Wilson missed a relatively easy late conversion. Still, it was a result worth a few extra schooners – with little chance of being molested going to or from the bar in polite Adelaide – because, under the convoluted Australian play-off system, it greatly improved Parramatta's chances of playing in the Grand Final, without eliminating Newtown. They would get their second chance the following weekend against Manly, who had eliminated fifth-placed Cronulla.

By then, we were in Alice Springs, having bused through a few hundred miles of nothing and spent a couple of days walking under, climbing up, running around, watching the sun rise and set upon, and generally experiencing Ayers Rock. Alice and the Rock were all aglow at the time with the Dingo Baby Case – the disappearance and death of Azariah Chamberlain and the fervid debate over whether it was the wild dogs or the mad parents what done it. One League commentator even got the immortal and sensitive phrase 'He swooped on that ball like a dingo on a baby' into his match call. Down in the dried-up bed of the Todd 'river', gnarled old blokes who looked as though any one of them could be John Ferguson's grandad sat in the shade of gum trees – dress restrictions doing a pretty thorough job of keeping Aboriginals out of the pubs – and shook their heads sagely. 'Dingo never'd take a kid,' they said. 'And Parramatta'll never get to the Grand Final with Stevens and O'Reilly in the team.'

But Parramatta did. This time the pub was full – pubs in Alice always were. But, after finding a spot within sight of an inaudible TV and directly under a precious ceiling fan, I could watch them beat Easts 12–8 after 20 minutes' extra-time, two penalties from Cronin eventually making the difference. Same pub, same crowd, same fan the following day, and Newtown too ignored the script. Manly were supposed to be the class act but, at the end of one of the great games of Rugby League, the inspired Blues had kicked them all the way back to the North Shore.

It was a game that began with the most almighty punch-up – greatly enjoyed by the punters in Alice, I recall. The first scrum erupted in a brawl, with Newtown's Steve Bowden and Manly's famously tough Kiwi, Mark Broadhurst, in the front line. Someone had a stopwatch on it at the Sydney Cricket Ground and timed it at two minutes from the first punch to the restoration of a semblance of peace. I can't vouch for that, but one bloke in Alice ordered and drank a beer, went to the dunny and came back to find that they were still at it. I'm looking now at a picture taken later in the match, and Broadhurst is in the background, looking like the Phantom of the Opera. Broady would never claim to have been the most photogenic of prop forwards, but anyone who could make him look that much worse than usual had landed some pretty effective shots. Bowden was sent off, along with Manly's hard-nut second-rower, Terry 'Igor' Randall.

The football, when it started, was of just as high a standard as the fighting. Newtown, with Sigsworth, Ryan and Gould out-standing, were always the better side, but they couldn't quite shake Manly off their coat-tails. They were 16-nil up on a side confi-dently predicted to beat them and were then hauled back to 16–10. Another try each way, with Manly's converted, brought the Sea Eagles within range, before Wilson's drop-goal saw Newtown home by 20–15.

That was it for Manly, but there was still the prospect of a Grand Final pitting fashionable stylists against Westie upstarts if Easts could beat Newtown the following week and thus qualify to meet Parramatta in the Grand Final. (Are you following all this? I'm not sure I am.) It was clear to everyone outside Newtown and

Marrickville that this was what was going to happen. But there were still things to do before the Final – so called, of course, because it is the penultimate match of the season – like sweating through Katherine, Mt Isa and Cairns, and visiting Arthur Beetson at his pub as essential research prior to watching him play the last serious match of his career for Redcliffe in the Brisbane Grand Final. For half an hour of the Sydney match on TV, it looked as though the world was right about Easts. They *were* going to get it right in the end. But, leading 5–2 just before the break, they were pegged back by a Ferguson try from a quickly-taken tap penalty, and were never in it in the second half as Gould and Blacklock added further tries. Fifteen-bloody-five! Newtown versus Parramatta. It was time to get back on the Greyhound and return home to Sydney in triumph.

Out of Sydney, out of mind. 'Mate, what we'd like you to do is watch the Grand Final from the Hill and give us your impressions of this great Australian institution,' said the saintly editor. (Translation: Oh shit, we've forgotten to organise a proper ticket for the Pommie bastard.) It was not, however, such a bad idea because, like much else in Sydney football, the Hill at the SCG was doomed. 1981 was not only the last year that the Premiership was confined to clubs from in and around the city – we got the leagues club crawl in just in time, because side trips to Canberra and Illawarra would have made it a long day on the grog, even for us. It was not only the last year before the Winfield Cup supplanted the trophy that had traditionally been awarded to the Premiers – the J. J. Giltinan Shield, a venerable artefact the size and shape of a small bookcase. It was also the last season before the Hill was emasculated in the name of modernising the Cricket Ground. Seven years later, the Grand Final would leave the SCG altogether, and it is highly debatable now whether there will ever be another involving two Sydney clubs.

But, back in 1981, Grand Final day was still a local, even a parochial obsession, with an intimacy that it was later to lose. And the Hill was still very much alive and well as the place from which the loud and the larrikin, the Ocker and the Westie shouted his team on. Even going there in the line of duty, you had to barrack for one side or the other, so there was a decision to be made. It was an underdog-fight for the affections. Parramatta, who had been trying without success to win the Premiership since coming into the competition in 1947? Or Newtown, out on their feet, but somehow staggering into their first Grand Final since 1955? In the end, it had to be the Bluebags. Parramatta were professional underdogs, sure enough, but Newtown were several notches further down the scale of canine suffering than that. They were the mangy mongrel on its last trip to the vet, inexplicably wagging its tail all the way.

There were a lot of blokes in Newtown socks on the Hill that day, and plenty in Parramatta socks as well. I notice from my Grand Final edition of *Big League* that the Under-23 final kicked off at 11 a.m. Most of my neighbours were long past caring about sartorial detail by that early hour. I don't believe that Australia as a nation could sue me for saying that its citizens are partial to a drink during and, indeed, before sporting occasions. But some of these on the Hill must have started half-way through the 1980 season and were already snoring under blankets, only the occasional protruding sock or flag clutched like a teddy bear revealing their loyalties.

Midway through the reserve-grade Grand Final – Parramatta were in all three grades, which should have been some clue as to the dynasty they were establishing – the second wave arrived. They had opted to do their preparatory drinking outside the ground and carried with them an essential item of equipment that I realised instantly I was going to regret being without. Why, oh why, had I not thought to bring a milk crate? Everyone else had one – even the comatose, I noticed on closer inspection, had one stashed away somewhere. The corner delis and grocers of Sydney must have had to find another way of organising their bottles that day. The crates were required for a more important use. Shortly before kick-off in the main match, men in Parramatta singlets or various items of royal blue – Newtown were not big on merchandising, and had only acquired a shirt sponsor half-way through the season – began to ascend their personal grandstands. No crate, no view. But a big, bearded bloke in blue detected a kindred spirit and lent me his spare, his mate being well beyond the standing-on-crates stage.

So that was it: I was standing on a Newtown crate, probably filched from outside a Vietnamese small-goods shop on the Marrickville Road. No wonder the Bluebag in me sang when Newtown led 11–7 early in the second half. For 20 minutes after that, they held out a resurgent Parramatta; but, 14 minutes from time, they cracked and eventually lost 11–20. The crate next to me was empty and forlorn by then.

You didn't, to be honest, get much of a view from the Hill, even with the help of the Australian dairy industry, but it had clearly been one hell of a match. And that night in Parramatta was a hell of a night, with an almost surreal quality. Jack Gibson walked up to the microphone in the leagues club and said, 'Ding dong, the witch is dead.' He was cheered to the echo by a delirious crowd who didn't know which witch and didn't care. By way of additional celebration, some of them went to the Cumberland Oval, the nearby home ground that Parramatta were due to leave for a new stadium, and burnt down the grandstand.

A year later, Parramatta had no new stadium, but six of the players who had carried off Jim Giltinan's bookcase formed the backbone of the Kangaroo squad who won every match on tour in Britain. There were none from Newtown. Of the players in the three grades that day, no less than 11 Eels eventually played for clubs in Britain, where for several seasons Parramatta became synonymous with Australian Rugby League. It wasn't quite the indestructible legacy it appeared to be, however. After winning further Premierships under Gibson in 1982 and 1983 and under John Monie in 1986, the Eels went into steep decline.

Not as steep as Newtown, though. Two years after being 14 minutes from the Premiership, they were voted out of the Winfield Cup when a proposed move to the satellite town of Campbelltown fell through. The Newtown and Marrickville areas had been given up as a hopeless case by the New South Wales Rugby League. The territory around the ground where I had stood soaking and cursing the oriental misadventures that had sent me there was now overwhelmingly oriental in its population and the game, whilst finally making inroads elsewhere in Australia, was less adept at attracting new ethnic groups in old Rugby League areas. Could they have kicked out the Bluebags if they had won in 1981, though? It seems highly doubtful.

By a deplorable irony, swanky old Easts finished up playing at grim old Henson when their Sports Ground home was ripped down to make way for the Sydney Football Stadium. But even that apparently final indignity didn't completely kill off Newtown. In 1991, they re-emerged, albeit as a team in the relatively low-key Metropolitan Cup. John Ferguson, the one former Newtown player to have made his mark in Britain, came out of retirement to play in their first match and then went back into retirement again.

The following year, with Shane Kelly – in whose wardrobe I

had once spent the Brisbane leg of a Lions tour – at prop, they won the Metropolitan Cup. It wasn't the J. J. Giltinan Shield, or even the Winfield Cup. But I put on my blue-and-white hooped socks, went to the garage to find a crate, and gave the Bluebags a cheer they might have heard in Newtown.

NO MORE WINTERS

Dave Hadfield, *May 1995*

Little did we suspect, as we were putting the final touches to *XIII Winters* a year ago, that within 12 months winter would be abolished. There will still be, I fear, a cold, wet, generally miserable time of the year, but it will not be winter in the true sense of the word. Its miseries will not be alleviated by the one thing that made it tolerable to the contributors to the book; there will, after the winter of 1995–96, be no professional rugby league.

It seems only yesterday that the proponents of summer rugby were a harmless little sub-sect, a set of flat-earthers who believed that the cosmos was carried on the back of an elephant and that all would be well at their largely roofless grounds if the game was played during the famously dry and reliable weather from March to September. The leading members of the Summer Tendency – Gary Hetherington of Sheffield Eagles, Chris Caisley of Bradford Northern and Jim Quinn of Oldham – were sent away to talk among themselves and stop interrupting the serious business. We didn't expect to be bothered by them again.

Early in the spring, however, something very strange began to happen. People who had previously dismissed the summer lobby as an annoying distraction started to hint that they might be onto something after all. If you had a nasty, suspicious mind, you might conclude that this constituted the first rumblings of the Super League bandwagon. If you had known or suspected that Rupert Murdoch was going to throw money at the British game in order to win his battle for control in Australia, it would not have taken a lot of foresight to work out that the masterplan would involve summer rugby. So the Three Stooges became the Three Wise Men and summer rugby became the new orthodoxy.

At the time of writing, the plans for the Super League have been several times around the houses and have settled down – who knows how permanently? – at the point at which we could and should have been five years ago, with something approximating to three divisions, each of 12 teams. After all the enthusiastic votes of chairmen in favour or mergers – at least for clubs other than their own – Wigan, wearied by the ease with which they beat teams like Oldham and Workington, are now quaking in their boots at the prospect of facing sides like, er, Workington and Oldham. The one really drastic change which has emerged from it all is the one which has never been properly debated at all; in future we will be mismanaging our game in summer instead of winter. Summer rugby rode in on the back of the Super League, unchallenged and barely remarked upon. The day the deed was done, my children captured, as they often seem to me to do, the mood of the time. A concerned deputation wanted to know the answers to two questions: Will you still have a job? and When will we have our holidays?

As a snapshot of a turbulent time in rugby league, it might be instructive to look at the effect that the whole Super League/summer rugby furore has had upon the clubs and, in some cases, the writers involved in *XIII Winters*. Let's start at the happy end of the spectrum. Wigan are thoroughly chuffed with the whole thing, although they might be less so if they lose too many more of their leading players to the Kerry Packer/Australian Rugby League backlash against the predations of Murdoch and his Super League. The London Broncos, successors to Fulham and the London Crusaders, can hardly believe their luck. No sooner have their parent company, the Brisbane Broncos, started muttering darkly about the London operation costing an arm and a leg than they get a glorious windfall – a place in the Super League and the money to go with it. For me, the popular North of

England sentiment that the game will never succeed in London is undermined by the fact that, in the early days at Craven Cottage, it did succeed and succeed spectacularly. Now they are getting their big chance to show that they can become part of the sporting fabric of the capital. If they blow it this time, it will be hard to argue for them in the future.

Swinton seem to me to be typical of a broad group of clubs for whom there seems little strategic advantage in either the Super League or summer rugby, but for whom large sums of money have talked and talked persuasively. There is nothing in this to help them recover lost glories, but the Murdoch pay-out will keep them going longer than would otherwise have been the case. And, although I don't know whether the brothers Kelner will regard this as reassuring or insulting, Swinton were one club never seriously regarded as merger candidates.

That brings us to Wakefield Trinity, a rare case of a club which, after consultation with its shareholders, was prepared to merge and become part of the proposed Calder conglomerate alongside Castleford and Featherstone Rovers. That should have been sufficient warning for anyone. As a rule of thumb, any club in such a dire state that it is prepared to merge is not the sort of club you should be merging with. Featherstone were certainly not interested, indeed the place became something of a symbol for the struggle of community clubs to retain their identities. Ian Clayton, the creator of *When Push Comes to Shove*, was in demand as never before as a spokesman for the 'Over our dead bodies' school of thought, in Featherstone and beyond. He had a wonderful sound-bite (or print-bite?) about the washing-lines from the village's back-to-backs being tethered to the rugby ground's perimeter wall. Merge the clubs, lose Post Office Road, and Featherstone's flannelette sheets and T-shirts will never be the same again. What interested me was the way that another dyed-in-the-wool Featherstonian, the XIII Winterman – if I can use that as a short-hand for our contributors – Chris Westwood, represented a subtly different viewpoint. He typifies the sort of rock-solid one-club loyalist who might nevertheless have been prepared to contemplate the unthinkable if asked rather than told. There is a moral in that somewhere. Featherstone members responded to the diktat by digging their heels in. If the price of being in the Super League was merger they would stay as they were – even to the extent of continuing to play in the winter. Then came the League's volte-face and the club's identity and the village's washing-lines were safe.

Hull is one of those places where the logic of pooling the resources of two clubs is blindingly obvious from fifty miles away. Once past the Humber Bridge, however, you are in a divided city where 'We're black, we're white, we'll never merge with shite' ranks among the more conciliatory greetings. The willingness of both boards to discuss the impossible was another illustration of that useful adage – never merge with anyone who wants to merge with you. For Whitehaven, meanwhile, there was a plan that would have made the bureaucrats who reorganised local government in the early '70s proud. Take a few places that look reasonably close together on a map and lump them into an administrative unit. A Cumbrian club strung out like Christmas-tree lights from Walney Island to the Solway Firth looked great apart from the inconvenient fact that none of the four existing clubs nor their communities wanted anything to do with it.

Leeds wanted nothing to do with summer rugby. They had made that plain repeatedly, so naturally they voted for it, leaping acrobatically from a position of implacable opposition to one of determination to entice the whole population of the city up to Headingley for afternoons of barbecues, Punch 'n' Judy and medieval jousting, with a game thrown in for good measure. On the warmest evening of last season, a fraction over 7,000 – their worst gate of the season against first-division opposition – saw them play Bradford Northern in the Premiership and there were several species of flying and crawling things in the press box. Summer rugby sucks – and bites and stings as well. These are the things they never tell you. XIII Winterperson Margaret Ratcliffe actually resigned from the writing business because she was so disgusted with the whole Super League farrago. It's always the wrong heads that roll.

One man's winter credentials remain unsullied. Peter Wilson and Tameside Borough will, like the rest of amateur rugby league, continue to do their stuff in winter. I anticipate queues around the block at Tameside International Stadium as dispossessed leaguies flock there for their winter fix.

And now for the really important consequences of the Winter of Discontent. How, I hear you ask, is it all going to affect what remains of Newtown and Blackpool Borough? Not long after the publication of *XIII Winters* in hardback, a representative of the Newtown club phoned me to update me on their current state of play and ask me to become their European representative. That is clearly the greatest honour that Rugby League has brought me, outshining even the Pennine League Division Six Winners' Medal 1983–84 that sits even now on the bookshelves to the right of this typewriter. With the Super League just starting to come to the boil in Australia, my first contribution to Newtown's future health and happiness was to suggest that they approached the Australian Rugby League to tell them: 'We now see that kicking us out in 1983 was all a terrible mis-understanding. If you ask us very nicely, we might just be prepared to come back and help you make your numbers up.'

'We've considered that,' said my Newtown contact. 'But we're not really financial enough.' A wonderful Australianism, that – 'financial' in the sense of having finance. Rugby League in Britain is now – although for how long? – financial; it has proved that by disbursing previously undreamed of sums of money to the likes of Chorley Borough, the club I have always regarded as the true descendants of Blackpool.

A very brief history of the game's various Boroughs is that, after a brief sojourn at Wigan Athletic, they split into Trafford and Chorley. If this amoeba-like method of reproduction had contin-ued, they would have been in the majority by now and would have been able to vote through anything they liked. Instead, Trafford eventually relocated to Blackpool as the Gladiators – or Gladioli, as I always find myself calling them – and both they and Chorley were kicked out of the league in 1993. It was one of those acts of self-mutilation that were popularly supposed to be the key to the future health of the game; a bit like plucking your eyebrows to cure paralysis in your legs. Unlike Blackpool, Chorley kept their act together moderately well in the National Conference and have now been invited back into the fold and given a big wad of money. That relatively straightforward outcome might not be the end of it. Already there is a stirring of opinion to the effect that nowhere in Britian is better suited to summer rugby than . . . Blackpool. Yes, I can see it now. Borough Park packed with holidaymakers sport-ing tangerine, black and white knotted hankies on their heads, gorging on cones and candyfloss as the Borough take on Paris. At the same time, the teeming millions in their flats in Manhattan and Kowloon tune into their Murdoch cable station and ask 'Who are these mighty men they call The Tangerine Machine? Where have they been all our lives?' Neither winter nor summer are ever going to be the same again.